THE LETTERS OF MARGARET FULLER

The Fuller family. Daguerreotype taken in the early 1850s. From the left: Arthur, Eugene, Ellen, Margarett Crane, and Richard. Courtesy of Elizabeth Channing Fuller and Willard P. Fuller, Jr.

THE LETTERS OF
Margaret Fuller

Edited by

ROBERT N. HUDSPETH

VOLUME III · 1842–44

Cornell University Press

ITHACA AND LONDON

PUBLICATION OF THIS BOOK WAS ASSISTED BY GRANTS FROM THE PROGRAM
FOR EDITIONS AND THE PUBLICATIONS PROGRAM OF THE NATIONAL
ENDOWMENT FOR THE HUMANITIES, AN INDEPENDENT FEDERAL AGENCY.

Copyright © 1984 by Cornell University Press

First published 1984 by Cornell University Press.
Published in the United Kingdom by Cornell University Press Ltd., London.

International Standard Book Number 0-8014-1707-4
Library of Congress Catalog Card Number 82-22098
Printed in the United States of America

*Librarians: Library of Congress cataloging information appears
on the last page of the book.*

*The paper in this book is acid-free and meets
the guidelines for permanence and durability
of the Committee on Production Guidelines for
Book Longevity of the Council on Library Resources.*

PREFACE

In the years 1842–44, Margaret Fuller established herself as a writer of impressive scope: she continued her literary criticism with essays in the *Dial* and the *Present* on contemporary drama, fiction (including that of her friend Nathaniel Hawthorne), and poetry (especially Tennyson's), and once again brought a German work to an American audience by translating Bettina von Arnim's *Günderode*. She wrote a sympathetic impression of the American Midwest in *Summer on the Lakes, in 1843*, and she finished these years with a provocative feminist analysis of American culture in *Woman in the Nineteenth Century*.

After the emotional tensions of the two preceding years, Fuller enjoyed greater inward calm: the crises with Sam Ward and Emerson were over, and she put her disappointment with both men behind her; nothing during these years approached the religious exaltation of 1840. By 1842 Fuller had created a vocation and accepted the limitations of her friends; she had a secure place as leader of her "conversations," and she continued to publish almost everything she wanted to publish.

The first major decision during these years came in the spring of 1842, when she gave up her editorship of the *Dial*. She saw that she was exhausting herself and that she was to get absolutely no monetary reward from the work. Reluctantly Emerson agreed to replace her. Although she was sorry to find that he wanted less variety in the journal, she was relieved to be free of the recurring deadlines. The next spring Fuller had the chance to fulfill a long-standing desire to see Niagara Falls. From there she went on to Chicago and the Plains area south of the city and north into the Wisconsin territory. The trip gave

5

her a subject for her travel book, and it prompted her to think about the American treatment of the Indians and of the very specific hardships the immigrants faced. The sights and the people were satisfying, but still she was glad to return to New England.

In addition to Fuller's public activities, there were domestic concerns: her sister-in-law Frances Fuller took an unwise trip to New Orleans with a small child; her mother went to Cincinnati to be with Margaret's sister, Ellen, and Ellen's husband, Ellery Channing; her brother Arthur bought a school in Illinois; her brother Richard began to study for his entrance to Harvard and then found that he did not meet his own high standards of scholarship; Ellen and Ellery moved to Concord, where their first child brought both delight and disruption to a small household. Through all of these upheavals Margaret offered advice, sympathy, and admonitions as the situations demanded. While she was not responsible for the risks the family members took, she always acknowledged the claims they made on her attention.

The leadership she exerted within the family, her wide reading, and her efforts to establish herself as a writer led to her critique of woman's role in America in her "Great Lawsuit" essay for the *Dial*. Fuller then devoted the fall of 1844 to a revision of the essay, and in November produced the manuscript that was published as *Woman in the Nineteenth Century*. She drew on what she had read and what she had experienced to define the ambivalence at the center of woman's life in American culture. She scolded Emerson when he said of the birth of Sam Ward's new daughter: "Though no son, yet a sacred event."[1] She dared to hope that Greta Channing, her namesake niece, would "have a better chance" in life than she had had.

During the time she was at work on her book, she decided to leave New England for New York. Horace Greeley had been so impressed by her writing that he had asked her to become his book reviewer for the *New-York Daily Tribune*. Without perhaps grasping the full meaning of the change, she moved outward into a bigger world, from exclusively literary writing to daily journalism, from a coterie of intellectuals to a mass audience. She freed herself of the immediate influence of Emerson; she ended her conversations with Boston women; she physically left the family; she assumed a role on the paper that hardly had precedent for a woman. The last letter in this volume finds Fuller poised for new flights, making plans with William Henry Channing

1. Ralph Waldo Emerson, *The Letters of Ralph Waldo Emerson*, ed. Ralph L. Rusk, 6 vols. (New York: Columbia University Press, 1939), 3:170.

for a visit to Blackwells Island which led her in 1845 to write on hospital and prison conditions. From literary reviews Fuller was turning to social criticism. The change was permanent: she never returned to her earlier interests, nor did she ever again live in New England.

Her letters from this period trace her new interests. No longer did she write long letters to James Clarke, for he had returned to Boston, and their mutual interest in German literature had cooled. Nor was Henry Hedge important in her correspondence, for his isolation in Bangor was complete, both physically and intellectually. Fortunately, her conversation with Emerson still took place by post. William Henry Channing, too, continued to be an important recipient of her letters, for his quest for spiritual growth, his unhappiness with the formalities of the church, and his passion for Christian reform made him her most sympathetic male correspondent during these years.

Of her women friends, Caroline Sturgis continued to be a steady correspondent when they were apart. Like Emerson, Elizabeth Hoar was conveniently near, yet far enough away to occasion letters. Sarah Shaw became increasingly a recipient of Fuller's letters, for she had a maternal warmth that Fuller found attractive. As she always did, Fuller played many roles in her letters—sister, critic, friend, editor, and judge—but she always gave herself freely to her correspondents.

Robert N. Hudspeth

State College, Pennsylvania

CONTENTS

Preface   5

Acknowledgments   17

Editorial Method   21
    Format, 22; Text, 22; Annotation and Index, 22

Editorial Apparatus   25
    Textual Devices, 25; Descriptive Symbols, 25; Location
      Symbols, 26; Short Titles and Abbreviations, 26

1842

345. 1 January, to Margarett C. Fuller   31
346. 6 January, to Richard F. Fuller   34
347. 8 January, to Margarett C. Fuller   35
348. 15 January, to Margarett C. Fuller   37
349. 15? January?, to Richard F. Fuller   40
350. 22 January, to Margarett C. Fuller   41
351. February, to William H. Channing?   42
352. 5 February, to Margarett C. Fuller   43
353. 10? February, to John S. Dwight   45
354. ca. 1 March, to ?   46
355. 8? March, to Elizabeth Hoar   46
356. 8 March, to Ralph Waldo Emerson   49
357. 15? March, to Ralph Waldo Emerson   52
358. 17? March, to Ralph Waldo Emerson   53

359. 20 March, to Elizabeth Hoar   54
360. April, to Caroline Sturgis   56
361. 7 April, to Mary Rotch   56
362. 9 April, to Ralph Waldo Emerson   57
363. 18 April, to Ralph Waldo Emerson   60
364. 22 April, to Richard F. Fuller   61
365. ca. May, to Mary Rotch   62
366. 12 May, to Richard F. Fuller   63
367. 4 June, to Sophia Peabody   65
368. 17 June, to William H. Channing   67
369. 19 June, to Elizabeth Hoar   68
370. 23? June, to William H. Channing?   69
371. 23 June, to Ralph Waldo Emerson   69
372. 25 June, to Richard F. Fuller   71
373. July, to Caroline Sturgis   72
374. July, to William H. Channing?   72
375. July, to William H. Channing?   75
376. 1 July, to Charles K. Newcomb   75
377. 25 July, to Ralph Waldo Emerson   77
378. 30 July, to Charles K. Newcomb   77
379. 31 July, to James F. Clarke   79
380. August?, to Elizabeth Hoar   79
381. August, to William H. Channing?   80
382. 5 August, to Richard F. Fuller   81
383. 10 August, to Ralph Waldo Emerson   83
384. 11 August, to Richard F. Fuller   85
385. 16 August, to Caroline Sturgis   87
386. 21 August, to Samuel G. Ward   88
387. 25 August, to William H. Channing?   90
388. September, to Ralph Waldo Emerson   92
389. September, to Charles K. Newcomb   93
390. 9 September, to Caroline Sturgis   94
391. 10 October, to Charles K. Newcomb   95
392. 16 October, to Ralph Waldo Emerson   96
393. November, to William H. Channing?   99
394. November, to Elizabeth Hoar   101
395. November, to Anna Huidekoper Clarke   101
396. 8 November, to Ralph Waldo Emerson   101
397. 4? December, to Ralph Waldo Emerson   102
398. 17 December, to George T. Davis   104

Contents

399. 17 December, to Frederic H. Hedge   106
400. 26 December, to Ralph Waldo Emerson?   110

1843

401. 1843, to James F. Clarke?   111
402. 1843, to ?   111
403. 16 January, to Elizabeth Hoar   113
404. 16 January, to Nathaniel Hawthorne   115
405. 30 January, to Elizabeth Hoar   118
406. 5 February, to Mary Rotch   119
407. 7 February, to Ralph Waldo Emerson   121
408. 16 February, to Mary Rotch   121
409. 3 May, to Henry W. Longfellow   122
410. 8 May, to Sarah Ann Clarke   123
411. 9 May, to Ralph Waldo Emerson   123
412. 22 May, to Charles K. Newcomb   125
413. 30 May, to Elizabeth Hoar   125
414. 30 May, to Sarah Shaw   127
415. 1 June, to Ralph Waldo Emerson   128
416. 16 June, to Ralph Waldo Emerson   129
417. 29 July, to Richard F. Fuller   132
418. 3 August, to Samuel G. Ward   134
419. 4 August, to Ralph Waldo Emerson   136
420. 7 August, to Albert H. Tracy   139
421. 9 August, to Mary Rotch   139
422. 16 August, to William H. Channing   141
423. 17 August, to Ralph Waldo Emerson   143
424. 7? September, to Richard F. Fuller   145
425. 20 September, to Maria Rotch   146
426. 25 September, to Henry D. Thoreau   148
427. 26 September, to Albert H. Tracy   149
428. 13 October, to Henry James, Sr.   151
429. ca. 16 October, to Ralph Waldo Emerson   152
430. 23 October, to Marianne Mackintosh Clarke   152
431. 27 October, to William H. Channing   153
432. 6 November, to Albert H. Tracy   155
433. 8 November, to William Emerson   158
434. 12 November, to Ralph Waldo Emerson   159

435. 5 December, to Abigail Allyn Francis   162
436. 12 December, to Ralph Waldo Emerson   163
437. 26 December, to Anna Barker Ward   164

1844

438. 1844, to ?   167
439. 10 January, to Sarah Shaw   168
440. 21 January, to Mary Rotch   168
441. 22 January, to Maria Rotch   170
442. 28 January, to Orestes A. Brownson   174
443. 28 January, to Ralph Waldo Emerson   175
444. 2 February, to Ralph Waldo Emerson   180
445. 2 February, to Richard F. Fuller   181
446. 14? February?, to Ralph Waldo Emerson   181
447. March?, to William H. Channing   182
448. 13 March, to Lydia Francis Child   183
449. 16 March, to Abigail Clarke Stimson   183
450. 21 March, to James F. Clarke   185
451. April?, to Elizabeth Hoar   185
452. 2 April, to Frances Hastings Fuller   187
453. 14 April, to Anna Barker Ward   189
454. 22 April, to Arthur B. Fuller   189
455. 28 April, to William H. Channing   193
456. 3 May, to Caroline Sturgis   193
457. 7 May, to Anna Loring   195
458. 9 May, to Ralph Waldo Emerson   196
459. 25 May, to Caroline Sturgis   196
460. 30 May, to Charles C. Little   197
461. June?, to William H. Channing   198
462. 3 June, to Caroline Sturgis   200
463. 3 June, to Little and Brown   200
464. 9 June, to Charles K. Newcomb   201
465. 14 June, to Barbara Channing   202
466. Summer, to ?   202
467. 3 July, to Arthur B. Fuller   202
468. 8 July, to Charles K. Newcomb   206
469. ca. 10 July, to Ralph Waldo Emerson   207
470. 11 July, to Richard F. Fuller   208
471. 13 July, to Ralph Waldo Emerson   209
472. 16 July, to Georgiana Bruce   210

Contents

473. 17 July, to Charles Lane   211
474. 20? July, to Ralph Waldo Emerson   213
475. 22 July, to Jane F. Tuckerman   217
476. 26 July, to Charles Lane   218
477. 4 August, to Caroline Sturgis   218
478. 15? August, to Sarah Shaw   221
479. 15 August, to Georgiana Bruce   221
480. 1? September, to William H. Channing   224
481. 1 September, to Sarah Shaw   225
482. 20 September, to Richard F. Fuller   227
483. 25 September, to Maria Rotch   229
484. 27 September, to Sarah Hodges   231
485. Autumn, to ?   232
486. Autumn, to ?   232
487. Autumn, to Christopher P. Cranch   233
488. 15 October, to Richard F. Fuller   234
489. 20 October, to Georgiana Bruce   235
490. 20 [28?] October, to Elizabeth Hoar   237
491. Early November?, to the women inmates at Sing Sing   238
492. 3? November, to William H. Channing   238
493. 17 November, to William H. Channing   241
494. 17 November, to Ralph Waldo Emerson   243
495. 20 November, to Sarah Shaw   245
496. 23 November, to Richard F. Fuller   247
497. 25 November, to Charles K. Newcomb   249
498. December, to ?   250
499. December?, to Georgiana Bruce   250
500. 3 December, to Ralph Waldo Emerson   251
501. 4 December, to William H. Channing   252
502. 12 December, to James F. Clarke   252
503. 26 December, to Elizabeth P. Peabody   253
504. 26 December, to Anna Loring   255
505. 29 December, to Samuel G. Ward   255
506. 31 December, to William H. Channing   257

Index   259

ILLUSTRATIONS

THE FULLER FAMILY	*frontis*
RALPH WALDO EMERSON	*51*
CAROLINE STURGIS	*73*
DR. WILLIAM ELLERY CHANNING	*100*
FREDERIC HENRY HEDGE	*107*
BROOK FARM	*113*
NATHANIEL HAWTHORNE	*116*
JAMES FREEMAN CLARKE	*186*
MOUNT AUBURN CEMETERY, CAMBRIDGE	*203*
MACKINAC ISLAND	*222*
SING SING PRISON	*239*

ACKNOWLEDGMENTS

I am grateful to John C. Fuller, Willard P. Fuller, Elizabeth Channing Fuller, Richard E. Fuller, and Willard P. Fuller, Jr., for permission to publish Margaret Fuller's letters. I also thank the following institutions and individuals for permission to publish the Fuller letters in their possession that appear in this volume: the Barnard College Library of Columbia University; the Boston Athenaeum; the Trustees of the Boston Public Library; the Cambridge Public Library, Cambridge, Massachusetts; the Columbia University Libraries; Gene De Gruson; the Fruitlands Museums; the Trustees of the Ralph Waldo Emerson Memorial Association, the Harvard College Library, and the Houghton Library, Harvard University; the Andover-Harvard Theological Library of Harvard Divinity School; the Long Island Historical Society, Brooklyn, New York; the Massachusetts Historical Society; the Middlebury College Library; the Henry W. and Albert A. Berg Collection, the New York Public Library, Astor, Lenox, and Tilden Foundations; the University of Notre Dame Archives; the Providence Athenaeum, Providence, Rhode Island; the Princeton University Library; the Arthur and Elizabeth Schlesinger Library, Radcliffe College; the University of Rochester Library; the Morris Library, Southern Illinois University at Carbondale; the American Authors and Literature Collection, Manuscripts Department, Division of Special Collections, Stanford University Libraries; the Sarah Margaret Fuller Collection, Barrett Library, University of Virginia Library; the Special Collections, Wellesley College Library; and Nelson C. White. I am grateful for permission of the Fruitlands Museums to publish also excerpts from Margaret Fuller's journal for 1844. Excerpts from letters of Margarett Crane Fuller, Richard F. Fuller, Eliza Rotch Farrar, Caroline Sturgis, and Nathaniel Hawthorne are reproduced by permission of the Houghton Library.

The following librarians have been generous with their time and attention: John Alden of the Boston Public Library; Patricia K. Ballou of the Barnard College Library; Edmund Berkeley, Jr., and Barbara C. Bettcher of the University of Virginia Library; Thomas E. Blantz, C.S.C., of the University of Notre Dame archives; William H. Bond, director of the Houghton Library, Harvard University, and of the Ralph Waldo Emerson Memorial Association; Robert Buckeye of the Middlebury College Library; Annie C. Cooke of the Providence Athenaeum; Rodney G. Dennis of the Houghton Library, Harvard University; Pawel J. Depta of the Cambridge Public Library; Kenneth P. Duckett of the Southern Illinois University at Carbondale Library; Malcolm Freiberg of the Massachusetts Historical Society; Hazel C. Godfrey of the Wellesley College Library; Anne M. Gordon of the Long Island Historical Society; William H. Harrison of the Fruitlands Museums; Jack Jackson of the Boston Athenaeum; Carolyn Jakeman of the Houghton Library, Harvard University; Clifton Jones of the John Hay Library, Brown University; Karl Kabelac of the University of Rochester Library; James Lawton of the Boston Public Library; Marguerite Lechiaro of the Cambridge Public Library; Kenneth A. Lohf of the Columbia University Library; Richard M. Ludwig of the Princeton University Library; Marian Marx of the Schlesinger Library, Radcliffe College; Sylvia Moubayed of the Providence Athenaeum; Jeanne Newlin of the Houghton Library, Harvard University; Eleanor L. Nicholes of the Wellesley College Library; Patricia J. Palmer of the Stanford University Library; Jean F. Preston of the Princeton University Library; Stephen Provizer of the Boston Athenaeum; Wanda M. Randall of the Princeton University Library; Richard S. Reed of the Fruitlands Museums; Stephen T. Riley of the Massachusetts Historical Society; Alan Seaburg of the Andover-Harvard Theological Library; Marte Shaw of the Houghton Library, Harvard University; Elizabeth Shenton of the Schlesinger Library, Radcliffe College; Lola L. Szladits, Berg Collection, New York Public Library; and Louis L. Tucker of the Massachusetts Historical Society.

I am grateful to the following individuals for help in securing illustrations for this and the previous volumes of Fuller letters: Marylou Birchmore of the Essex Institute; Joyce M. Botelho of the Rhode Island Historical Society; Jane S. Byrne of the Metropolitan Museum of Art; George Dimock of Smith College; Suzanne Embree of the National Portrait Gallery, the Smithsonian Institution; Jayne K. Gordon of the Louisa May Alcott Memorial Association, Concord, Massachu-

Acknowledgments

setts; Jonathan Harding of the Boston Athenaeum; Allen Hamilton of the Boston Public Library; Euginia Kaledin of the Massachusetts Institute of Technology; Robin McElheny of the Schlesinger Library, Radcliffe College; Laura Monti of the Boston Public Library; Marcia E. Moss of the Concord Free Public Library, Concord, Massachusetts; Sally Pierce of the Boston Athenaeum; Carl Seaburg of the Unitarian Universalist Association; Elizabeth Shenton of the Schlesinger Library, Radcliffe College; Roger E. Stoddard of the Houghton Library, Harvard University; John Wright of the Essex Institute; and Roberta Zonghi of the Boston Public Library.

Among the scholars who have answered my many queries are Patricia Barber, Charles Blackburn, Paula Blanchard, Arthur W. Brown, Lynn Cadwallader, Joseph Jay Deiss, Russell E. Durning, Alfred R. Ferguson, Elizabeth Maxfield-Miller, Howard N. Meyer, Margaret Nussendorfer, Bruce A. Ronda, Carl F. Strauch, and Richard P. Wunder. I am particularly grateful for the generous advice of Eleanor M. Tilton and Madeleine B. Stern. Kathy Fuller of the Division of Research Programs at the National Endowment for the Humanities was generous with her help; Karen Szymanski discovered several holographs for me; Stephen Riley of the Massachusetts Historical Society kindly gave me access to the large, uncatalogued collections of Channing and Clarke family papers at the Society's library. I am glad to be able to acknowledge the patient support extended me by my departmental chairmen: Robert B. Heilman and Robert D. Stevick of the University of Washington, and David Stewart, Arthur O. Lewis, Robert Worth Frank, Jr., and Wendell V. Harris of the Pennsylvania State University. I have received valuable advice from colleagues, most notably John D. C. Buck, Gary Collison, Robert D. Hume, John Moore, and James Rambeau, of the Pennsylvania State University. Wilma R. Ebbitt gave her time and knowledge on many occasions; Charles Mann, the Rare Books and Manuscripts Librarian of the Pennsylvania State University, has helped me gather source materials for the edition. I make special note of the help and encouragement that I have received from Joel Myerson of the University of South Carolina. His work on Fuller has been constantly valuable to me; he has gone out of his way to give me access to his materials.

It is a distinct pleasure to acknowledge the help given me by several very skilled research assistants. Iris Malveau helped with my calendar of Fuller letters; Carolyn Kephart read manuscripts to me and worked on the annotations; Charles Hackenberry read manuscripts, hunted down elusive quotations, and applied himself to problems of bibliography; Larry Carlson and Ann Hostetler both undertook major assignments with the annotations and repeatedly pierced obscurities. Once more Robert D. Habich has been unfailingly tireless and patient as he checked the final draft, helped with the proofs, and took on some of the most puzzling references. Barbara Salazar, senior manuscript editor of Cornell University Press, saved me from many errors and gave me her expert advice. To my wife, Kay Hudspeth, I owe more than my acknowledgment will convey.

This volume of Fuller letters has received financial support from the University of Washington Graduate School Research Fund; the Pennsylvania State University College of Liberal Arts Research Fund, administered by Thomas Magner; and the Pennsylvania State University Institute for the Arts and Humanistic Studies, administered by Stanley Weintraub. I am grateful for this support. The preparation of all of the volumes in this edition was made possible in part by grants from the Program for Editions of the National Endowment for the Humanities, an independent federal agency.

R. N. H.

EDITORIAL METHOD

This edition brings together for the first time all of the known extant letters written by Margaret Fuller. The texts are presented in their entirety in chronological order. Only conservative emendations, as outlined below under "Text," have been incorporated in the text; all others are recorded in textual notes. The text has been prepared from holographs whenever possible. When a holograph is lacking, the text is based on a manuscript copy of the lost holograph. When two manuscript copies of the same letter survive in the absence of a holograph, the more nearly complete version has been chosen. If both are of the same length, I have chosen the copy prepared by the Fuller family, because a spot comparison of other family copies with their surviving holographs shows them to be more nearly accurate than copies by other hands, if not exact. Only those letters with no manuscript authority have been taken from printed sources. Those letters dated by year only appear at the head of the year; those dated only by month, at the head of the month; undated letters come at the end of the edition, arranged alphabetically by recipient when known.

To establish the text, I first gathered microfilm or photocopies of all the manuscript letters and then made typed copies of these photoreproductions. I also typed all of the letters that now exist only in printed versions. I then corrected the typescript twice: first an assistant read aloud to me all of the photoreproductions and the printed versions of the letters; later, two other assistants (working with me at different times) accompanied me to the libraries that hold the original manuscripts and read those manuscripts aloud to me as I again corrected the typescript. (Three letters were not read during this second check, for I was unable to visit three libraries.)

The final text derives from the corrected typescript, and proof was read aloud.

Format

The letters are numbered chronologically and the recipients identified in uniform headings. All dates, locations, salutations, and signatures are regularized in the following manner: dates and locations are set flush against the right margin, salutations flush against the left margin; signatures are set in large and small capitals and indented from the right margin at the bottom of the letter; when two or more initials are used in a signature, they are regularized with a space between each pair.

Text

The text is presented as faithfully as possible with conservative emendations. Fuller's spelling, capitalization, and punctuation are retained, as are her occasional slips of the pen (e.g., *and and*). Her end punctuation is often ambiguous, for her period resembles a comma. In all instances this mark is preserved as a period. Punctuation is supplied in brackets only when its absence leads to confusion. A paragraph is often indicated in the holographs only by a space at the end of the preceding line. In all such instances the following paragraph is silently indented. Fuller used the dash as an all-purpose mark of punctuation; her dashes are consistently retained. Abbreviations are not expanded save in those instances where ambiguities might otherwise result. When expanded, the additions are enclosed in square brackets. Cancellations are omitted from the text, and interlined additions are lowered; all such emendations are reported in the textual notes. Cross-hatching (Fuller occasionally turned the sheet and wrote at a right angle across her letter) and all symbols, notes, and marks added by later hands are emended and unreported. The German ß is set as "ss"; "&" becomes "and." Unless otherwise noted, the matter canceled by a later hand in the collection at the Boston Public Library has been recovered. All the letters and fragments taken from Emerson's "Ossoli" journal (MH: bMS Am 1280 [111]) are in his hand.

Annotation and Index

The text of each letter is followed by a provenance note that indicates the source of the text, any surviving manuscript copies, any previous publishing history, the name and address of the recipient as written by Fuller, the postmark, and the recipient's endorsement, if any. A brief biography of the recipient follows the provenance note to the first surviving letter to him or her, unless the recipient has already been identified. Then come textual notes listing editorial emendations, Fuller's cancellations, and her interlined insertions. Fuller's words here are set in roman type; editorial interpolations are set in italics.

The numbered annotations that follow the textual notes identify all people mentioned in the letter except those well known to readers (e.g., Dante, Shakespeare, Milton) and those previously identified, and all books, literary and historical allusions, and quotations that can be established. Brief biographies of well-known individuals who are not identified in the notes can be found in *Webster's Biographical Dictionary.*

Citations to the Massachusetts vital records office take two forms. Citations to nineteenth-century records refer only to volume and page numbers. Thus "MVR 129:84" cites page 84 of volume 129 of the death record. Beginning in this century, the reference has a preceding date. Thus "MVR 1910 15:108" cites the death record for 1910, volume 15, page 108. Unless otherwise noted, all citations are to death records.

Publication data come from the *National Union Catalog* of the Library of Congress or, when necessary, from the *British Museum General Catalogue of Printed Books.* Occasional notes explain ambiguities in the text, summarize events in Fuller's life, or refer the reader to other letters. The surviving letters written to Fuller have provided explanatory material for many of the annotations. Unidentified items are usually silently passed over.

An appendix in the final volume lists chronologically the letters Fuller is known to have written but which have not survived.

Each volume of the letters has a separate index. A comprehensive index appears in the final volume.

Editorial Apparatus

Textual Devices

The following devices are used in the text:

[Square brackets] enclose editorial additions.
[*Italics*] indicate editorial comments.
[I] [II] [III] indicate sections of a letter recovered from various sources.
[   ] marks matter missing from the text.
Superscript^n refers the reader to a textual note.
Superscript^1 refers the reader to an explanatory note.

The following devices are used in the textual notes:

⟨Angle brackets⟩ identify recovered cancellations.
⟨?⟩ identifies unrecovered cancellations.
↑ Opposed arrows ↓ indicate interlined insertions.
Italics indicate editorial comments.

Descriptive Symbols

AL	Autograph letter, unsigned
ALC	Autograph copy of a letter
ALfr	Autograph letter fragment, unsigned
ALfrS	Autograph letter fragment, signed with name or initial(s)
ALS	Autograph letter, signed with name or initial(s)
AMs	Autograph manuscript; may not be a letter for the reason stated
EL	Edited letter, as previously published; holograph now lost
ELfr	Edited letter fragment, as previously published; holograph now lost

MsC   Manuscript copy of a Fuller letter in a hand other than Fuller's; unless otherwise indicated, the holograph has not been recovered

MsCfr   Manuscript copy of a fragment of a Fuller letter in a hand other than Fuller's; unless otherwise indicated, the holograph has not been recovered

Location Symbols

CSt	Stanford University Library
ICarbS	Southern Illinois (Carbondale) Library
IND-Archives	University of Notre Dame Archives
MB	Boston Public Library, Department of Rare Books and Manuscripts
MBAt	Boston Athenaeum Library
MC	Cambridge Public Library
MCR-S	Radcliffe College, Schlesinger Library
MH	Harvard University, Houghton Library
MH-AH	Harvard Divinity School, Andover-Harvard Theological Library
MHarF	Fruitlands Museums, Harvard, Massachusetts
MHi	Massachusetts Historical Society
MWelC	Wellesley College Library
NBLiHi	Long Island Historical Society
NjP	Princeton University Library
NN-B	New York Public Library, Henry W. and Albert A. Berg Collection
NNC	Columbia University Library
NNC-B	Barnard College Library
NRU	University of Rochester Library
RPA	Providence Athenaeum
ViU	University of Virginia Library
VtMiM	Middlebury College Library

Short Titles and Abbreviations

Appletons' Cyclopaedia: *Appletons' Cyclopaedia of American Biography*, ed. James Grant Wilson and John Fiske, 6 vols. (New York: D. Appleton, 1888–89).

Briggs, *Cabot Family*: L. Vernon Briggs, *History and Genealogy of the Cabot Family*, 2 vols. (Boston: C. E. Goodspeed, 1927).

Bullard, *Rotches*: John M. Bullard, *The Rotches* (New Bedford, Mass.: Privately published, 1947).

CC: *Columbian Centinel* (Boston).

Charvat, "Emerson's Lecture Engagements": William Charvat, "A Chronological List of Emerson's American Lecture Engagements," *Bulletin of the New York Public Library* 64 (1960):492–507.

Chevigny: Bell Gale Chevigny, *The Woman and the Myth: Margaret Fuller's Life and Writings* (Old Westbury, N.Y.: Feminist Press, 1976).

CVR: *Vital Records of Cambridge, Massachusetts, to the Year 1850*, 2 vols. (Boston: Wright & Potter, 1914–15).

DAB: *Dictionary of American Biography*, ed. Allen Johnson and Dumas Malone, 20 vols. (New York: Scribner's, 1928–36).

DNB: *Dictionary of National Biography*, ed. Leslie Stephen and Sidney Lee, 22 vols. (London: Oxford University Press, 1937–38).

Edgell, "Bronson Alcott's 'Autobiographical Index'": David P. Edgell, "Bronson Alcott's 'Autobiographical Index,'" *New England Quarterly* 14 (1941): 704–15.

Frothingham, *Memoir of William Henry Channing*: Octavius Brooks Frothingham, *Memoir of William Henry Channing* (Boston: Houghton Mifflin, 1886).

Greeley Family: George Hiram Greeley, *Genealogy of the Greely-Greeley Family* (Boston: F. Wood, 1905).

Harding, *Days of Henry Thoreau*: Walter Harding, *Days of Henry Thoreau* (New York: Knopf, 1965).

Harding, *Emerson's Library*: Walter Harding, *Emerson's Library* (Charlottesville: University Press of Virginia, 1967).

Heralds: Samuel A. Eliot, *Heralds of a Liberal Faith*, 3 vols. (Boston: American Unitarian Association, 1910).

Higginson, *Descendants of the Reverend Francis Higginson*: Thomas Wentworth Higginson, *Descendants of the Reverend Francis Higginson* ([Cambridge?, Mass.]: Privately published, 1910).

Higginson, *MFO*: Thomas Wentworth Higginson, *Margaret Fuller Ossoli* (Boston: Houghton Mifflin, 1884).

Hodges Family: Almon D. Hodges, Jr., *Genealogical Record of the Hodges Family of New England, Ending December 31, 1894* (Boston: Privately published, 1896).

JMN: *The Journals and Miscellaneous Notebooks of Ralph Waldo Emerson*, ed. William H. Gilman et al., 16 vols. (Cambridge: Belknap Press of Harvard University Press, 1960–82).

Kirby, *Years of Experience*: Georgiana Bruce Kirby, *Years of Experience* (New York: Putnam, 1887).

Letters of JFC: *The Letters of James Freeman Clarke to Margaret Fuller*, ed. John Wesley Thomas (Hamburg: Cram, de Gruyter, 1957).

Memoirs: *Memoirs of Margaret Fuller Ossoli*, ed. R. W. Emerson, W. H. Channing, and J. F. Clarke, 2 vols. (Boston: Phillips, Sampson, 1852).

Miller: *Margaret Fuller: American Romantic*, ed. Perry Miller (Garden City, N.Y.: Doubleday, 1963).

MVR: Massachusetts vital records, Boston.

Myerson, "Margaret Fuller's 1842 Journal": Joel Myerson, "Margaret Fuller's 1842 Journal: At Concord with the Emersons," *Harvard Library Bulletin* 21 (1973):320–40.

Myerson, *New England Transcendentalists and the "Dial"*: Joel Myerson, *The New England Transcendentalists and the "Dial"* (Rutherford, N.J.: Fairleigh Dickinson University Press, 1980).

NEHGS: The New England Historic Genealogical Society, Boston.

OCGL: Henry and Mary Garland, *The Oxford Companion to German Literature* (Oxford: Clarendon Press, 1976).

Pope, *Loring Genealogy*: Charles Henry Pope, *Loring Genealogy* (Cambridge, Mass.: Murray & Emery, 1917).

Randall, *Poems*: John W. Randall, *Poems of Nature and Life*, ed. F. E. Abbot (Boston: G. H. Ellis, 1899).

Rusk, *Letters of RWE*: *The Letters of Ralph Waldo Emerson*, ed. Ralph L. Rusk, 6 vols. (New York: Columbia University Press, 1939).

Shepard, *Pedlar's Progress*: Odell Shepard, *Pedlar's Progress* (Boston: Little, Brown, 1937).

Sturgis of Yarmouth: *Edward Sturgis of Yarmouth, Massachusetts*, ed. Roger Faxton Sturgis (Boston: Privately published by Stanhope Press, 1914).

Tennyson, *Poems*: Alfred Tennyson, *Poems*, 2 vols. (Boston: William D. Ticknor, 1842).

Tharp, *Peabody Sisters*: Louise Hall Tharp, *The Peabody Sisters of Salem* (Boston: Little, Brown, 1950).

VR: vital records.

Wade: *The Writings of Margaret Fuller*, ed. Mason Wade (New York: Viking Press, 1941).

WNC: Margaret Fuller Ossoli, *Woman in the Nineteenth Century, and Kindred Papers*, ed. Arthur B. Fuller (Boston: John P. Jewett, 1855).

Works: Manuscript copybooks, Fuller family papers, 3 vols., in Houghton Library, Harvard University.

Works of George Herbert: *The Works of George Herbert*, ed. F. E. Hutchinson (Oxford: Clarendon Press, 1941).

THE LETTERS OF MARGARET FULLER

345. To Margarett C. Fuller

Saturday 1st Jany
1842.

I wish you a happy new year, dear Mother. May the coming months bring you hope, clear knowledge, and a point of support in life.

I sent you two letters by post, one from Ellen, one from Uncle A.—[1] The first, I thought, would please you. As to going to Cincinnati if they should decide to remain there; it would be, in some respects, a pleasant home for you, but if the climate has a tendency to create bile would it not be dangerous, as these attacks of yours seem to be of the nature of bilious cholic?

I thought you would be highly pleased at the idea of selling Easton *without* the wood lot. Send to my care by Mr Cleverly your answer to Uncle A.[2]

Letters from Arthur and Richard show them well and happy.[3] A paper from Eugene to say he is well, and that W. H. will write directly to Uncle H. about reconveying the property.[4] I shall think myself fortunate if it ends by my only having all this trouble for nothing.

My week has fled as all my weeks do with the speed of lightning. When I wrote to you I was exceedingly fatigued but Sunday was a day of rest and meditation and I have been better ever since. In the eveg I went again to hear the" Messiah. Braham[5] was gone, but the music was there and I enjoyed it greatly. With all the fatigue and interruption I decidedly prefer living in town during the winter, if only for this that I can in the eveg hear fine music which raises my spirits and refreshes me in the best way.

On Tuesday eveg the Wards had Rakemann to play for them at Chickering's rooms on the very finest piano I *ever* heard.[6] E. Cumming and B. and M. had the pleasure of hearing him too.[7] I went home with Anna and staid all night, had a pleasant time with them. The baby grows more and more lovely. Has not Fanny's improved very much.[8] I wish she would write me about it, and about herself. Tell her she must not fail this time. Anna asked a great deal about her, and about the baby. Has she given its name decisively yet, and what is it *Frances Ellen*? Is not grandmother pleased with this first great grandchild.[9]

Uncle William has lost his wife. She died of consumption— His child is well.[10]

William Channing [was] at Mr E's lecture, and wa[lke]d with me to Anna Shaw's who [ha]d a party after it.[11] He s[eeme]d well and bright, asked e[speciall]y after you: it is the only time [I] have seen him this week, but [exp]ect to tonight.

One o clock. Re[turn]ing home I found several pretty presents, among others a beautiful vase, and more beautiful bouquet one from M Ward, the other from A. Shaw.[12] I wish you were here to see my flowers Find also a letter from Eugene dated 20th Decr, he is well, for the rest tells only what you know about W. and his wishing Fanny to join him. About this I can have nothing to say.

I send Charles Crane's Dial; his name put down Cram by W and J. thought I might as well save" his postage.[13] Also a Dial for you." They had not credited him as having paid, which is just a specimen of their way of carrying on business Praise Allah! it is now transferred. I send some nice tea, with which you may regale yourself in company with Grandmother and Aunt.[14]

Don't fail to write me all about yourself, and send back Charles O Malley,[15] your always affectionate

M.

I have tried the drawers; they fit perfectly. Many thanks both to you and F. I forgot the tape when out; will send it next week if not now.

ALS (MH: fMS Am 1086 [9:80]); MsC (MH: fMS Am 1086 [Works, 2:555–61]). *Addressed*: Mrs [Margarett Fuller] / Canton / Mass / Politeness / Mr Cleverly.

Her mother was Margarett Crane Fuller, daughter of Peter and Elizabeth Crane of Canton, Massachusetts.

The sheet has been cut to remove her mother's name from the address.

hear the] hear ↑ the ↓
as well save] as well ⟨pay⟩ ↑ save ↓
Also a Dial for you.]   ↑ Also a Dial for you. ↓

1. Fuller's sister, Ellen Kilshaw Fuller, married the poet Ellery Channing in 1841. The couple was living in Cincinnati, where Ellery was working for a newspaper. Abraham Williams Fuller, Margaret's uncle, was a Boston lawyer and businessman who was the executor of her father's estate. His handling of the money was a continual source of irritation for Margaret and her mother.

2. Asa Cleverly, a Universalist minister who lived in Boston, was preaching in Canton on Sundays. His wife was Rebecca Whiton Cleverly of Hingham.

3. Margaret's brother Arthur Buckminster was then a student at Harvard; her brother Richard Frederick was in Concord preparing for college.

4. Her eldest brother, Eugene, was a businessman in New Orleans; her brother William Henry, a failed businessman, was planning to move to New Orleans. Their uncle Henry Holton Fuller was a lawyer in Boston.

5. John Braham (born Abraham) was a popular tenor who often sang in Boston.

6. In 1839 Fuller was in love with Samuel G. Ward, an aspiring painter who became a banker instead. In 1840 he broke off from Fuller to marry her good friend Anna Barker. Frederic William Rackemann was a German-born pianist who began his Boston career in 1839. The firm of J. Chickering, Piano Maker, moved to Boston from New Hampshire in 1818 (Christine Ayars, *Contributions to the Art of Music in America by the Music Industries of Boston, 1640 to 1936* [New York, 1937], pp. 111–12).

7. Elizabeth Randall Cumming and her sisters, Belinda and Maria Randall, were Fuller's close friends. They were the daughters of Dr. John Randall of Boston.

8. Anna Barker Ward, the Wards' first child, was then three months old. Fuller's niece, Cornelia, daughter of William Henry and Frances Hastings Fuller, was born on 23 October 1841.

9. Her grandmother Crane.

10. Mary Fletcher (1813–41), daughter of Nathaniel and Sarah Fletcher of Kennebunk, Maine, married Fuller's uncle William Williams Fuller on 16 August 1840. She died during the first week of December 1841 (Robert Fletcher, *Fletcher Genealogy: An Account of the Descendants of Robert Fletcher, of Concord, Mass.* [Boston, 1871], p. 188; Harvard archives).

11. William Henry Channing was one of Fuller's most frequent correspondents. A nephew of the celebrated Dr. William Ellery Channing, William Henry graduated from Harvard in 1829 and was ordained in the Unitarian ministry. In 1836 he married Julia Allen (1813–89), daughter of William and Maria Allen of Rondout, New York (Higginson, *Descendants of the Reverend Francis Higginson*, p. 32). Never completely settled in his early ministry, he had recently resigned his pulpit in Cincinnati. For many years Mrs. Fuller had been impressed by his ability. Emerson delivered "Manners," the fifth lecture of his series "The Times," on 30 December 1841 (Charvat, "Emerson's Lecture Engagements," p. 504). Anna Blake Shaw, daughter of Robert Gould Shaw, was Fuller's close friend. She later married William Batchelder Greene.

12. Mary Ward, the daughter of Thomas Wren and Lydia Ward, later married Charles Hazen Dorr.

13. The firm of Weeks & Jordan in Boston was the first publisher of the *Dial*, the literary journal Fuller, Emerson, and their friends began in 1840. She was at this time coming to the end of her two-year editorship of the magazine. Fuller's cousin Charles P. Crane, son of Simeon and Elizabeth Crane of Canton, married Elizabeth Watson, daughter of William and Mary Watson of Nantucket, in 1846 (Nantucket VR).

14. Abigail Crane, Margaret's aunt, lived in Canton.

15. Charles James Lever (1806–72), *Charles O'Malley, the Irish Dragoon* (Dublin, 1840–41). An American edition of the novel was published in Philadelphia.

33

346. To Richard F. Fuller

Thursday eveg
6th Jany. [1842]

My dear Richard,

I could not last week find the letter from Ellen which I now send you, accompanied by my last[n] from mother, Send both back next week.

I have since recd another from Ellery and Ellen but have mislaid it. There is no important news in it. Also a specimen number of Ellery's newspaper, the Cincini Gazette. It must give him a great deal of drudgery, being a weekly, triweekly, and daily paper.— If you have not already written, I wish you would to them directly. Ellen seems so to long to hear oftener from her family.

Mr Keats, Emma's father, is dead;[1] to me this brings unusual sorrow,[n] though I had never yet seen him, but I thought of him as one of the very few persons known to me by reputation whose acquaintance might enrich me. His character was a sufficient answer to the doubt whether a merchant can be a man of honor; he was like your father, a man all whose virtues had stood the test;[2] he was no "Word-Hero."— Emma loses a friend in her father, his other children lose all; they have no relatives on this soil, and I understand his affairs were embarrassed; that is to say they were in such a state that he would have cleared them, if he had lived, but agents are not likely to make his claims available.

Do you keep Lloyd in your[n] thoughts as Mother hoped.[3] I begin to think with anxiety what can be done for him in the Spring. He made me a little visit the other day. I do not know what to make of him, or what can be done with him. He seemed very sweet, but every thing he said was so unreal.

You can visit Mr Alcott sometimes with profit, but keep your eyes open and steady to look at him on all sides.[4]

I will not write any more tonight, for I have been ill, and am still weak and languid so that the pen is not good for me. With prayerful best wishes your affectionate sister

MARGARET.

Write to Lloyd next week, if you can and send by Mr E. I expect to go out and see him on Friday.

ALS (MH: fMS Am 1086 [9:87]); MsCfr (MH: fMS Am 1086 [Works, 2:671–75]). *Addressed*: R. F. Fuller / Concord Mass. / Mr. Emerson.

by my last] by ⟨one⟩ ↑ my last ↓
unusual sorrow,] unusual⟨ly⟩ sorrow,
in your] in ↑ your ↓

1. George Keats, the poet's brother, was a businessman in Cincinnati. He sent his daughter Emma to school in New England, where she was Fuller's pupil.
2. Timothy Fuller, Margaret's father, had been a lawyer, congressman, and farmer. After serving in the U.S. House of Representatives he retired, moved to Groton, and died of cholera in 1835.
3. Her youngest brother, James Lloyd Fuller, appears to have been slightly retarded.
4. A. Bronson Alcott, a self-taught philosopher, writer, and teacher, had conducted experimental schools in Philadelphia and Boston (where Fuller had been his assistant) before turning to reform as his vocation. He was at this time living in Concord. Fuller had a wary friendship with Alcott, whose ideas she distrusted.

347. To Margarett C. Fuller

Boston.
8th Jany, 1842.

Dear Mother,

I did not know till just now that Mr Cleverly was not going to Canton, or I should have written last night, for I know you will be disappointed at not hearing from me before Monday.

Uncle H. has this week recd a letter from Wm requesting to have the property reconveyed to me.— He writes in good spirits, had his books made up, and expects his creditors will agree to a compromise.

As to Fanny's going out, the case is plain.[1] Beside the risk to the baby, she *must* live much more expensively because beside[n] the difference in the rate of living she must take a nurse. I do not doubt her situation is very fatiguing and dull, yet *not a few* but *very many* women, as young and untried, have found strength from a sense of duty to go through far more with cheerfulness. But, as you say, the want of steadiness and clear judgement in W. H. is a great excuse. I entirely agree with you that they must take their own course. I think you ought to make F fully aware from your greater experience of any dangers to her unforseen to which she may expose the infant, and *then*, if she *is* to go, why *the sooner the better*; why should she stay to make herself and others useless suffering. If she began to prepare *now* she could not join Wm before the middle of Feby. Do not show her this letter, if it will pain her uselessly; she is a sweet girl, and I am disposed as you desire to *"pity not blame."*

I have a letter this week from the two Es of Cincini, which I will

35

send you next oppory. All well;— Ellen is to sit for her picture with part of the money the Wards sent her. I shall be glad to have one of her at this time of loveliness and happiness. *Yours* dating from the same age and same position was a great pleasure to me as it hung in my chamber[n] last winter. I hope Fanny's too will be carefully pre-served I wish there had been one taken of dear Eugene at 18 when he was so beautiful.

I have been quite ill, and nothing could exceed the kindness of Aunt M. and S. Clarke.[2] Uncle H. and Aunt M. are most kind to me, considering my comfort in every way and doing little things for me. I think you, usually too indulgent, are not sufficiently so in your esti-mate of Aunt M. I will tell you when I come what I think of it.[3]

Mrs Clarke has not yet left her chamber.[4] I would send love, if she knew I was writing. I gave your message to M. Jackson who is now better, she seemed pleased[5] Belinda was here yesterday; she wanted to know if you were not coming and I gave your message. E. is much better lately.[6] I have not seen her since Sunday, when at my invite she went with a party of us to hear Rakemann play Beethoven's music, and afterwards to the beautiful new church to hear the organ tried.[7] Lloyd came into town while I was ill (by the way I forgot to mention that I am well now) and Aunt M. went out and bought the stuffs for him. Mrs R. says she will see to having the clothes made.—[8] I want you to send me an order for Uncle A. to furnish me money when I want it for boys— dont forget this.— Will write about Easton when every thing is settled liked your letter very much.

Mr. Keats is dead!— He died on the 29th Dec of rapid consumption. It is said he has left his affairs in an embarrassed state, though if he had lived he would have cleared them up. Thus will wife and children have much to feel in his loss, beside that which I, for one, deeply feel of the loss of his presence in the world. I wish we had met and be-come friends, as I am sure we should maugre all unpleasant circum-stances that have intervened. Farewell. Love to Grandmother. I thank her for her affectionate thoughts of me and hope to see her ere long. Love to Aunt Abby and no less to Fanny, and a kiss to the dear little baby. Most affetly your daughter

MARGARET.

Have just recd a bundle from the Kuhns for you.[9] Shall send it, if Miss Kinslay knows of an oppory.

ALS (MH: fMS Am 1086 [9:98]); MsC (MH: fMS Am 1086 [Works, 2:561–69]). *Ad-dressed:* Mrs Margaret Fuller / Canton / Mass.

because beside] because ⟨she⟩ beside
my chamber] my cham⟨p⟩ber

1. Frances Fuller, William Henry's wife, was planning to join her husband in New Orleans. Both Margaret and her mother feared for the health of Fanny and her child.

2. Aunt M. is Mary Stone Fuller, Henry Holton Fuller's wife. S. Clarke is Sarah Clarke, one of Fuller's closest friends. She was a painter who had studied with Washington Allston.

3. In her response, Mrs. Fuller said of her sister-in-law: "You judge from your experience, and I from mine. I do know that never any person had less of *personal kindness*, I will not say *heart felt sympathy* than I have received from my husband's family since his death" (Margarett Crane Fuller to Margaret Fuller, n.d., MH).

4. Probably her mother's good friend Marianne Mackintosh Clarke, who is mentioned in several letters. The daughter of Peter and Dorcas Mackintosh, she married Thomas Clarke of New Orleans in 1837.

5. Marianne Jackson, daughter of Judge Charles T. Jackson of Boston, had been Fuller's pupil.

6. Elizabeth Randall Cumming.

7. On 31 December 1841 the new building of the Central Congregational Church was dedicated in Boston. The *Boston Daily Evening Transcript* called it "one of the most beautiful buildings in the city" (10 December 1841). The church was led by the Reverend William Matticks Rogers (1806–51) (William B. Sprague, *Annals of the American Pulpit* [New York, 1859], 2:730–32).

8. Lloyd was staying at Brook Farm, the experimental community established in Roxbury by George and Sophia Dana Ripley. Though never a member of Brook Farm, Margaret often visited there.

9. Nancy Weiser, Mrs. Fuller's half sister, married George Kuhn, a Boston businessman.

348. To Margarett C. Fuller

Boston, 15th
Jany. [1842]

Dear Mother,

I do hope this lovely day finds you better, but notwithstanding all you say I know very well you cannot have comforts where you are, good food and quiet at home, exercise and pleasant objects abroad such as your now delicate health requires. I intreat you to take every care of yourself for my sake and that of the children, if for nothing else.

Sam Ward recommended the Life Assurance company, as a perfectly safe place where to invest your money, and one where at his request they would probably receive it, though, he said, they did[n] not like the care of small sums. I think I had better not invest it till the other is recd also which you said would be due about this time. Worcester rail-road stock pays higher interest, but is not so certain. N England bank stock about the same, write, if you have any preference among these three.—

Have you heard of the death of Eleanor Shattuck, of Russell Freeman—[1] and of Mr Bussey.— It is said that the beautiful place at J. P. is bequeathed to Mrs Motley during her life. I hope she will allow as free entrance to the beautiful wood as her grandfathers did.[2]

All our friends are well. Mary Channing said she should bring here a letter for you, if recd in time I shall inclose it.[3] I send one from me to Eugene which, having read, please put into the post-office next time you send. Return Richard's.— The Channings had a letter from Ellen this week; no news of importance, I believe.

I could not but sympathize with your tender feeling about poor Fanny yet I feel that it would have been much better for Wm as well as herself, if she could have seen clearly the right, and persisted in her own view. He would have seen with her by and by. However I do not wish to say any more. I suppose she will go.

I expect to come to Canton the first week in Feby, probably the latter part of the week, but will write again about it.

I am very much grieved to hear of your ague, pray take all possible care against cold.

I will give you my diary since F. was here.

Tuesday p. m. Lesson from half-past three till five, S. Howes, a fine generous English sort of girl who interests me much.—[4] Half-past five tea at Mrs Bancroft's. Sir John Caldwell there an elderly Engh Baronet who has become much interested in the Science of the Soul.[5] To Mr Walker's lecture with them.[6] Immense crowd up to the very roof of the Odeon. Lecture in a truly large noble and gentle spirit. Finished little before 9. Home to Mrs B's Mr Eames of N. York there, a showy but also really "talent-full" young man who is lecturing here.[7]

Wednesday. Walk after breakfast; Lesson M. Ward from ten to half-past eleven. Dress— class from twelve till two— pretty good time. P. M. wrote awhile then lay down. Mr Eames's lecture, went with Bancrofts and Baronet, like himself showy but brilliant. To Peabody's[n] where Mr and Mrs Grattun were to meet me.[8] Charles Sumner tells me his far famed stories of Prince Metternich[9] Mr and Mrs Grattun.— Mr a jocose bon vivant— Mrs a sweet and kind woman who has read a great deal and thought somewhat— Home *too* tired.

Thursday— walk, lessons from ten till one, very tired, walk and go see Mrs Farrar a moment.[10] P. M.— Mrs Cleverly, now recovered, puts all the obstacles she can in the way of my reception evening. Left Aunt M and Sarah C. to Mary and went to give a lesson half past three till five. Lay down a short time, Mrs Symonds made me tea in my room got dressed in time for lecture After lecture a large and brilliant circle, Wards, Shaws, Greenoughs Sturgiss many pleasant men Eames the lecturer, Eames the painter, Sir John flying about with busy delight James Clarke concocting bon mots in a corner.[11] Mr E. enjoyed it[12]

ALfr (MH: fMS Am 1086 [9:99]); MsCfr (MH: fMS Am 1086 [Works, 2:263–69]).

they did] they ⟨pai⟩ did

To Peabody's] To Pea⟨?⟩body's

1. Eleanor Elizabeth Shattuck, daughter of George and Amelia Shattuck, died on 5 January, aged 23. Her father was the most prominent doctor in Boston (*CVR: DAB*). Russell Freeman (1782–1842), son of the Honorable Nathaniel and Tryphosa Freeman, was a lawyer in Sandwich. He died suddenly of a heart attack on 9 January. In 1817 he had married Eliza Jackson Sturgis (1793–1870), a distant cousin of Caroline Sturgis (Frederick Freeman, *Freeman Genealogy* [Boston, 1875], pp. 120, 202; *Sturgis of Yarmouth*, p. 38).

2. Benjamin Bussey (1757–1842) died on 13 January. A Revolutionary War soldier, a silversmith, and a horticulturalist, the very wealthy Bussey developed Woodland Hill, a 300-acre estate in Roxbury. He willed one-half of the estate to Harvard, which later used the bequest to establish the Bussey Institute, a school of practical agriculture and horticulture. On 24 August 1780 Bussey married Judith Gay (1762–1849), daughter of Joshua and Sarah Gay of Dedham (Francis S. Drake, *The Town of Roxbury* [Roxbury, 1878], pp. 53, 440; *Twentieth Century Biographical Dictionary of Notable Americans* [Boston, 1904]); Roxbury VR; Dedham VR). Mrs. Motley was Bussey's granddaughter, Maria Antoinette Davis (1814–94), daughter of Charles and Eliza Bussey Davis, who married Thomas Motley, Jr. (1812–64), in 1834. In 1842 the Motleys were living at Woodland Hill (*CVR*; MVR 447:347, 176:67; *CC* 15 November 1834).

3. Ellery Channing's sister Mary Elizabeth later married Fuller's biographer, Thomas Wentworth Higginson.

4. Susan Howes (1822–1907), daughter of Frederick and Elizabeth Burley Howes of Salem, married Joseph S. Cabot (1796–1874) in 1852 (Salem VR; MVR 1907 10:26; Briggs, *Cabot Family*, pp. 647–48).

5. Fuller was on good terms with George Bancroft despite their small confrontation in 1834, when they disputed the character of Brutus in the Boston press. His wife, Elizabeth Davis Bancroft, was a member of Fuller's Conversations. Sir John Caldwell (1775–1842), a Canadian lawyer, had served as the receiver general of Lower Canada until he was dismissed during a scandal in 1823 (W. Stewart Wallace, *The Macmillan Dictionary of Canadian Biography*, 3d ed. [London, 1963]).

6. James Walker (1794–1874), Harvard's Alford Professor of Natural Religion, began a course of twelve lectures on "natural religion" on 11 January. The son of John and Lucy Johnson Walker of Burlington, Massachusetts, he graduated from Harvard in 1814 and from the Divinity School in 1817. After serving as minister at Charlestown, he joined the Harvard faculty and edited the *Christian Examiner* from 1831 to 1839. He was president of Harvard from 1853 to 1860. In 1829 Walker married Catharine Bartlett (1797–1868), daughter of George and Mary Gorham Bartlett (Harvard archives; *CC* 23 December 1829; MVR 212:98; *DAB*).

7. Charles Eames (1812–67) graduated at the head the Harvard class of 1831. First known as a lecturer, he became a diplomat under presidents Polk and Pierce before making a fortune in admiralty law. The *Boston Daily Advertiser* announced several lectures by Eames in Boston, the most recent of which had been at the Lyceum on Thursday, 13 January, the same night Emerson delivered a lecture, "Man's Relation to Nature," at the Masonic Temple (Harvard archives).

8. The Peabodys were Dr. Nathaniel Peabody of Salem; his wife, Elizabeth; and their daughters, Mary, Elizabeth Palmer, and Sophia. Mary married Horace Mann; Elizabeth Palmer had a bookstore on West Street, where Fuller conducted her Conversations; Sophia was an artist who later married Nathaniel Hawthorne. Thomas Colley Grattan (1792–1864), an Irish writer who had written for several British reviews, was the British consul to Massachusetts from 1839 to 1846. He was admired as a speaker and storyteller. In 1818 he married Eliza O'Donnel (*DNB*).

9. Charles Sumner met Prince Klemens von Metternich in the autumn of 1839. Apparently his discussion with the Austrian diplomat concerned Jared Sparks's biography of George Washington (Edward L. Pierce, *Memoir and Letters of Charles Sumner* [Boston, 1877], 2:129).

10. Eliza Rotch married Professor John Farrar, a Harvard mathematician. She was an early and devoted friend of Fuller's.

11. Fuller's circle included the families of Sam Ward, Frank Shaw, Horatio Greenough, William Sturgis, and Joseph Alexander Ames (1816–72) of Roxbury, a self-taught painter. Fuller later knew Ames and his wife, the sculptor Sarah Clampitt Ames (1817–1901), when they were in Italy in 1848. James Freeman Clarke, Sarah's brother, was minister of Boston's Church of the Disciples. He had known Fuller, his distant relative, from the 1820s. The two had studied German together and had a long and deep friendship.

12. Despite his preoccupation with his own lectures, Emerson attended Fuller's party (Rusk, *Letters of RWE*, 3:3).

349. To Richard F. Fuller

[I] Saturday
[15? January? 1842?]

No time, dear Richard, to write this week. No news from any of the family except Mother, she is tolerably well

I wish you had said distinctly how much money you want. I send five dollars which perhaps is not enough. Yet this makes twenty I have sent you since Mother went away, so you see even your frugality does not enable you wholly to dispense with the circulating medium you so much dispise and whose use, when you have thought more deeply on these subjects, you will find to have been indispensable to the production of the arts, of literature and all that distinguishes civilized man. It is abused like all good things, but without it you would not have had your Horace and Virgil[n] stimulated by whose society you read the woods and fields to more advantage than Stilman Lawrence, or Edward Rice[1] [II] well, enjoy your fields and trees, supplicating the Spirit of all to bring you clear light and full sight.

Your always affectionate Sister

MARGARET

I: ALfr (MH: fMS Am 1086 [9:77]); II: MsCfr (MH: fMS Am 1086 [Works, 2:703]); MsC (MH: fMS Am 1086 [Works, 2:701–3]). Published in part in Higginson, *MFO*, p. 106. *Addressed:* R. F. Fuller, / Concord.

and Virgil] and Virgi(s)l

1. Edward Rice (b. 1824) was the son of William and Charlotte Rice of Sudbury (Andrew Henshaw Ward, *A Genealogical History of the Rice Family* [Boston, 1858], p. 239).

350. To Margarett C. Fuller

Saturday 22d Jany 1842.

Dearest Mother,

I have received this week no letters from the children, with the exception of Richard. I hope you have from Ellen, if so do send it me.

I have been shut up, this week and lost much time in consequence of sore throat. It came on with symptions of fever, but a blister drawn on the throat reduced inflammation, though a remedy so irritating has sometimes seemed as bad as the disease.

George Kuhn has been to see me. The rest of the money will be received in a few days and shall then be invested.

I am going to day to Spring St. and to see Lloyd, and to stay a day or two with the Ripley's and Mrs. Russell, so shall not hear from you till Tuesday night or Wednesday morning which seems a long time.[1] I want to hear that you have not had a return of the ague, or attack of any kind of pain.—

I intend to come to Canton a week from next *Monday* in the afternoon cars and stay till *Wednesday* afternoon. I shall bring one dress I should like to have made. Hope you will be able to give me all your time while I stay, for it is very inconvenient for me to come, and I should only do it from wishing to see just how you are situated, and to see F. and the baby in case of her going. But for this I should have deferred it till Spring, for cutting up my time now and postponing some lessons [   ] work upon me when I return.

Ask aunt to let me know how much Cambric I shall need for lining skirt and sleeves of the dress (my black Mousseline) and how much silk to pipe it. I intend to have folds on the boddice, which will require piping, also what kind of silk.

Do you want any thing I can get for you;

Mary Channing never brought a letter. Barbara has been staying

41

with the Ripley's two or three weeks and enjoys it highly.—[2]

I have a bouquet of most beautiful flowers, sent to me by Mrs. R. G.—the other night when I was quite unwell, they did me a world of good, all little sweet flowers such as you would like, tea-rose, helitrope, daphne, and a lovely branch of heath. I wish you could see them.

I send to day's Boston Notion that you may see all about Elder Knapp who is rousing the Community at such a rate.[3] The [   ] from New York express I thought would amuse you, but keep them with care and give them me when I come as they belong to Thomas.

Little Mary has got almost well and Mrs. Clarke down stairs.[4]

Love to Grandmother and Aunt A, I am glad I shall see them so soon, love to F.

I write in greatest haste, having every thing to do this morning.

Very affectionately yours,

MARGARET.

MsC (MH: fMS Am 1086 [Works, 2:569–73]).

1. Spring Street was in West Roxbury, the location of Brook Farm and the home of several of Fuller's friends. The Ripleys are George and Sophia Dana Ripley, founders of Brook Farm. Fuller had known them since her youth in Cambridge. She was also going to visit Sarah Shaw Russell (1811–88), daughter of Robert Gould and Elizabeth Shaw, and wife of George Robert Russell (1800–1866), a founder of the firm of Russell & Sturgis, one of the greatest China trading houses in America (John Russell Bartlett, *Genealogy of That Branch of the Russell Family Which Comprises the Descendants of John Russell of Woburn, Massachusetts, 1640–1878* [Providence, 1879], p. 52; MVR 393:279).

2. Mary and Barbara (1816–80) Channing, Ellery's sisters.

3. The *Quarto Boston Notion or Roberts' Weekly Journal of American and Foreign Literature, Fine Arts, and General News* for 22 January had several columns denouncing Jacob Knapp (1799–1874), a fiery itinerant evangelist, who had been invited to preach in Boston by the Church in Bowdoin Square. The *Notion* claimed that Knapp had driven several people to insanity and that he was being sued in Providence for slander (*Appletons' Cyclopaedia*).

4. Marianna Elizabeth Clarke (b. 1838), oldest daughter of Marianne Mackintosh Clarke, with whom Fuller was staying (John Clarke, *Records of the Descendants of Hugh Clark, of Watertown, Mass., 1640–1866* [Boston, 1866], p. 101).

351. To William H. Channing[?]

February 1842

I am deeply sad at the loss of little Waldo, from whom I hoped more than from almost any living being.[1] I cannot yet reconcile myself to the thought that the sun shines upon the grave of the beautiful blue-eyed boy, and I shall see him no more.

Five years he was an angel to us, and I know not that any person was ever more the theme of thought to me. As I walk the streets they swarm with apparently worthless lives, and the question will rise, why he, why just he, who "bore within himself the golden future," must be torn away? His father will meet him again; but to me he seems lost, and yet that is weakness. I *must* meet that which he represented, since I so truly loved it. He was the only child I ever saw, that I sometimes wished I could have called mine.

I loved him more than any child I ever knew, as he was of nature more fair and noble. You would be surprised to know how dear he was to my imagination. I saw him but little, and it was well; for it is unwise to bind the heart where there is no claim. But it is all gone, and is another of the lessons brought by each year, that we are to expect suggestions only, and not fulfilments, from each form of beauty, and to regard them merely as Angels of the Beauty.

ELfr, from *Memoirs*, 2:62–63.

1. Waldo Emerson, the poet's first child, died the evening of 27 January. The following day Emerson wrote Fuller: "My little boy must die also. All his wonderful beauty could not save him. He gave up his innocent breath last night and my world this morning is poor enough. He had Scarlatina on Monday night. Shall I ever dare to love any thing again. Farewell and Farewell, O my Boy!" (Rusk, *Letters of RWE*, 3:8).

352. To Margarett C. Fuller

Saturday 5th Feby, [1842]

Dearest Mother,

I suppose Charles[1] told you what a race we ran to reach the cars which, by good luck we accomplished in time. But it was, indeed, *by good luck*, for when I reached B. I found my watch, which was half an hour in advance of *your* time, twenty minutes slow of *B.*

I trust F. has heard something decisive by this time. I was much touched by her sweetness, naturalness, and perfect sincerity; I felt that she and W. H. are of age, that their characters are cast in a different mould from mine and that they had best take their fate entirely in their own hands.— Still should F. be detained here, contrary to her wishes, I trust she will look on the bright side, will feel that Heaven may have over ruled her wishes and judgment for the best.

Every one thinks that if her lovely infant survives the voyage, yet the change of climate will be dangerous for it, at this period," and whatever their feelings may be at present, I cannot think that either parent could look on the death of the child without remorse. I think both would feel that they had fallen very short of the responsibilities assumed by those who have put themselves in a position to become the guardians of a living soul. I feel sure that you and I could convince W. H. of the true nature of his conduct, and that they might meet again in more peace perhaps for the delay. I feel that, though there is a good deal of reason for F's course, she is also much influenced by her feelings. Still I do not wish, even if I could, to influence her, too vain have been my efforts to preserve others from error. I feel that each must encounter such ills as spring from his own character before they can be convinced. I think continually of the passage "He is of age, ask *him*"— Heaven will do so.

I inclose a letter from Ellen and Ellery I ventured to open it, as it was sent via me, and if you will excuse this *I feel sure they would.* I cannot help feeling much encouraged about them by these letters, though I do not wish to encourage hopes hastily. But Ellen does seem very sweet, equable, and so really satisfied, and four months of "close communion have passed now. I have just written to them, will you write next week?

I have also a parcel from Eugene with a sweet little note He says— "My address is Rose Hill, Amite County, Mississipi" (I hope you will write to him immedy— It is *Williams* who has got the place at *Clinton*.)" There will be no society or only that of unlettered cottonplanters, and I *must* remain *a year* with the recompense of about six hundred dollars a year beside all my expenses paid. The sum I mention I shall have in Jany— 43. I shall be lonely at first, but become reconciled to it very soon. Beside earning the money I shall try to improve my leisure time which will be considerable, as I have Saty and Sunday to myself I commence on Monday 17th Jany.

Braham has returned as if on purpose for you. I do not know how long he will stay, but probably not less than a fortnight. He is to sing tomorrow night at the oratorio and probably, also, a week from tomorrow night.[2] I want you then to come to town a week from today.— Mrs Cleverly will let you have the attic which is a neat room, and has in it a good bed, for three dollars and a half a week. You are offered Aunt M's parlor, Mrs Clarke's parlor or the other parlor to sit in *ad libitum* when you cannot be in my room, or you can have a fire in your own whenever you please as I have wood. The difference between [   ]

ALfr (MH: fMS Am 1086 [9:81]); MsC (MH: fMS Am 1086 [*Works*, 2:275–85]).

it at this period,] it ↑ at this period ↓ ,

1. Charles Crane, with whom Mrs. Fuller was staying in Canton.

2. The *Boston Daily Evening Telegraph* followed with warm approval the several concerts that Braham gave at this time. After a secular recital on Saturday, 5 February, he sang with the Handel and Haydn Society on the sixth and again on the thirteenth. He gave operatic concerts in Boston and other Massachusetts towns until the end of February.

353. To John S. Dwight

Thursday
[10? February 1842]

My dear Mr Dwight,

I enclose the sum I vainly attempted to rob from the musical public under cloak of your reputation.—[1] I shall not be able to hear your lecture as it is the last eveg my sister Fanny passes with us before a separation like to be a long one; but trust you will give your audience as much pleasure as you did last time.— The expressions of obligation that I heard were numerous. If there is a concert or rehearsal at the Odeon on Saty eveg will it be convenient for you to escort Caroline and myself?[2]

With regard

S. M. FULLER

ALS (Collection of Gene De Gruson).

John Sullivan Dwight was living at Brook Farm, where he wrote and lectured on music. A graduate of Harvard and of the Divinity School in Cambridge, Dwight became a music critic and editor.

In a letter of 6 February (MH), Fuller's mother noted that Frances Fuller was going to Boston the next day to prepare for her New Orleans trip (the one Margaret mentions in this letter). Although the exact date of her departure is unclear, Frances probably left the following week, thus making the date here the tenth.

1. The *Boston Daily Evening Transcript* for 29 January announced Dwight's "course of 8 lectures on the life and genius of some of the great music composers and on the departments of music which they represent." He lectured each Thursday evening beginning on 3 February.

2. The *Transcript* of 12 February announced Braham's concert at the Melodeon for that evening. Caroline Sturgis, daughter of William Sturgis of Boston, was Fuller's closest friend. She contributed poetry to the *Dial* and wrote children's books later in life.

354. To [?]

[ca. 1 March 1842]

[   ] to my feelings, for I was really thinking more of him[n] and of you than of myself. I thought of you much, but I have not yet thought well on this subject, because not deeply, and in quiet; but the letter will give you one or two of my first feelings.

You ask me questions—of Ellen and Ellery—I feel encouraged as to their mutual happiness and aid to one another. The great trust shown by Ellen has assured Ellery's heart, long shut by distrust and a grotesque irony of mind, he will I trust refine the dross, retain the gold, and be no less the nature, and the genius, for being more the man. If I may judge from Ellen's letters the development of gentleness, good sense and true generosity in her is proceeding. But I can tell you more by and by. They are to remain in Cincini and Mother is going to them at their urgent request. This step has given me great anxiety. Mother's health is much shaken; she [   ]

ALfr (MHarF).
Dated from Fuller's reference to the Channings.
more of him] more of ⟨y⟩ ↑ him ↓

355. To Elizabeth Hoar

[I] [8?] March 1842

Carrie I see little. I have not time, and we were so much together in the summer, that it needs not, at present. She, however, has come forth into life, seeking in the details of study and observation, fuel for her flame. But neither love nor duty offer yet with any bounty, occasions which can much aid her, and she is learning, at present, I believe, grain of sand on grain of sand, as Schiller said.[1] She is much with Anna Shaw, whose free and noble ardour suits her now. &c. &c. Thus the orbs weave their dance.

Sam and Anna I see little, but take more pleasure in them when I do than before. They are more open to genial and inspiring themes. Still we are in different regions. Just as I put off the operation on Arthur's eye till they set off on their bridal tour, and on that first day of divine October beauty was with him and the surgeon, while they were together, so is it now, as to circumstances between us.[2] I do not like to tell them what I am thinking and doing; they can tell one another what they think and do. It is all well, if they will live worthily.

[II] [   ] if she survives the voyage and change of climate I shall never see that look again.[3] F. was surprized by the beauty of her infant; she did not care for it at first, but seemed to be like a little girl, longing to^n get rid of a burden and run out into the free fields, and lie beneath the bushes, but as the child began to show its loveliness she grew very fond of it. If it had been mine I should have done nothing else, but take care of it. There was so much to see in it. The difference between infants of the earliest age is heaven wide, there was as much between these two as between Anna W. and Cary.

Well! it will not do to write all night, yet how much I should like to tell you. My inward life has been rich and deep, and of more calm and musical flow than ever before. It seems to me that Heaven, whose course has ever been to "cross-bias me" as Herbert hath it, is no niggard in its compensations.[4] I have, indeed, been forced to take up old burdens from which I thought I had learned what they would teach, the pen has been snatched from my hand, just as I most longed to give myself to it, and fancied I was ready, my new^n fund of health and strength dissipated, seemingly to little purpose. I have been forced to dissipate when I wished to concentrate, to feel the hourly pressure of others mental wants when it seemed otherwise I was just on the point of satisfying my own. "Some natural tears I shed"[5] to be sure at the first prospect of all this, for all the sweet feelings of the summer seemed forced back upon me, as yet unrealized by thought. But I had scarcely begun when a new page was turned and an era began from which I am not yet sufficiently remote to describe it as I would. I have lived a life, if only in the music I have heard and one development seemed to follow another therein as if bound together by destiny, and all things done for me. All minds, all scenes have ministered to me. Nature has seemed an ever open secret, the Divine a sheltering love, Truth an always spraying fountain, and my own soul more alone and less lonely, more hopeful, more patient and above all more gentle and humble in its living.

New minds have come to reveal themselves to me, though I do not wish it, for I feel myself inadequate to the ties already formed. I have not strength or time to do anything as I would, or meet the thoughts of those I love already. But these new have come with gifts too fair to be refused and which have cheered my passive mind.

I wish much, dear Elizabeth, I could write to you well and often both because I always am sure of your justness of perception, and now that you will meet me as much as if I were cold, and, also, because I should like to bring before you the varied world-scene [III] you cannot so well go out to unfold for yourself. But it was never permitted me even where I wished it most. I think less than a daily offering of thought and feeling would not content me so much seems to pass unspoken each day But the forest leaves fall unseen and make a soil on which shall be reared the growth and fabrics of a nobler era. This thought rounds off each day. Your letter was a little golden key[6] to a whole volume of thoughts and feelings. I cannot make the one bright drop, like champagne in ice, but must pour a full gush if I speak at all, and not think whether the water is clear either.

Richard read me something from the Greek, for he did not wish to talk about little Waldo. It was to this effect: "All things return to thee, o Prosperpine! But all things that go to the earth become beautiful. Venus poured out her tears for Adonis's wounds, yet all was turned to flowers; for each drop of blood, a rose; for each tear, an anemone."

I: MsCfr (MH: bMS Am 1280 [111, pp. 165–66]); II: ALfr (MHarF); III: MsCfr (MH: bMS Am 1280 [111, pp. 180–84]). Published in part in *Memoirs*, 1:285–86, 309–10, and *JMN*, 11:487, 488–89.

Elizabeth Sherman Hoar of Concord had been engaged to Emerson's brother Charles when he died. Thereafter Elizabeth was regarded as one of the Emerson family. She and Fuller had a close, enduring friendship.

longing to] longing to ⟨like⟩
my new] my ⟨let⟩ new

1. From the final stanza of "Die Ideale":

> Die zu dem Bau der Ewigkeiten
> Zwar Sandkorn nur für Sandkorn reicht,
> Doch von der grossen Schuld der Zeiten
> Minuten, Tage, Jahre streicht.

Edward Bulwer-Lytton translated the passage (in *Poems and Ballads of Schiller* [Edinburgh, 1844], 1:97):

> Tho' but by grains thou aid'st the pile
> The vast Eternity uprears,
> At least thou strik'st from Time the while
> Life's debt—the minutes, days and years.

2. For Arthur Fuller's injury, see letter 82.
3. Fuller is discussing her sister-in-law, Frances Hastings Fuller.

4. From "Affliction" in George Herbert's poem "The Church": "Thus doth thy power crosse-bias me, not making / Thine own gift good, yet me from my wayes taking" (*Works of George Herbert*, p. 48).

5. Probably a modification of Milton's description of Adam and Eve as they left the garden: "Some natural tears they dropped, but wiped them soon" (*John Milton: Complete Poems and Major Prose*, ed. Merritt Y. Hughes [New York, 1957], p. 468).

6. Milton, *Comus*:

> Yet some there be that by due steps aspire
> To lay their just hands on that Golden Key
> That opes the Palace of Eternity: [Ibid., p. 90]

356.   To Ralph Waldo Emerson

Boston, March 8th, 1842.

Dearest Waldo,

My letter comes along tardily, but I have been ill much of the time, and the better days so full in consequence of the enforced indolence of the bad days that thoughts and feelings have had no chance to grow for the absent;[n] Yet that is not all, there has been a sort of incubus on me when I looked your way, it disappears when we meet, but it returns to prevent my writing. Your letter (of 1st March, but not received till today) drives it away for the present.[1] I have thought of you many times, indeed in all my walks, and in the night, with unspeakable tenderness, in the same way as I see you in your letter[n] and of that time when you were in N York, two years ago, so much that I have been trying to go to Cambridge and get your letter in which after seeing the ships go by, you turn to the little dead flowers of the year before that grew upon the wall[n]—[2] But I suppose you have forgotten all about it.— I will not follow this path;

I have to day a dear letter from dear Elizabeth. It came with yours. She says the right words as[n] always when she speaks, the words which meet my heart, and I felt very grateful to her for writing when I could not to her.—

Mr Alcott came last Sunday and spent some hours in talking with me His need seemed to be to make "a clean breast on't." He told me that he looked with less approval on the past year than on any former of his life, how he had pined for sympathy, had vainly sought it in the society of crude reformers, found them limited as the men they opposed, had sunk into moody musing and then "found himself on the borders of frenzy"— But, said he, perhaps it has not been in vain. I

49

have learned to know my limitations,— the need man has of a gradual education through circumstances and intercourse with other men; And "I have gained the greatest gain of my life in the magnanimity of a friend" And then, as he spoke of what you had done and "above all the manner of doing it" he wept a plenteous shower of gracious tears.[3]

I must say, I envied your faith in him, your fidelity to him, as I saw his calm face watered by those tears. Indeed I have always prized them even when I could not sympathize and wished you valued sight less and character more. But we are always elevated when we see any fidelity, any love that suffereth long and is kind.[4]

He then spoke of me, how he had often distrusted me from the very first, and, at times, did so still. I told him that was nothing peculiar to him; it seemed the friends I loved best and had supposed my vowed fellow-pilgrims did the same, but the fault, in his case, was, he never showed distrust to me, but spoke of it to others,— now that he had spoken of it to myself, all was well.

This interview did not increase my confidence in him, nor did I feel that I could respond to his expressions of wish[n] for sympathy. I still saw the same man, seeing states in the intellect which he will not humbly realize in heart and life. He had been to see W. Channing, he was going to West Roxbury, and I felt that after he had talked out this ne[w] phase to a dozen people, it would have done its work, and truth be left unembodied as far as depends on him. Yet I see, too, he is sincere in his own way, and that it is very hard for me to be just to him. I will try to be more gentle and reverent in my thoughts of him, if only because he has felt you at this moment.

Caroline, Sam, and I, all have letters from Ellery, theirs full of verses, mine of whimsies. I liked mine. My Mother now expects to go to Cincini and live with the two children a year.

Anna W. is confined to her bed; she has over-exerted herself and the physician says she must lie there a fortnight. I have been able to go to see her only a few minutes— Sam passes the evegs in her chamber painting. Each eveg he conceives and executes some little sketch, which may, I fear, prove less for the good of his eyes than of his mind.

Cary is well. I see her but little, yet this last week more than usual and in much sweetness. She, too, seemed to find difficulty in writing to you and for the same reason, to one loved it is needful to give all the life, or else the best.— Charles was here and we had the divine musical evening together.[5] He had been fostered by your sympathy into yet more courage and will give Dolen for the Dial—[6] I finished

Ralph Waldo Emerson. Steel engraving by Stephen Alonzo Scheff, after
Samuel Worcester Rowse. National Portrait Gallery, Smithsonian Institution, Washington, D.C.

the 1st no Günderode last night, it will be out early next week. The two vols are to be translated in four numbers.[7] I have just got into the spirit of writing to you as the paper ends, perhaps I will write again tomorrow if I do not it will be because I have not time

Always yours

MARGARET.

Tell me more about those dim New Yorkers.

ALS (MH: bMS Am 1280 [2362]). Published in part in Higginson, *MFO*, pp. 168–69, and Rusk, *Letters of RWE*, 2:263; published entire in Rusk, *Letters of RWE*, 3:28–29. *Addressed:* R. W. Emerson / care William Emerson Esq / Wall St / New York. *Postmark:* Boston Mss Mar 8. *Endorsed:* Margaret Fuller / March 1842.

the absent;] the absen⟨ce⟩t;

in the same way as I see you in your letter] ↑ in the same way as I see you in your letter ↓

words as] words ⟨which⟩ a⟨r⟩s

of wish] of ⟨regard⟩ wish

1. Emerson described his meeting with Horace Greeley, the editor of the *New-York Daily Tribune*: "I saw my fate in a moment & that I should never content him." He also described with dismay the Fourierite Albert Brisbane (1809–90), who had been lecturing in Philadelphia and New York on behalf of Fourierite reform (*DAB*). Presumably these are the "dim New Yorkers" Fuller mentions at the end of the letter (Rusk, *Letters of RWE*, 3:19–20).

2. On 17 March 1840 Emerson wrote Fuller, describing a number of ships he saw from Fort Tompkins on Staten Island. He concluded: "and yet I saw nothing as affecting as the little jaunty tops & tassels of last year's grass that nodded on the top of the wall in which they had contrived to cast their little roots" (Rusk, *Letters of RWE*, 2:262–63).

3. Probably a reference to Emerson's proposal of early 1841 to have the Alcotts live with the Emersons. Alcott accepted the offer, but his wife adamantly refused (Rusk, *Letters of RWE*, 2:382, 389).

4. 1 Cor. 13:4: "Love suffereth long, and is kind."

5. Both Fuller and Emerson admired Charles King Newcomb of Providence. He spent some time at Brook Farm, wrote a little for the *Dial*, but never became the writer that his friends had expected.

6. Newcomb's essay "The Two Dolons" appeared in *Dial* 3 (1842):112–23.

7. Elizabeth Peabody published Fuller's translation of Bettina von Arnim's *Günderode*. Fuller completed only one of the four planned numbers, however.

357. To Ralph Waldo Emerson

15 [?] March 1842

It is to be hoped, my best one, that the experiences of life will yet correct your vocabulary, and, that you will not always answer the burst of frank affection by the use of such a word as "*flattery*."[1]

Thou knowest, oh all seeing Truth, whether that hour is base or unworthy thee, in which the heart turns tenderly towards some beloved object, whether stirred by an apprehension of its needs, or of its present beauty, or of its great promise, when it would lay before it, all the flowers of hope and love, would soothe its weariness, as gently as might the sweet South, and *flatter* it by as fond an outbreak of pride and devotion, as is seen on the sunset clouds. Thou knowest whether these promptings, whether these longings, be not truer than intellectual scrutiny of the details of character; than cold distrust of the exaggerations even of heart. What we hope, what we think of those we love, is true, true as the fondest dream of love and friendship that ever shone upon the childish heart The faithful shall yet meet a full eyed love, ready as profound,— that never needs turn the key on its retirement, or arrest the stammering of an overweening trust.

MsCfr in Emerson's hand (MH: Os 735Laa 1842.3.15). Published in *Memoirs*, 1:285.

1. Answering her previous letter on 10 March, Emerson unguardedly said: "You know best of all living how to flatter your friend, both directly & by finest indirections" (Rusk, *Letters of RWE*, 3:28). He apologized on 18 March: "Yet blotted be every word written of mine & oblivion fall on every spoken word if any such have ever been which doubted your sincerity" (Rusk, *Letters of RWE*, 3:32).

358.   To Ralph Waldo Emerson

[17? March 1842]

My dear Waldo,

I requested Miss P to write to you, but, after looking over her letter, I want to add some lines myself. I hoped they would get at these particulars before you returned from N. York, that you might hear them on your way and not be teazed as soon as you arrived at your quiet home, but you came earlier than I had expected. Yesterday I found myself so unwell, and really exhausted, ·letters recd from the family made my stay here so uncertain that I wrote the little notice with regard to the possibility of suspending the Dial for a time, feeling that I must draw back[n] from my promise that I would see to the summer no.— But this morng after J. Clarke and Miss P. had at last the means of almost entirely examining the accounts, they give me the[n] result you find in her letter to you, which makes it impossible for me to go on at all.[1]

I could not do it, in future, if I have the same burden on me as I have had before, even as well as I have done. There is a perceptible diminution of my strength, and this winter which has been one of so severe labor I shall not recover fully from for two or three months. Then if I must take up a similar course next winter and have this tie upon me for the summer I think I should sink under it entirely.

I grieve to disappoint you after all the trouble you have taken. I am also sorry myself, for if I could have received a maintenance from this Dial, I could have done my duties to it well, which I never have all this time, and my time might have been given to my pen, while now for more than three months I have been able to write no line except letters. But it cannot be helped. It has been a sad business.

I think perhaps[n] Mr Parker would like to carry it on even under these circumstances.[2] For him, or for you it would be much easier than for me, for you have quiet homes, and better health. Of course if you do carry it on, I should like to do any thing I can to aid you.[3]

There must be prompt answer as the press will wait.

Your affectionate

MARGARET.

ALS (MH: bMS Am 1280 [2361]). Published in Higginson, *MFO*, pp. 168–69. *Addressed:* Mr Emerson. *Endorsed:* Margaret Fuller / March 1842.

draw back] draw ⟨p⟩ back
give me the] give me ⟨that⟩ the
I think perhaps] I think ↑ perhaps ↓

1. Elizabeth Peabody and James Clarke had examined the accounts of Weeks & Jordan, the previous publishers of the *Dial*, and found that the firm had overstated the paying subscribers to the magazine. The result was that Fuller could expect no payment for either past or future work for the *Dial* (Myerson, *New England Transcendentalists and the "Dial,"* pp. 73–74).

2. Theodore Parker, the minister of the Unitarian church in West Roxbury, was a learned young radical, the only major critic of conservative Unitarianism who remained in the pulpit. He was one of the most prolific writers for the *Dial*.

3. In his reply on 18 March Emerson cautiously agreed to "promise for the July Number, but I am not ready tonight to say I will take it for a year." Three days later he agreed to take full responsibility: "After thinking a little concerning this matter of the Dial, I incline to undertake it for a time, rather than have it stop or go into hands that know not Joseph" (Rusk, *Letters of RWE*, 3:34, 35). Emerson continued as editor until the magazine's end in April 1844.

359. To Elizabeth Hoar

March 20th. 1842,
Sunday eveg

My dear Elizabeth,

I have wanted to write to you this day a good letter, in reply to yours which was so dear to me Sunday is my only day of peace, and how often, as in Providence, have I blest again and again the "sweet day of sacred rest."— My Sundays have been golden, only all too short, but unfortunately to day I am not well. I am tired out now so that there is constant irritation in my head which I can only soothe by keeping it wet with cold water, and pain, such as formerly, in the spine and side, though not so acute. I have also a great languor on my spirits, so that the grasshopper is a burden, and though as each task comes I borrow a readiness from its aspect as I always do brightness for the moment from the face of a friend, yet as soon as the hour is past I am quite exhausted, feel as if I could not go a step further, and the day, as a whole, has no joyous energy.— I do not suffer keen pains and spasms as I used to do, but on the other hand have not[n] half the energy in the intervals I supposed *then* in fact I never used to get well, but be always in a state of tension of nerves, while now I am not.— Then I constantly looked forward to death; now I feel there has been a crisis in my constitution. It is a subject of great interest to me as connected with my mental life, for I feel this change dates from the era of illumination in my mental life.[1] If I live I shall write a full account of all I have observed. Now that my mind is so calm and sweet, there seems to be no fire in me to resist or to consume, and I can neither bear nor do what I could while much more sick, but am very weak. No doubt this finds its parallel in what we know of the great bodily strength of the insane.

This word reminds me of a little thing I wished to tell you. Mother passed the afternoon at the insane asylum at South Boston and there she saw a black woman who was in a high state of mind. She told Mother "there was no church but the body, if men went into built churches with any purpose except to learn better how they might keep the body an undefiled temple, they only burnt chaff and stubble before the Lord."— "When I lived in the world," said she, "I had not much time to go to churches and worship; as my family was large and poor,[n] but we kept a cow, and when we could spare any milk, I gave it to the hungry; that was my act of worship."— One other incident Mother told which pleased me, but it is too long to be written down here.

I saw yesterday in a book a story of an insane priest which reminded me of Mr Alcott I will[n] show it to you sometime.[   ]

ALfr (MHarF); MsCfr (MH: bMS Am 1280 [111, pp. 146–48]). Published in part in *JMN*, 11:484.

hand have not] hand ↑ have not ↓

worship as my family was large and poor,] worship ↑ as my family was large and poor, ↓

I will] I ↑ will ↓

1. Her religious experience, which she describes in letter 273, occurred in 1840.

360. To Caroline Sturgis

Apr. 1842

It is somewhat sad that two friends must become uninteresting to one another, because they have arrived at a mutual good understanding, yet this very thing makes the beauty as well as the sadness of music.

MsCfr (MH: bMS Am 1280 [111, pp. 15–16]). Published in *JMN*, 11:461.

361. To Mary Rotch

Boston,
7th April 1842.

My dear Miss Rotch,

I am ashamed to see I have kept your letter by me unanswered for three weeks. The only reason of my delay has been that, as you touched on a great topic, I felt I might perhaps find the right hour to say a few words in answer. But such an one has never come. The fag-end of the winter is all broken by engagements, errands[n] and visits that have been postponed, beside I am now much fatigued, and my mind so languid that I am disinclined to write an unnecessary line. I will not then say any thing till I see you and Miss Gifford[1] at your home, which I hope to do the last week in May or the first in June; most probably the latter, if it depends on me, but I should like by and by to write again about it. I am going to the country to be in absolute retirement and stillness, thus I hope to be again braced and raised by the quiet flow of thought— Having given out from myself now every day and all the day for nearly six months, books too will be most acceptable for a while. But by the time the trees are in full leaf, I doubt not I also[n] shall feel fresh and ready once more.

My winter has, indeed, been very pleasant. Destiny which still "cross biases me" as Herbert said it did him, refusing me what I desired, solitude and quiet in which to concentrate my powers, has[n] rewarded my submission to her guidance with more and fairer gifts than I could have deemed the due of any one, with many new and sweet thoughts, an extending hope, and a clearer faith.— I will not mar any subject by such utterance as I should just now give it but hope when I am with you we shall find intercourse satisfying. There are many topics I should like to talk over with you, but *all* topics are in relation to the one mentioned in your letter. Mrs Farrar says the time I mention is as likely to suit her as any. Till that time, then, I will postpone my words and remain with best regards to your friend, dear Miss Rotch, affectionately yours,

MARGARET F.[n]

AL (MH: fMS Am 1086 [9:70]); MsC (MH: fMS Am 1086 [Works, 1:25–27]); MsC (MH: bMS Am 1280 [111, p. 128]). Published in part in *JMN*, 11:480. *Addressed:* Miss Mary Rotch / New Bedford / Mass. *Postmark:* Boston Ms Apr 8.

Mary Rotch, of New Bedford, was Eliza Farrar's aunt. A Quaker, Rotch was drawn to the ideas of Emerson and his friends. Both he and Fuller called her "Aunt Mary."

engagements, errands] engagements, ⟨and⟩ errands
I also] I ↑ also ↓
powers, has] powers, ↑ has ↓
affectionately yours, Margaret F.] *Added from the manuscript copy, for the signature has been cut out.*

1. Mary Gifford (1796–1875), daughter of Warren and Tabitha Gifford of Dartmouth, Massachusetts, was Mary Rotch's companion at her home in New Bedford (MVR 274:132; Bullard, *Rotches*, pp. 92–93).

362. To Ralph Waldo Emerson

Boston,
9th April, 1842.

Dear Waldo,

I understand you have given notice to the Public, that, the[n] Dial is to be under your care in future, and I am very glad of this for several reasons, though I did not like to express my feeling as you seemed reluctant to bind yourself in any way. But a year is short time enough for a fair trial.

Since it is now understood that you are Pilot, it is not needful for me to make the observations I had in view. The work cannot but change its character a good deal, but it will now be understood there is a change of director, too." The only way in which this is of importance to me is that I think you will sometimes reject pieces that I should not. For you have always had in view to make a good periodical and represent your own tastes, while I have had in view to let all kinds of people have freedom to say their say, for better, for worse.

Should time and my mood be propitious, I should like to write some pages on the amusements here this past winter, and a notice[n] at some length of Hawthorne's Twice told tales.[1] I was much interested by the Gipsey book, but dont incline to write about it—[2] Longfellow sent us his poems, and if you have toleration for them, it would be well to have a short notice written by some one (*not* me)— I will have them sent to you and the little prayer book also.[n3] If you do not receive the latter, it will be because I could not get it, not because I have forgotten your wish. Please mention in your next, whether you did not find "Napoleon." I do not see it among[n] my papers, and think I must have given it you.[4]

As to pecuniary matters, Miss Peabody I have found more exact and judicious than I expected, but she is variable in her attention, because she has so many private affairs. She will do very well under your supervision, but a connection with her offers no advantages for the spread of your work whatever it may be. But you have always thought the Dial required nothing of this kind. Much, much do I wish for myself I could find a publisher who is honest, and has also business talents. Such a connexion ought to be permanent. But I can hear of no person in Boston or elsewhere that it is desirable to be connected with, so I suppose I must still jog on as before, this dubious[n] pace. But if ever you get any light in this quarter, pray impart.[5]

I should think the Dial affairs were now in such a state that you could see clear into the coming year, and might economize about it considerably.

Well! I believe this is all I have to say, not much truly.

I leave town Monday eveg and go to Cambridge for a few days. On Friday or Saturday I go to Canton to board with an Aunt of mine for four or five weeks. I think I shall be there perfectly retired and quiet; it suits my convenience in many respects to go. I wish I could feel as if the Muse would favor me there and then, but I feel at present so sad and languid, as if I should not know an hour of bright life again. It will be pity if this hangs about me just at the time when I might obey[n] inspirations, if we[n] had them, but these things are beyond control, and the demon no more forgets us than the angel. I will make myself no more promises *in time*. If you have any thing to say to me I should receive a letter here as late as Friday morng, if directed to Miss Peabody's care. Afterward direct to me at Canton. Care Charles Crane.

I thank you and Lidian[6] for your invitation and know well your untiring hospitality. Should it seem well so to do, I will come. I cannot now tell how I shall feel. After Canton I shall go to Providence, for a few days, then to N. Bedford to pass a week with Aunt Mary Rotch. Farewell, dear Waldo, yours as ever,

MARGARET.

I still have thoughts of going to the West, but shall not know about it for some weeks.

ALS (MH: bMS Am 1280 [2363]). Published in Rusk, *Letters of RWE*, 3:45–46, and Wade, pp. 558–59. *Addressed:* R. W. Emerson / Concord / Mass. *Postmark:* Boston Apr 10. *Endorsed:* SMF / April 1842.

that, the] that, ↑ the ↓
change of director, too.] change ↑ of ⟨direction⟩ director, too ↓ .
winter, and a notice] winter, and a⟨n⟩ notice
book also.] book ↑ also ↓ .
it among] it ⟨amid⟩ ↑ among ↓
this dubious] this du⟨po⟩bious
might obey] might ⟨?⟩ obey
if we] if ⟨they⟩ ↑ we ↓

1. Fuller's "Entertainments of the Past Winter," *Dial* 3 (1842):46–72 and her review of Hawthorne's *Twice-Told Tales*, ibid., pp. 130–31.
2. With his letter of 2? April, Emerson had sent Fuller George Borrow's *The Zincali* (London, 1841), which he reviewed in *Dial* 3(1842):127–28 (Rusk, *Letters of RWE*, 3:42–43).
3. Fuller probably refers to Henry Wadsworth Longfellow's *Ballads and Other Poems* (Cambridge, Mass., 1841), which had been published in late December (*The Letters of Henry Wadsworth Longfellow*, ed. Andrew Hilen [Cambridge, Mass., 1966], 2:363–64). Longfellow (1807–82) was at this time on the faculty at Harvard (*DAB*). Although she knew his wife, Frances Appleton, Fuller was not a member of their circle. Fuller's next letter to Emerson names Dorothea Dix as the author of the "prayer book." The reference is probably to *Meditations for Private Hours*, published in 1828 and often republished. Neither the Longfellow nor the Dix book was reviewed in the *Dial*.
4. In his reply of 10 April Emerson identifies the author of the poem as Benjamin Franklin Presbury (1810–68) of Taunton. However, no poem such as this was published in the magazine (Rusk, *Letters of RWE*, 3:46). Presbury, the son of Seth and Sarah Pratt Presbury, did contribute two poems to the second volume of the *Dial*. He later wrote for the *Atlantic* and became an active abolitionist (Joseph Waite Presby, *William Presbrey of London, England, and Taunton, Mass., and His Descendants, 1690–1918* [Rutland, Vt., 1918], p. 41).
5. Beginning with the January 1842 issue, Fuller and Emerson changed publishers. Elizabeth Peabody published the *Dial* until July 1843 (Myerson, *New England Transcendentalists and the "Dial,"* pp. 71, 90).
6. Emerson's second wife was Lydia Jackson of Plymouth, whom he and all his friends called Lidian.

363. To Ralph Waldo Emerson

Canton, 18th April. [1842]

Dear friend,

I received your letter before I left Boston, but in the hurry of the last hours could not write even a notelette with the parcel I requested S. Clarke to make up for you of Borrow, Longfellow, some more shreds of Dial, including the wearifu' Napoleon, and the Prayer Book, if Dorothea Dix could be induced to grant the same. What awkward thing could I have said about your advertisement? I cant think.— All was understood, except that you had said "I should put my name on the cover and announce myself as Editor only that I am not sure I can bind myself for so *long*[n] as a year" &c so when I saw the advertisement I was glad, and only so far surprized as that I had not felt sure you would do it.—[1] How many tedious words!

I think I shall like being here much and find the rest I seek. The country is tolerably pretty, gentle, unobtrusive—within the house plain kindness, and generally, a silence unbroken except by the sounds from the poultry, or the wind, to appreciate which blessing one should have lived half a year in a boarding house with as infirm a head as mine, and none to ward off interruptions sick or well.

I will not write more to you now, as what time I have I must give to letters for Cincini. My Mother goes on Wednesday. With love to your mother, Lidian, and Elizabeth and good wishes to Mr Alcott on his voyage (I was sorry to be obliged to cut short his last visit for a lesson)[2]

Your affectionate

MARGARET.

Let me before I forget it guard you, if need be, against trusting E. P. P. to write the slightest notice or advertisement. I never saw any thing like her for impossibility of being clear and accurate in a brief space. She wrote one notice about "the importance of public[n] patronage to secure the *identity* of Editors" which I fortunately arrested on the way and I see she has advertised Günderode as[n] "Correse of Bettine Brentano with a *Nun*" as if people could not make mistakes enough of themselves without putting the grossest in their way.

I shall perhaps[n] let Lloyd put this into West-Roxbury post-office just for the convenience of today, but there is one in Canton to which I shall send every day in future, so write at pleasure, but dont exert thyself for mine.

ALS (MH: bMS Am 1280 [2364]); MsC (MB: Ms. Am. 1450 [77]). Published in part in Higginson, *MFO*, pp. 169–70. *Addressed:* R. W. Emerson / Concord / Mass. *Endorsed:* S. M Fuller / Apr 1842.

so *long*] so *lo⟨g⟩ng*
importance of public] importance of ⟨securing⟩ public
Günderode as] Günderode ↑ as ↓
shall perhaps] shall ↑ perhaps ↓

1. Fuller was surprised only that Emerson had made a public announcement of his editorship, not that he had undertaken the work.

2. On 8 May Alcott sailed for England, whence he returned on 21 October (Shepard, *Pedlar's Progress*, pp. 303, 342).

364. To Richard F. Fuller

Canton 22d April
1842.

My dear Richard,

I want you now to go to Mrs Farrar see when Mr Metcalf expects to receive Lloyd and what is to be done about his room, clothes &c.[1]

If he needs any particular dress for his work, it might be made at West-Roxbury and I should like to have you settle it all when you go there a week from tomorrow.

What he needs can be removed to his room at Mr Metcalf's and the rest to the house at C. Port, and I want to have *all* the things left scattering at Jamaica removed at the same time, that all may be together at last.

Mrs Ripley was desirous of buying one of the bedsteads, but Mother seemed inclined to keep it rather, I will leave this to your judgment, and also about other things, if they wish to keep them. His old bureau may be worth something there and is hardly worth bringing away. But both the matrass and feather bed shd be brought.

There are things of Mother's in Lloyd's care, such as sheets and napkins, which I wish to have carefully put away at the C. P. house.

I will commend to your discretion the removal of these things at as little cost as may be, and to settle Lloyd in his new position under the circumstances best adapted to give him a fair chance.

If you can take this guardianship of his affairs now and act for him as well as or better than I could, you will indeed do[n] a friendly and brotherly service to me, for this is the only thing I have to trouble me at present.

I dare not feel trust that he will succeed, but let us not say a word to discourage him, but do all we can for him.

I should like to have you write me exactly and fully on this subject. Say to Mr and Mrs Ripley that I shall write to them when I know about his going and that I shall pay what is again due for him when I return to Boston. And give them my best regards.

Mention in your letter what money you shall want for moving the things &c.

Dear Mother went in a smiling, though also half tearful mood. It rained after you went till Wednesday noon, but the beautiful white clouds[n] were all floating over the sunlight when she went. The last thing she sent her love to you boys. Mine to Arthur.

Your sister and friend

S. M. FULLER.

P.S. I have enjoyed these two days of stillness and fine weather very much, and begin to fancy myself well already.

Do not buy a chest for Lloyd. I have one for him here, which I shall send after he gets to Cambridge. My love to him.

ALS (MH: fMS Am 1086 [9:88]); MsC (MH: fMS Am 1086 [Works, 2:695–701]). *Addressed:* R. F. Fuller / Cambridge / Mass.

indeed do] indeed ⟨t⟩do
white clouds] white ⟨glo⟩ clouds

1. Lloyd, who had been living at Brook Farm, was to begin a trial as an apprentice in the printing firm founded by Charles R. Metcalf (1797–1877) of Cambridge. Richard reported in his letter of 1 May (MH) that the trial period was to be six weeks, not the four months Margaret had wanted (Lucius R. Paige, *History of Cambridge, Massachusetts, 1630–1877: Supplement and Index* [Boston, 1877], p. 507; *Boston Daily Advertiser*, 11 August 1877).

365. To Mary Rotch

Canton [ca. May] 1842

I have enjoyed the solitude and silence. It has been a thotful, tho' not a thinking time. I incline thus to characterize the two phases of life. At such times, however, with the great subjects lying mountainous and distant as ever in the horizon, it seems a farce to pretend one has ever been thinking or living at all, or, far more, that one has ever been fatigued with such child's play as that of last year. The growths of the last year which seemed at the time a rich and various mantle, have recurred to mother Earth, and, all that remains is some pictures, seeds, and a few more hieroglyphics indicating the way to truths that promise a perennial spring.

MsCfr (MH: bMS Am 1280 [111, pp. 26–27]). Published in *JMN*, 11:463–64.

366. To Richard F. Fuller

Canton, 12th May
1842.

My dear Richard,

I have had a very pleasant letter from Mother. She was eight days on her journey which she seems highly to have enjoyed. She finds every thing very pleasant so far, and likes Ellery. This was a short letter, the next will be more full. I should send them to you and Arthur, but that there are little things, intended for me alone. When I come to Cambridge I shall read them to you.

I had supposed you would come to see me. We might enjoy going into the fields, now it is so beautiful. But perhaps so long a walk is too great a price to pay, if so I would not have you come. I shall be here but two Sundays more.

I am sorry Mr Metcalf will not try Lloyd more than six weeks, and fear that time will not be sufficient. Do you however settle him as well as you can, and do all you[n] can to encourage and help him to the best. You can never perform a more important duty; this is probably, the crisis in his youth, and no one could be of such benefit[n] to him as a brother near his own age.

As you may not come here and I may not be in Cambridge for four or five weeks I inclose ten dollars, for you and ten for Arthur, also three for moving Lloyd's things. You said you thought you could do it for *two*, but inclose this lest more should be needed. Please make out a little account for him and also one for yourself. I depend on Arthur too keeping some account of his money, as I am but a steward at present, but of this money I wish you and Arthur both to give your Aunt Kuhn some to buy linen for your shirt bosoms. No one here understands how you wish them made whether you wish to have bosoms and collars sewed on or separate, and you must each leave with her separate[n] precise written directions, signed with your separate names or they will not be done so as to suit you.

Elizabeth Hoar has been making[n] me a little visit which I much enjoyed. I have found out what book she would like and shall get it for her, as you desired, when I come to Boston.

As to what you say of your rank, I doubt not you will find, if you persevere, that it will be steadily higher. I can well understand that no effort on your part can at once place you on a footing with persons who have been carefully instructed at the Latin or other as good schools. The finishing touches in any kind of culture must be slowly attained.— When your father and Uncles were in college not nearly so much was expected of students as now; however your father and Uncle Henry were probably, gifted by nature with greater quickness than you. Your father had beside very great power of attention. I have never seen any person who excelled him in that. You are equally capable of it.[1]

I entirely agree in what you say of *tuition* and *intuition*.[2] The two must act and react upon one another to make a man, to form a mind. Drudgery is as necessary to call out the treasures of the mind, as harrowing and planting with those of the earth. And beside the growths of literature and art are as much Nature as the trees in Concord woods, but Nature idealized and perfected.

While here I have been reading (only in translation, alas!) the Cyropaedia and other works of Xenophon[3] and some dramas of Euripides, and, were envy[n] ever worth our while, I should deeply envy those who can with convenience gain access to the Greek mind in its proper garb. No possession *can* be more precious than a knowledge of Greek.

Adieu, dear Richard. I wish I could see you. Write to me as early as the 22d if not earlier. My love to Arthur. Why does he not write to me. I want both of you to write to your Mother if you have not already done so. Write a letter together if you have not time or materials for two. With much affection your sister

MARGARET.

I wish you and Arthur would now and then send newspapers to Eugene. Those large ones as the Yankee Nation.[4] I will repay what you spend for this.

When you move the things, ascertain from Mr Henry whether the *Lemon tree* as well as the other plants is in Mr Balch's greenhouse.[5] Mother wishes them all left there and I think the Lemon was sent elsewhere to be bedded.

Do not leave this note unless Mrs Farrar has returned from her journey. If she is still absent ask when she will return and call again with it then.

64

Let Aunt K. know if tiers[6] have been provided for L. as, if not, she will see to it.

Friday morng   Since writing the above more linen has been found but I doubt whether enough for all the shirts. Aunt K. will be able to tell you.

ALS (MH: fMS Am 1086 [9:89]): MsC (MH: fMS Am 1086 [Works, 2:685–95]). Published in part in Higginson, *MFO*, p. 105. *Addressed:* R. F. Fuller / Cambridge / Mass.

all you] all ⟨that⟩ you
such benefit] such ↑ benefit ↓
her separate] her ↑ separate ↓
been making] been ⟨?⟩making
were envy] were en⟨o⟩vy

1. In his letter of 1 May (MH), Richard had bitterly described his mediocre performance at Harvard, saying that he had "been pretty zealously engaged in the ignoble strife for marks." He was particularly aware of his inability to measure up to the standard he felt that his father would have expected: "It was my hope, on coming here that I should be able to show that my fathers blood circulated in at least one of his sons. . . . I think the judgement of a number of learned men quite decisive as to what one is, and it seems to me that, when my father and uncles were such excellent scholars, it shows a shameful degeneration from the virtues of the parent stock that all my father's sons should be but middling ones."

2. In closing, Richard said: "I have discovered that mere love or admiration of the beautiful, without culture makes but a rude thinker after all; and that perhaps there is danger that while we are lovers of exterior beauty, of setting too low a value upon this tuition, as I might call it, naming the other intuition."

3. Xenophon (ca. 428/7 B.C.–ca. 354 B.C.) was an Athenian soldier and author. His *Cyropaedia* was a historical "novel" that discussed statecraft and family life.

4. The *Universal Yankee Nation* was a Boston weekly begun in 1841 by John N. Bradley (Mary Westcott and Allene Ramage, comps., *A Checklist of United States Newspapers* [Durham, N.C., 1932], 2:264.

5. Joseph Williams Balch of Jamaica Plain was a prominent insurance executive.

6. Aprons.

367.   To Sophia Peabody

Saturday June 4th. [1842]

My dear Sophia,

After reading your letter I wanted to write a few lines, as we met in such a hasty, interrupted fashion.[1] Yet not much have I to say, for great occasions of bliss, of bane,— tell their own story, and we would not, by unnecessary words, come limping after the true sense. If ever mortal was secure of a pure and rational happiness which shall grow and extend into immortal life, I think it is you, for the love that binds you to him you love is wise and pure and religious, it is a love given not chosen, and the growth not of wants and wishes, but of the demands of character. Its whole scope and promise is very fair in my eyes. And for daily life, as well as in the long account, I think there will be great happiness, for if ever[n] I saw a man who combined delicate tenderness to understand the heart of a woman, with quiet depth and manliness enough to satisfy her, it is Mr Hawthorne. How simple and rational, too, seems your plan of life. You will be separated only by your several pursuits and just enough daily[n] to freshen the founts of thought and feeling; to one who cannot think of love merely in the heart, or even in the common destiny of two[n] souls, but as necessarily comprehending intellectual friendship, too, it seems the happiest lot imaginable that lies before you. But, if it should not be so, if unexpected griefs or perils should arise, I know that mutual love and heavenly trust will gleam brightly through the dark. I do not *demand* the earnest of a future happiness to all believing souls. I wish to temper the mind to believe, without prematurely craving *sight*, but it is sweet when here and there some little spots of garden ground reveal the flowers that deck our natural Eden,— sweet when[n] some characters can bear fruit without the aid of the knife, and the first scene of that age-long drama in which each child of God must act to find himself is plainly to be deciphered, and its cadences harmonious to the ear.

I wish you could have begun your new life so as to have had these glorious June days in Concord. The whole earth is decked for a bridal. I see not a spot on her full and gold bespangled drapery. All her perfumes breathe, and her eye glows with joy. I saw a *rose* this morning, and I fear the beautiful white and Provence roses will bloom and wither before you are ready to gather them.

My affectionate remembrance to your friend. You rightly felt how glad I should be to be thought of in the happy hour and plan for the future. As far as bearing an intelligent heart I think I deserve to be esteemed a friend. And thus in affection and prayer dear Sophia yours

MARGARET F.

ALS (NN-B). *Addressed:* Miss Sophia Peabody / West St / Boston. *Endorsed:* Margaret Fuller.

if ever] if ⟨if⟩ ever
enough daily] enough ⟨to⟩ daily
of two] of ↑ two ↓
sweet when] sweet ⟨that⟩ ↑ when ↓

1. Peabody's letter undoubtedly discussed her engagement to Nathaniel Haw-

thorne, whom she married on 9 July at the Peabody home on West Street, Boston. James Clarke performed the ceremony (Tharp, *Peabody Sisters*, pp. 149–51).

368. To William H. Channing

17 June [1842]

[   ] I did not say how happy I felt last Sunday but you knew it, I suppose. Especially the prayers touched the inmost heart. Anna[n] S. said there were tones mysterious to her, indescribable except that they spoke of pain—this is true, he is not yet serene and triumphant, except at moments, yet all kindled with the spirit. Is it my defect of spiritual experience, that while that weight of sagacity which is the iron to the dart of genius is needful to satisfy me, the undertone of another and a deeper knowledge does not please, does not command me. Even in Handel's Messiah, I am half incredulous, half impatient, when the music of the second part comes to check, before it interprets, the promise of the first, and the strain "Was ever sorrow like to his sorrow" is not for me, as I have been, as I am.

In my quiet retreat I read Xenophon, and became more acquainted with his Socrates.[1] I had before known only the Socrates of Plato, one much more to my mind. Socrates took the ground that you approve; he conformed to the Greek Church, and it is evident with a sincere reverence, because it was the growth of the rational mind. He thought best to stand on its platform, and illustrate though with keen truth[n] by received forms; this was his right way, for his influence was, naturally, private, for individuals, who could, in some degree, respond to the teachings of his "demon", it made no difference to him he knew the multitude would not understand him, but it was the other way that Jesus took, preaching in the field, and plucking ears of corn on the Sabbath day.[2]

I intend to send you by and by some notes I made on Xenophon, if in looking them over, they do not seem too slight.

I was surprized to hear you speak in your sermon[n] as if the extent of the Christian triumph proved its superiority; that of other faiths is numerically greater; and their hold as strong in the nations they rule.[n]

Confusius and Socrates were sages, not missionaries[n] of religion. You spoke, too, as others do as if Europe was the world, merely because civilization is more active there.

[   ] them but not yours. Adieu, dearest friend. I shall hope to hear from you while at N. Bedford; in the course of a week you may find "something to say." Write how Mr Parker answered to your proposition[3] Write to me some times of your little boy, as he does new things;[4] it gives me peculiar pleasure when you speak of your children—and of all children I think what we learn from them [   ]

ALfr (MB: Ms. Am. 1450 [50]). Published in part in *Memoirs*, 2:87, and Higginson, *MFO*, 309–10. *Addressed:* Rev. W. H. Channing / Nashua / New Hampshire. *Postmark:* Cambridge Ms Jun 17. *Endorsed:* ⟨July⟩ June 17th 1842. Cambridge.

Anna] *The remainder of this sentence has been canceled by a later hand.*

illustrate though with keen truth] illustrate ↑though with keen truth↓

speak in your sermon] speak ↑in your sermon↓

greater; and their hold as strong in the nations they rule.] greater; ⟨?⟩ ↑and their hold as ⟨to⟩ ⟨?⟩ strong in the nations they rule.↓

not missionaries] not ⟨pre⟩ ↑missionaries↓

1. A member of the Socratic circle in Athens, Xenophon wrote often on the philosopher in *Apology, Memorabilia*, and *Symposium*.

2. Matt. 12:1, Mark 2:24, and Luke 6:2.

3. On 9 June Channing wrote Parker to compliment him on the publication of his *Discourse of Matters Pertaining to Religion* (Boston, 1842). At the end of the letter Channing opened a new topic: "I have very much that I want to talk to you about. Amongst other things it seems to me that a time has come for strenuous and determined action. . . . I will tell you in a word what I want, and what I think the age calls for. It is the establishment of 'an order of the sons of God.' I wish no direct severance from the Unitarians, but a completion of that movement. . . ." Channing quickly drew back, however: "This letter has been accidentally delayed, and I open it to say all this is too enthusiastic. . . . Let us unite with the Unitarians; they may do much" (Frothingham, *Memoir of William Henry Channing*, pp. 173, 175–76).

4. Francis Allston Channing, who was born in 1841, later became an English baron.

369. To Elizabeth Hoar

New Bedford
19 June 1842

You must have been happy too that you had lived long enough to do all you did for them.[1] You filled just the place to which Goethe wished to train his Meister.[2] What you knew and were, bore full upon the case, and there was no other person for whom your office of helping raising and interpreting seemed appointed. You helped to make bad not only better, but good. When we do this, we have not paid too dear for our schooling.

MsCfr (MH: bMS Am 1280H [41, p. 114]). Published in *JMN*, 8:184.

1. In his journal Emerson identifies Maria Randall as Fuller's subject. She died on 25 May (Randall, *Poems*, p. 42; *JMN*, 8:184).

2. Goethe's novels *Wilhelm Meisters Lehrjahre* and *Wilhelm Meisters Wanderjahre* were among Fuller's favorite books.

370. To William H. Channing[?]

[23?] June 1842

Why must children be with perfect people, any more than people wait to be perfect to be friends? The secret is,—is it not?—for parents to feel and be willing their children should know that they are but little older than themselves; only a class above, and able to give them some help in learning their lesson. Then parent and child keep growing together, in the same house. Let them blunder as we blundered. God is patient for us; why should not we be for them? Aspiration teaches always, and God leads, by inches. A perfect being would hurt a child no less than an imperfect.

It always makes my annoyances seem light, to be riding about to visit these fine houses. Not that I am intolerant towards the rich, but I cannot help feeling at such times how much characters require the discipline of difficult circumstances. To say nothing of the need the soul has of a peace and courage that cannot be disturbed, even as to the intellect, how can one be sure of not sitting down in the midst of indulgence to pamper tastes alone, and how easy to cheat one's self with the fancy that a little easy reading or writing is quite work. I am safer; I do not sleep on roses. I smile to myself, when with these friends, at their care of me. I let them do as they will, for I know it will not last long enough to spoil me.

I take great pleasure in talking with Aunt Mary. Her strong and simple nature checks not, falters not. Her experience is entirely unlike mine, as, indeed, is that of most others whom I know. No rapture, no subtle process, no slow fermentation in the unknown depths, but a rill struck out from the rock, clear and cool in all its course, the still, small voice. She says the guide of her life has shown itself rather as a restraining, than an impelling principle. I like her life, too, as far as I see it; it is dignified and true.

ELfr, from *Memoirs*, 2:63–64.

371. To Ralph Waldo Emerson

New Bedford,
23d June, 1842.

Dear Waldo,

I feel like writing to you, yet cannot perceive that there is much of a letter lying in my mind. It does not agree with my humor just now to be going about and seeing so many people, and I dont thrive under it. It is not Aunt Mary's fault, that I do not exactly as I please, for she is a nonpariel of a hostess in her combination of quiet, courteous attention to the comfort of her guest, with theⁿ desire to let alone, whenever it is best.[1] But the visits of others dissipate my thoughts, and there are no beautiful walks, no places where I can go and feel as I did in the real country. I stay in my room some hours each day, but little comes of it. I have had good talks with Aunt Mary; her range of experiences is not familiar to me, but where we meet we meet truly. She says, though, that, in comparing her life with others, she finds the guideⁿ of hers had been a restraining not an impelling power. She has known peace and assurance, but not energy, not rapture. She is unacquainted with the passions and with genius. She is strong and simple, a vestal mind, transmitting the oracle in purity, but not the parent of new born angels.

I have seen all the others here, but you know them well enough. I go to Providence on Saturday. Beyond that my future is yet in nubilus, but I shall write again.

I finished correcting my proof while in Boston. The little notices do you take charge of, if you will, and make any corrections you see fit. I think with pleasure of the coming out of this Dial. I, too, shall find something fresh in it, this time, and not have the thoughts of my friends indissolubly associated, with proof reading, post-office, or printer's ink. I do not even know what you have written there. Charles writes me that *this* Dolon is a new one. Did you have a pleasant visit from Charles?[2]

In Boston I heard W. Channing preach and saw him, beside; had a good visit from Sam, and made a visit to his house which was pleasant, though in a different way, and looked at my leisure, at many beautiful engravings of John Randall's, which I have never seen before, and hope you *will* see. One of Dominichino I wish I could show you myself, and the Rape of Europa, by a German painter whose name is not familiar to me took my fancy too.[3] The four horses I should like to have you see.

The new colonists will be with you soon.[4] Your community seems to grow. I think you must take pleasure in Hawthorne when yo[u] know him. you will find him more *mellow* than most fruits at your board, and of distinct flavor too. Now, if you would sell us for some two thousand dollars a house and small farm, and promise that a frugal subsistence could there be obtained, my mother Ellen and Ellery might live in Concord, too, they might keep there my goods, my pen and paper, and I might find a home there whenever I could pause from winning lucre. And I think we should be better friends, if such an arrangement could take effect, for I should not plague you with my business affairs, we should meet often, and naturally, and part as soon as we had done. I think, too, I should like to live with Ellery a part of the time, and I now feel confidence in him that if he do not win a foothold on this earth, it will not be that he deprives himself of it, by indulgence in childish freaks. A cow we own to give us milk, but would Concord yield brown bread and salt? I fear not. But dont plague yourself to answer these suggestions on paper. When we meet is time enough, indeed. I scarce think fate wills me ever to live in Concord, though I should like it now. Your affectionate

MARGARET.

I like Aunt Mary's dry humor. Have you ever seen *that*?

ALS (MH: bMS Am 1280 [2360]). Published in Rusk, *Letters of RWE*, 3:72–73. Addressed: R. W. Emerson, / Concord / Mass. *Postmark:* New Bedford Ms Jun 24. *Endorsed:* Margaret Fuller / June 1842.

guest, with the] guest, ⟨and her⟩ ↑ with the ↓
the guide] the ⟨genius⟩ ↑ guide ↓

1. Fuller was visiting Mary Rotch in New Bedford.
2. Emerson had been deeply moved by Newcomb's "Two Dolons" manuscript: "Let it be his praise that when I carried his MS story to the woods, & read it in the armchair of the upturned root of a pinetree I felt for the first time since Waldo's death some efficient faith again in the repairs of the Universe, some independency of natural relations whilst spiritual affinities can be so perfect & compensating" (*JMN*, 8:179).
3. John Randall, Jr., was the son of Dr. John Randall of Boston. Il Domenichino (1581–1641) was a Bolognese painter.
4. Nathaniel and Sophia Hawthorne were moving to the Old Manse in Concord.

---

372. To Richard F. Fuller

Saturday

June, 25th. [1842]

Dear Richard

If you hear nothing to the contrary from me, let Lloyd go to Canton a week from next Monday. I may find a place for him in Providence, if so, I shall either return to C. a week from today and let him know, or write. Look into the post office, daily.

If I do not return, use your best judgment as to his arrangements. He need not take many things to Canton, as if[n] I can make any

71

other[n] arrangement, I shall not leave him there more than a few days. He had best take some book, pens and paper to amuse himself there. Perhaps it may not be necessary for him to go. I hope not.

No letter from Mother while here, but a pleasant one from Eugene. A pleasant visit here.

I hope you got your money safe, and have your clothes by this time. Write to me at Providence, if any thing is to be said, care Mrs R. Newcomb.[1] With love to Arthur and Lloyd, your affectionate sis[ ]

M.

ALS (MH: fMS Am 1086 [9:84]); MsC (MH: fMS Am 1086 [Works, 2:683–85]). *Addressed:* R. F. Fuller / Cambridge / Kindness / Mrs Farrar. *Endorsed:* June 25th / 42.

as if] as ↑if↓
any other] any ↑other↓

1. Rhoda Mardenbrough Newcomb, Charles's mother, was a member of the group of intellectuals whom Fuller knew in Providence when she taught at the Greene-Street School.

373.   To Caroline Sturgis

July 1842

it is because of the recoils and positive repulsions which have attended every stage of your development and been most manifest in my direction.[1]

MsCfr (MH: bMS Am 1280 [111, p. 164]). Published in *JMN*, 11:487.

1. This may be a fragment of Fuller's answer to Sturgis's letter of 21 July (MH), in which she complains of being lonely and misunderstood: "I am glad that you trust me but even you do not trust me enough. I wish some one in the world would have real faith in me & then I should not feel so lonely."

374.   To William H. Channing[?]

July 1842

A letter at Providence would have been like manna in the wilderness. I came into the very midst of the fuss, and, tedious as it was at the time, I am glad to have seen it.[1] I shall in future be able to believe

Caroline Sturgis. Courtesy of Daphne B. Prout.

real what I have read with a dim disbelief of such times and tendencies. There is, indeed, little good, little cheer, in what I have seen: a city full of grown-up people as wild, as mischief-seeking, as full of prejudice, careless slander, and exaggeration, as a herd of boys in the play-ground of the worst boarding-school. Women whom I have seen, as the domestic cat, gentle, graceful, cajoling, suddenly showing the disposition, if not the force, of the tigress. I thought I appreciated the monstrous growths of rumor before, but I never did. The Latin poet, though used to a court, has faintly described what I saw and heard often, in going the length of a street.[2] It is astonishing what force, purity and wisdom it requires for a human being to keep clear of falsehoods. These absurdities, of course, are linked with good qualities, with energy of feeling, and with a love of morality, though narrowed and vulgarized by the absence of the intelligence which should enlighten. I had the good discipline of trying to make allowance for those making none, to be charitable to their want of charity, and cool without being cold. But I don't know when I have felt such an aversion to my environment and prayed so earnestly day by day,—"O, Eternal purge from my inmost heart this hot haste about ephemeral trifles," and "keep back thy servant from presumptuous sins; let them not have dominion over me."[3]

What a change from the almost vestal quiet of "Aunt Mary's" life, to all this open-windowed, open-eyed screaming of "poltroon," "nefarious plan," "entire depravity," &c. &c.

ELfr, from *Memoirs*, 2:64–65.

1. Fuller was in Providence during the height of the Dorr Rebellion, when Rhode Island had two governments, one legal and one revolutionary. Thomas Wilson Dorr (1805–54) formed a "People's Party" in Rhode Island, almost the only state in 1841 that did not have practical manhood suffrage, and the only state that had no written constitution. His party submitted a constitution to the people in an extralegal referendum in December 1841. After its overwhelming approval, the legislature rejected the action and submitted its own constitution to the voters, who rejected it in March 1842. The People's Party then elected an entire state government with Dorr as governor. Governor Samuel King proclaimed martial law and jailed Dorr and many of his followers (Richard B. Morris, *Encyclopedia of American History* [New York, 1953]; *DAB*).

2. Fuller refers to Dido's suicide in bk. 4 of the *Aeneid*:

> then rumour ran amok through the shocked city.
> All was weeping and wailing, the streets were filled with a keening
> Of women, the air resounded with terrible lamentations.

[*The Aeneid of Virgil*, trans. C. Day Lewis (New York, 1952), p. 91]

3. Ps. 19:13: "Keep back thy servant also from presumptuous sins; let them not have dominion over me: then shall I be upright, and I shall be innocent from the great transgression."

375. To William H. Channing[?]

July 1842

I have been entertaining the girls here with my old experiences at Groton. They have been very fresh in my mind this week. Had I but been as wise in such matters then as now, how easy and fair I might have made the whole! Too late, too late to live, but not too late to think! And as that maxim of the wise Oriental teaches, "the Acts of this life shall be the Fate of the next."

ELfr, from *Memoirs*, 2:65.

376. To Charles K. Newcomb

Providence,
1st July, 1842.

My dear Charles,

I am like to die of ennui here without you, and so I think I will write a few lines. I had no idea what a difference it would make not to find you, indeed we have often met here in a way so interrupted and uncongenial, that I thought it would be quite as well not to have you at all, but to give the few days, entirely to others, in *their* way. But I do not find it so. If you had been here, we could have walked out into the green fields and woods, which I would not alone, at this time and I would have been refreshed from the din and excitement and the hot, staring streets. And you would have been amused with the same slight things that I am, and would not have needed to explain. The few with whom no explanation is needed; that is all our society: is it not Charles?

When I see you, I shall have many things to tell about this period, but there is no time or space to write them.

Your sisters are to me sweet, and fair in their several ways, as formerly.[1] Intercourse with your M[other], I find more pleasant. She is, I see, much improved, more wise and self-possessed, and I do not think I shall feel painful constraint in acquaintance with her, henceforth. As always, she is a tender and intelligent parent to you.

I was very glad you so enjoyed your visit to Mr E (whom I love always more truly and largely) and to see that you mentioned pleasure,

75

in seeing E. Hoar.[2] E. H. is a rare being; she is one not only pure and of noble intent, but of real refinement *both* of character and intellect. Her character is one of rose colored crystals, her mind one of many, though minute flowers, and golden grain is seen there too, well ripened, fit for bread, yet still waving in the wind.

I will tell you just what I think of the new Dolon. I hope you will keep the other two just as they are. Sometime, I want to hear them read again. I hope the Dial will never perish, but be, as you say, the common ground of friendship, and the means of development to us all. To you, may the summer be fruitful!

You would, probably have seen me at Brook Farm next week, but that I find your mother proposes going there. This will take up the room, and, beside, I had rather be there by myself.— But ascertain from Mrs Ripley, and write to me whether there will be room if I come on a little visit, the week after, or the week after *that*.— I wish you would say to her, too, or to Mr R. as you think best, and request them not to mention it, that Lloyd's experiment has not been successful, and that, if I must remove him and cannot place him to my mind, elsewhere, whether he can be received back, or whether his place is now filled up.

Just, as I had written this, your mother found I was writing and thought she would send you a message, instead of writing by me. She will come to Brook Farm on Saturday next, and go a journey with you afterward[n] This gives me time enough for my visit, and, if agreeable to Mrs Ripley, I will come *Tuesday, p. m.* I wish you could come to Cambridge and fetch me, as then we might have a beautiful drive, but suppose there is full employment for the farm[n] steeds. Mr Farrar will bring me, or I will come by omnibus. Write to me by post, to say whether it will be convenient to have me, and put it into the mail on Sunday, unless you can send to Cambridge direct, care Prof. Farrar. *Do not* speak about L. since I am to come myself. I hope it will be convenient to have me, visits if postponed are so likely not to be made at all. Your friend

M. F.

ALS (MH: fMS Am 1086 [10:136]). *Addressed:* Charles K. Newcomb. / West Roxbury / Mass. *Postmark:* Providence Jul 1 R I.

and go a journey with you afterward] ↑ and go a journey with you afterward ↓
the farm] the ⟨fr⟩ farm

1. Two of Charles's sisters, Elizabeth and Charlotte, had been Fuller's pupils at Jamaica Plain.

2. Emerson invited Newcomb to Concord on 8 June. He came, stayed until 19 or 20 June, left his manuscript of "The Two Dolons," and impressed not only Emerson but also Elizabeth Hoar and Thoreau (Rusk, *Letters of RWE*, 3:61, 64, 65, 67).

377.   To Ralph Waldo Emerson

White Mts July 25, 1842

You say that Nature does not keep her promise: but surely she satisfies us now and then, for the time.[1] The drama is always in progress, but here and there she speaks out a sentence, full in its cadence, complete in its structure, it occupies for the time the sense and the thought. We have no care for promises. Will you say, it is the superficialness of my life, that I have known hours with men and nature that bore their proper fruit, all present ate, and were filled, and there were taken up of the fragments twelve baskets full.[2] Is it because of the superficial mind, or the believing heart that I can say this?

MsCfr (MH: bMS Am 1280 [111, pp. 130–31]). Published in *Memoirs*, 1:264–65, and *JMN*, 11:481.

1. In his letter of 19 July, Emerson said to Fuller: "Ah promising promising flattering Nature! when to perform so much as is convenanted by a ray from a dewdrop or the night lamp of a firefly?—" (Rusk, *Letters of RWE*, 3:73).

2. The feeding of the multitude described in Matt. 14:20 ("And they did all eat, and were filled: and they took up of the fragments that remained twelve baskets full"), Mark 6:43, and Luke 9:17.

378.   To Charles K. Newcomb

Cambridge
30th July, 1842.

Well, dear Charles, how did your journey prosper?— Did you see beautiful things? Did you have leisure and peace to enjoy them? Have you garnered up new thoughts therefrom? I want much to hear from you, both of these things and of your health, for you seemed to me quite unwell during my week at Brook Farm.

I, too, have been with some friends to the White Hills, and "from the brain of the purple mountain" flowed forth cheer to my somewhat weary mind.[1] Could I have returned light and musical, making my own course and decking its borders as easily as the streams do, it would have been still better, but the journey home was one of dust and other annoy, relieved however by the kind and pleasant companionship of those who can both speak and be silent.

The mountains seemed very hospitable and familiar. Their aspect is grand, commanding but not sublime. Neither are there the beautiful and mysterious features we read of in the Alpine and Welsh mountains, not sudden chasms, and precipices, not[n] wild torrents, nor peak towering above peak to scale the sky,[n] but noble swells of lands tossed and heaped up wavelike, here and there suddenly rebounding, but oftener sloping down as with smooth though sharply outlined watery crest. All is now overgrown with wood, except where now and then a water course, or abraded descent gleams in the sun. The woods are most alluring, in many places full of fallen trees, lying negligently across one another and covered with calm-looking moss. In the streams there is a very beautiful moss, with a waxen leaf, such as I have not elsewhere seen. The changing hues upon the mountains were beautiful beyond my thought. There are, also, very graceful waterfalls amid the hills, and caves of more dignity than that at Brook Farm!— From "Edith" gleams of magical light, intimations of deep promise come upon my thought.[2] I am very glad you read me that. I like to hear your thoughts from your own tones of profound and timid sensibility far better than to read them myself, yet I cannot recal all I would.

You know my final feeling was that your mind must fashion its own garb. Yet it is right to tell you that, as usual, I hit exactly on the average impression most minds would receive from Dolon. Its redundant and involved style displeases, and hides, not drapes the thought. On a third reading I am more than ever sensible that you must learn the art of choosing among your thoughts, and prune as well as water your vine, if it is ever to give forth the express, the ruby wine from its clusters. Even the perfect Raphael chose amid his thoughts as may well be seen by looking through his Studies, and more and more as he grew older. Your mind is worthy and able to discipline itself. I know you wish to refuse exaggerated and premature praise, and you have promised me that you will not permit critiques which must, from their nature, be superficial to interfere, to your prejudice[n] but you may borrow from them useful suggestion.— I have a letter this morning from Caroline. I wish we had talked more fully on her subject. She regrets to feel any gap between her and souls which have been allied with hers, but she feels that she must go her free path, and does not wish prematurely to explain even to herself the stages of her progress.[3] Trust her, my dear Charles, that she *must* keep herself true to her aim. She is not the ideal figure you have made from her. But the genius of Nature is nobler than the genius of any one man, and those who are true to their inward light become fairer poems (in a long, indeed, Oh how long, scope) than they can suggest. Trust her for your own sake, since she could so move you to think and create.

Farewell, may light and life be yours!

MARGARET F.

78

ALS (MH: fMS Am 1086 [10:139]). *Addressed:* Charles K. Newcomb / West Roxbury / Mass.

and precipices, not] and pre⟨s⟩cipices, no⟨r⟩t

nor peak towering above peak to scale the sky,] ↑ nor peak towering above peak to scale the sky, ↓

to interfere, to your prejudice] ↑ to ↓ interfere, ↑ to your prejudice ↓

1. Tennyson, "The Poet's Mind":

> In the middle leaps a fountain
> Like sheet lightning,
> Ever brightening
> With a low melodious thunder;
> All day and all night it is ever drawn
> From the brain of the purple mountain
> Which stands in the distance yonder:
>
> [Tennyson, *Poems*, 1:51]

2. A story Newcomb had written.

3. In her letter of 21 July (MH), Sturgis said of Newcomb and Emerson: "Why will they not let me develope myself in my own way—because it lies through persons & almost any person will stand between any other two? I wish no one would ever ask me why I like another—I never can tell why the question always seems to me presumptuous."

379. To James F. Clarke

31 July 1842
Cambridge

I said I was happy in having no secret. It is my nature, and has been the tendency of my life, to wish that all my thoughts and deeds might lie, as the "open secrets" of Nature, free to all who are able to understand them. I have no reserves, except intellectual reserves; for to speak of things to those who cannot receive them is stupidity, rather than frankness. But in this case, I alone am not concerned. Therefore, dear James, give heed to the subject. You have received a key to what was before unknown of your friend; you have made use of it, now let it be buried with the past, over whose passages profound and sad, yet touched with heaven-born beauty, "let silence stand sentinel."

ELfr, from *Memoirs*, 1:74.

380. To Elizabeth Hoar

Cambridge [August?] 1842

E[llery] has written to you. We have had several good hours to-

gether.¹ he is unequal and uncertain but in his good moods, of the
the best for a companion, absolutely abandoned to the revelations of
the moment, without distrust or check of any kind, unlimited, and
delicate, abundant in thought, and free of motion, he enriches life,
and fills the hour.

MsCfr (MH: bMS Am 1280 [111, p. 95]). Published in part in *Memoirs*, 1:210; published entire in *JMN*, 11:475.
1. Leaving Ellen in Cincinnati, Channing returned to Boston, where he planned for them to live. Margaret saw him often during August and early September, especially when they visited Emerson in Concord (Myerson, "Margaret Fuller's 1842 Journal," pp. 320–40).

381.   To William H. Channing[?]

August 1842
Cambridge

Few have eyes for the pretty little features of a scene. In this, men are
not so good as boys. Artists are always thus young; poets are; but the
pilgrim does not lay aside his belt of steel, nor the merchant his pack,
to worship the flowers on the fountain's brink. I feel, like Herbert, the
weight of "business to be done,"¹ but the bird-like particle would skim
and sing at these sweet places. It seems strange to leave them; and
that we do so, while so fitted to live deeply in them, shows that beauty
is the end but not the means.

I have just been reading the new poems of Tennyson.² Much has
he thought, much suffered, since the first ecstasy of so fine an organization clothed all the world with rosy light. He has not suffered himself to become a mere intellectual voluptuary, nor the songster of
fancy and passion, but has earnestly revolved the problems of life,
and his conclusions are calmly noble. In these later verses is a still,
deep sweetness; how different from the intoxicating, sensuous mel-
ody of his earlier cadence! I have loved him much this time, and
taken him to heart as a brother. One of his themes has long been my
favorite,—the last expedition of Ulysses,—and his, like mine, is the
Ulysses of the Odyssey, with his deep romance of wisdom, and not the
worldling of the Iliad. How finely marked his slight description of
himself and of Telemachus. In Dora, Locksley Hall, the Two Voices,
Morte D'Arthur, I find my own life, much of it, written truly out.

ELfr, from *Memoirs*, 2:66.

1. From George Herbert, "The Church-Porch": "Let thy minde still be bent, still plotting where, / And when, and how the businesse may be done" (*Works of George Herbert*, p. 20).

2. Fuller reviewed Tennyson's 1842 two-volume edition of poems in *Dial* 3 (1842):273–76, where she said:

> So large a proportion of even the good poetry of our time is ever over-ethical or over-passionate, and the stock poetry is so deeply tained with a sentimental egotism, that this, whose chief merits lay in its melody and picturesque power, was most refreshing. What a relief, after sermonizing and wailing had dulled the sense with such a weight of cold abstraction, to be soothed by this ivory lute! [P. 273]

382. To Richard F. Fuller

Cambridge,
5th August, 1842.

Dear Richard,

I want to hear how you enjoyed your journey, and what you think of the world as surveyed from mountain-tops, but suppose you are waiting to hear from me.[1] The heat during my journey was extreme. I suffered from fatigue, and the times I enjoyed were those when we were staying amid the mountains. I feel satisfied, as I thought I should, with reading these bolder lines in the manuscript of nature. Merely gentle and winning scenes are not enough for me. I wish my lot had been cast amid the sources of the streams, where the voice of the hidden torrent is heard by night, where the eagle soars, and the thunder resounds in long peals from side to side, where the grasp of a more powerful emotion has rent asunder the rocks, and the long purple shadows fall like a broad wing upon the valley. All places like all persons[n] I know have beauty which may be discovered by a thoughtful and observing mind, but only in some scenes, and with some people can I expand, and feel myself at home. I feel this all the more for having passed my childhood in such a place as Cambridge. Port. There I had nothing except[n] the little flower garden behind the house, and the elms before the door. I used to long and pine for beautiful places such as I read of. There was not one walk for me, except over the bridge. I liked that very much, the river, and the city glittering in sunset, and the lovely undulating line all round, and the light smokes, seen in some weathers.

I did not incline to stay at the White Hills after the others had gone,

81

both because it was too[n] expensive, for at these mountain houses they bring what is wanted from so great a distance that they are obliged to ask as much as at a city hotel, and because there are so many people coming and going that I should have needed the protection of a gentleman.— I wish that you and I could afford to go to some of the finest places and stay there awhile, for I should like to be with you better than with any one almost. I have thought, if we have money, perhaps we may go to Niagara another summer, for, hacknied thoroughfare as it is now, I have a great desire to see that wonder under circumstances that will not disturb my pleasure in it. It is a great deal to have these things to remember, though you do not live in them at the time, this indeed you can rarely expect, time is limited and the whole expedition conducted in a business way, not favorable to the right mood coming up.

I now hope to settle my mind for a while. I have grown weary of dissipation. You, too, I hope are happy in thought and study. Books are good in this: they do not excite as men and nature do[n] one can half-slumber in their company and dream no useless dream.

Arthur returned from R. I. a few days since and is now gone to Duxbury. He much enjoyed his visits, and had gleaned many things pleasant to hear. Lloyd is now settled, for the present, at Brook Farm and pretty happy. Yet keep him in your thoughts, if you may see any thing better for him: they send me word nothing can be done at P. now. Ellery is here, he wants to see you. I have had one pleasant visit from him. He thinks he shall board at Concord with Ellen, and employ himself in writing through the winter. He has written for Mother and Ellen to come on early in Septr. I saw Uncle Abra just before I went away; he expressed great delight in you, observed he heard the best accounts of your progress, and that[n] I knew you had always been *his favorite*!! which I did not dispute, though I could not recal any signal proofs he had given of this partiality. Farewell, write me a long letter tell about yourself, your journey and how all looks in Groton. Is the vine still flourishing on the piazza?

Direct to me here Care Prof Farrar, and do not pay your postage, as I shall not mine. Affey your sister

M.

ALS (MH: fMS Am 1086 [9:90]); MsC (MH: fMS Am 1086 [Works, 2:711–19]). Published in part in *WNC*, pp. 365–66, and Miller, pp. 4–5. *Addressed:* Richard F. Fuller / Groton / Mass. *Postmark:* Cambridge MS. Aug. 5.

places like all persons] places ↑ like all persons ↓
nothing except] nothing ex⟨p⟩cept

was too] was ↑ too ↓
nature do] nature ↑ do ↓
and that] and ⟨observed⟩ that

1. On 19 July Richard and Thoreau set off for a walk to Wachusett mountain. Thoreau later described the expedition in "A Walk to Wachusett" (Rusk, *Letters of RWE*, 3:75; *The Writings of Henry David Thoreau* [Boston, 1893], 9:163–86). Margaret was on cordial terms with Thoreau, though she had rejected his essays when she edited the *Dial*.

383. To Ralph Waldo Emerson

Cambridge
10th August, 1842.

Dear Waldo,

I have been waiting to write to you till Mr and Mrs Farrar should decide whether to go a journey they had in view. If they had gone, I was to have staid here during their absence for this would have ensured me several weeks of stillness and solitude, so that I could have fixed my mind on writing. But they have given up this journey, and I should like to come to you next week, if you please. Now I want you to be perfectly frank in answering what I shall say. I am tired to death of dissipation; I do not enjoy it, nor find any repose in mere observation now I long to employ myself steadily. I have no inspiration now, but hope it might come, if I were once fixed in some congenial situation. Should you like it should be with you, that I should come and really *live* in your house a month, instead of making a visit, as I should here. Would it entirely suit Lidian's convenience?[1]

Do not regard hospitality in your answer for if I am[n] to feel quite happy and at my ease it must be perfectly pleasant for you. I must feel that I shall not be in any one's way. I am always sensitive about encamping on your territories, for I think so many tax your hospitality without mercy. Beside I have put off my visit to suit myself, and it may not now suit you. Then, though I feel as if I should like to be with you now, yet as regards convenience, they will give me a room at Brook Farm, if I wish, let me do as I please, and I think if I went there to stay, I could keep by myself, and employ myself, if there is any force in my mind.—[2] Beside, I will not give up seeing you. If you do not want me to stay in this unlimited fashion, I will come for two or three days, on a visit (technically speaking. But I want to know before hand which it shall be for if I come to stay, I shall bring my papers &c, but if not, I shall leave them here, write to Brook Farm to engage my room, and go there as soon as I have seen you satisfactorily.

Now, dear friend, be entirely frank, and induce Lidian to be so. I should be with you.

Whether for the long, or the little stay, I can come any day next week after Tuesday that you will appoint. As to your coming for me, I have bethought me, that you may purpose coming to the Commencement exercises the[n] following week, and may not wish to come so soon before. I should still like to have you, insomuch as I should enjoy riding with you, and seeing you first so, but unless you have other *errands* to do and would altogether like to come, you must not, because I suggested it, but write, and, if you dont wish it so, I will come in the stage.

I should be glad to get an answer on Saty if possible. This I meant to send by Ellery who goes today to Concord, but cannot get it to Boston, however, it will reach you almost as soon as he. Ellery wants to try the boarding place, himself, before Ellen comes, and I am glad he is going to do so, beside he is as anxious to get settled as I am, and more impatient. Why is Mrs Thoreau's recommended, rather than Mrs Pritchard's?[3] I thought the latter was much the pleasantest family, and the windows look over the meadows and river.— My love to Elizabeth. Say I wrote to her, but I did not like the letter and put it into my portfolio.[4] I shall talk better than I wrote I hope. All other things postponing till we meet yours as ever

MARGARET.

ALS (MH; bMS Am 1280 [2366]). Published in part in Higginson, *MFO*, p. 182, and Rusk, *Letters of RWE*, 3:79–80. *Addressed:* R W. Emerson / Concord / Mass. *Postmark:* Cambridge MS Aug 10. *Endorsed:* Margaret F / Aug. 1842 . Cambridge.

for if I am] for ↑if I am↓
exercises the] exercises ⟨nex⟩ the

1. Emerson immediately responded: "Well, now please to come, for this I have always desired that you will make my house in some way useful to your occasions & not a mere hotel for a sleighing or summering party" (Rusk, *Letters of RWE*, 3:80).

2. In good humor, Emerson promised to let her alone: "I admire the conditions of the treaty, that you shall put on sulkiness as a morning gown, & I shall put on sulkiness as a surtout, and speech shall be contraband & the exception not the rule" (Rusk, *Letters of RWE*, 3:80).

3. Henry Thoreau's mother, Cynthia Dunbar Thoreau (Harding, *Days of Henry Thoreau*, pp. 8–10). Jane Hallett Prichard was the wife of Moses Prichard, a failed businessman in Concord.

4. Perhaps letter 369 above, which Emerson copied into his journal.

384.   To Richard F. Fuller

Cambridge
11th August, 1842.

Dear Richard,

I dont see any way I can do about your money, unless to inclose it in a letter. I am sorry to do this, as you will have to pay double postage, probably, next time you must take enough to secure you against emergencies. If this sum is not enough, (I could not judge from your letter,) you might borrow a small sum from Mr Lawrence, and send it to him on your return, but I hope this will not be necessary.

Your letter was very pleasant to me, and as to the journal[n] I shall be glad to read, ay, and correct it, too! You do not speak of Groton. That place is very beautiful in its way, but I never admired it much, both because the scenery is too tamely smiling and sleepy, and because it jarred my mood. My associations with the place are painful. The first passage of our lives there was Arthur's misfortune, my first weeks there were passed in Arthur's chambers. These darkened round as the consequences of our father's ill-judged exchange, ill-judged at least as regarded himself, your Mother, and myself.[1] The younger ones were not violently rent from all their former life and cast on toils for which they were unprepared. There your Mother's health was injured and mine destroyed; there your father died, but not till the cares of a narrowed income, and collisions with his elder sons which would not have ended there had so embittered his life and made him so over anxious that I have never regretted that he did not stay longer to watch the turning of the[n] tide, for his life up to 1830 had been one of well-earned prosperity, which, after that time, was rapidly ebbing from him, and I do not think adversity would have done him good, he could not reconcile himself to it, his feeling was that after thirty years labor and self-denial he was entitled to peace and he would not have had it.

You were too young to feel how trying are the disorders of a house which has lost its head, the miserable perplexities which arose in our affairs, the wounds your mother underwent in that time of deep dejection from the unfeeling and insolent conduct of many who had been kept in check by respect for your father, her loneliness and sense of unfitness for the new and heavy burden of care. It will be many years yet, before you can appreciate the conflicts of my mind, as I doubted whether to give up all which my heart desired for a path

85

for which I had no skill, and no call, except that *some one* must tread it, and none else was ready. The Peterborough hills, and the Wachusetts are associated in my mind with many hours of anguish, as great I think as I am capable of feeling. I used to look at them, towering to the sky, and feel that I, too, from my birth had longed to rise, but I felt crushed to earth, yet again a nobler spirit said *that* could never be. The good knight may come forth scarred and maimed from the unequal contest, shorn of his strength and unsightly to the careless eye, but the same fire burns within and deeper ever, he may be conquered but *never subdued.* But if these beautiful hills, and wide, rich fields saw this sad lore well learned they also saw some precious lessons given too, of faith, of fortitude, of self-command, and a less selfish love. There too in solitude the mind acquired more power of concentration and discerned the beauty of a stricter method. There the heart was awakened to sympathize with the ignorant, to pity the vulgar, and hope for the seemingly worthless, for a need was felt of realizing the only reality, the divine soul of this visible creation, which cannot err and will not sleep, which cannot permit evil to be permanent or its aim of beauty to be eventually frustrated in the smallest particular.—

Ellery is gone to Concord to stay, and you can see him there at any time. He now expects to pass the winter there in writing. Mother and Ellen will return by the middle of Septr. If you defer your visit till the end of the week, or till you are on your way back to Cambridge, you may see me too.[2] I shall probably be there next week. I am glad you like your books. I have been reading Herodotus. I find these Greeks, though I can only read them in translations the most healthful and satisfactory companions. I keep one of them by me always now. You should not have tried Cousin on Locke but his Introduction[3] Affectionately your sister

M.

Ought I not to say that my younger brothers too laid here the foundations of more robust enterprizing and at the same time self denying character than the elder had been led to by more indulgent nurture.

ALS (MH: fMS Am 1086 [9:83]); MsC (MH: fMS Am 1086 [Works, 2:719–27]). Published in part in Higginson, *MFO*, pp. 59–61; Miller, pp. 34–35; and Chevigny, p. 172. Published entire in Wade, pp. 560–61. *Addressed:* Richard F. Fuller / Groton / Mass. *Postmark:* Cambridge MS. Aug. 12.

and as to the journal] and ↑ as to the journal ↓
of the] of ⟨?⟩the

1. Arthur suffered a severe injury to an eye shortly after the Fullers moved to Groton in 1833. The "ill-judged exchange" was her father's decision to leave his law practice and become a farmer.

2. Richard visited her at the Emersons (Myerson, "Margaret Fuller's 1842 Journal," p. 327).

3. Victor Cousin discussed Locke in his lectures on eighteenth-century philosophy, which were published as the second volume of *Cours de l'histoire de la philosophie* (Paris, 1829). Caleb Sprague Henry had published a translation, *Elements of Psychology: Included in a Critical Examination of Locke's Essay on the Human Understanding* (Hartford, Conn., 1834).

385.   To Caroline Sturgis

16th August, 1842.

I hope the book, dear Cary, does not come too late for your wishes. I have only just now been able to get it. Have you not liked much Tennyson's new poems?

I have had pleasant meetings with Ellery. He seems frank, even *direct*, and gentle. In his eye is most sweet expression. He has gone to board in Concord. I am going there tomorrow to stay some time and shall then see him often, and I hope to find pleasure in it.[1]

Jane I saw yesterday.[2] She too soon goes to Concord on a visit. She is *modestly* happy, is much better, and looks prettier than I have seen her for a long time.

I saw Anna Shaw just before she went on her[n] journey, and she looked like a tall lily on which the rain had beaten too hard. However the ills are all from *without* and very bearable with so much happiness. Indeed she seemed glad of some bitter with so much sweet.

Charles has been very ill (in the same way as you were)—near death, I hear, but they think him out of danger now. Perhaps you hear from Brook Farm.

At the gallery are Murillo's "boys with grapes and melons" which I should like to have you see.[3] There are few good pictures.

Write to me at Concord, if you can. I want to know if the sands of Nashoun look golden still.

M.

Caroline, these with haste as in haste written.

ALS (MH: bMS Am 1221 [245]). *Endorsed:* 16th Aug. 1842.

went on her] went on ⟨a⟩her

1. Fuller described her visit to Emerson and meetings there with Ellery Channing in her journal (Myerson, "Margaret Fuller's 1842 Journal," pp. 320–40).

87

2. Jane Tuckerman, daughter of Gustavus Tuckerman of Boston, had been Fuller's pupil. She was a good friend of Caroline Sturgis.

3. Bartolomé Esteban Murillo (1617–82), the Spanish painter. His *Dos niños comiendo fruta* was painted ca. 1650.

386. To Samuel G. Ward

Concord
August 21st 1842

The Sunday came with its usual contracts of sunlight, coolness, and pleasure. But you came not with it, at which I did not grieve, for I have nothing to offer you, or any one, in society, though God knows I do bear you with me in my heart. I am under a painful weight of debt to you for large store of kindnesses in the past, and in the present, and am glad to find my faith does not diminish in your bounty, or my affection grow cold in absence. I think you stand well among the figures on my canvass,— a reasonable man, whom the demon of vanity has not led into idleness or contempt for his kind. I am free to carry you as a recollection which I am past doing for many, and only wonder you have escaped all the nonsense of our day so well and stand steadily drudging at your broker's shop, like many another son of Adam. Whence came that broad prudence which has made its nest in your brain, unless from Minerva herself?

I shall never pay off even the interest of this large debt I owe you, of fine thoughts, of noble deeds, now running on so many years, but if there is any God who meets men face to face, and knows their merits, I believe your goodness to me will not go unbalanced. I was born to a fortune, though not of pence, for which last, truly, I cannot bow. I came in, to meet the splendid hearts of friends, who have matched their earliest gifts, every day down to this present; I have been conquered out of my desperate monodies, by the sounds of their cheerful speech. Yet, though I love them more, I am every day more careless of them, being but a poor creature at the best, and my only mercy with any at the nib of the pen. My speech to men has failed to pay its dividends, yet my capital stock is not withdrawn.

I will confess, once for all, I had longed to see you a painter, and not a merchant out of the intolerable stupidity of my nature, which still owns a treacherous inkling for pictures and poems, and I have not even so far cured this miserable vanity, as not now and then to scribble some paltry line. I used to gaze on you, and say to myself, this

man must needs be the painter of our country, and as one in the ser-
ried ranks of his friends, I shall witness his victories over the immortal
beauty, with some little satisfaction, as high as my nature will go in
that line, which I do confess is not lofty. The very mould of this man's
face was built for the life of statues, buildings, and splendid landscapes. He will set the century on fire, with the beauty of his conceptions, and burn up the stubble of our degeneracy in a flame which
shall lick away the stars. Once in five hundred years, God sends some
pitiful figure to convince us that we are only dead bones in his presence, and life springs into charming, from the touch of his finger, as
if he did create.

I had linked these silly thoughts with you, and many times, in imagination, have I[n] sat in your studio, and wept over my inadequate
strength to grasp the greatness of your landscapes or statues in my
eye, and played some comic part among your creations which went
nigh to lunacy. Yet, it was not without a touch of ravishment, when I
saw you spring on shore after your Italian voyage, as light as some
creature of the element, and the translation of all the beauty of many
centuries.[1] I felt it was a glad hour for art, and that our Prometheus
still held the divine fire on the point of his pencil. Of course, it was
that you must be the Painter of the time, redeem our souls from their
Lethean slumber, and waft us into the upper airs of felicity. Such
were the silly tricks, my fatuous imagination played with the honest
domain of common sense, for even then I had a pitiful snickering after verse, and already had made some wretched rhymes.

When I learned you were to become a merchant, to sit at the dead
wood of the desk, and calculate figures, I was betrayed into some unbelief, as if this information was the lusus of a report, the shadow of
the chimney's smoke. Yet it came true, as many another unbelief of
mine has.

I would you had starved yourself lean, for two-score years, over a
few shavings in some garret, and therein fixed an iron spear in the
hard breast of Art, and forced it to yield its elixir. I would that Art
had crushed you in its bronze vice, until your life ran out a rich wine
of beauty. Had only a great despair passed its stained fingers across
your temples, and drawn therein ten perpetual furrows. Had want
showered early over your classic form its grey mantle of cloud, had
you wept bitter tears, over five hundred failures of your pencil stung
your palm, as though it had carried an asp to its handle

So wretched a mendicant am I, at the great gate of riches, and so
low are my conceptions of that ripe prudence which tarries in your intellect, as if fourscore years had unladen their mighty freights of ex-

perience in your mind, I feel assured, both by the honor I bear your deeds, and by the respect I feel that the path you now creep in is the best.

I do but paint the shadows which intrude momentarily in my being and pass forever more over the fathomless lake of my existence. Yet I have been fortunate, and plucked some sunny spring-flowers, which shake their blue bells over this ruin that I was. It matters not, in this brief and flying moment, which we call life, after all, what we accomplish. Unresting nature bathes each infant as he rises out of the visionless sea with these fair, gentle influences, and does not demand back even the husks of our joys. Ever swings at th' other end, the melancholy portal at which we exit, a line of shadow between two worlds of spotless beauty.

> Who paints not here,
> Paints in that other sphere,
> And bends his line
> With forms divine.

By the stroke of the clock, I see the meridian hour sits full upon the fields. Yon stately[n] elm, with its central shadow, else sheeted in this crown of sunlight, which ever day wears for the full noon hour, emblems again the picturesqueness of our fate. I see the tasselled corn ripening in the glorious warmth; I do note the green turf of the bank below me, and the blue of the peaceful sky. So infinitely genial may also fall the noon-hour of your life, and the gratitude of your poor friend be[n] like some little birds' song in the grand meridian concert. With which I also conclude myself, yours in love

AMs (MH: fMS Am 1086 [9:91]). *Endorsed* in Fuller's hand: E to Rafaello.

The letter probably is a copy made by Fuller.

have I] ⟨I⟩ have ↑ I ↓
Yon stately] Yo⟨u⟩n stately
friend be] friend⟨s⟩ be

1. In the mid-1830s Ward had gone to Europe with John and Eliza Farrar, a trip Fuller would have made had not her father died.

387. To William H. Channing[?]

25 August 1842
Concord

Beneath this roof of peace, beneficence, and intellectual activity, I

find just the alternation of repose and satisfying pleasure that I need.
[   ]

Do not find fault with the hermits and scholars. The true text is:—

> "Mine own Telemachus
> He does his work—I mine."[1]

All do the work, whether they will or no; but he is "mine own Telemachus" who does it in the spirit of religion, never believing that the last results can be arrested in any one measure or set of measures, listening always to the voice of the Spirit,—and who does this more than [Waldo]?[2]

After the first excitement of intimacy with him,—when I was made so happy by his high tendency, absolute purity, the freedom and infinite graces of an intellect cultivated much beyond any I had known, —came with me the questioning season. I was greatly disappointed in my relation to him. I was, indeed, always called on to be worthy,— this benefit was sure in our friendship. But I found no intelligence of my best self; far less was it revealed to me in new modes; for not only did he seem to want the living faith which enables one to discharge this holiest office of a friend, but he absolutely distrusted me in every region of my life with which he was unacquainted. The same trait I detected in his relations with others. He had faith in the Universal, but not in the Individual Man; he met men, not as a brother, but as a critic. Philosophy appeared to chill instead of exalting the poet.

But now I am better acquainted with him. His "accept" is true; the "I shall learn," with which he answers every accusation, is no less true. No one can feel his limitations, in fact, more than he, though he always speaks confidently from his present knowledge as all he has yet, and never qualifies or explains. He feels himself "shut up in a crystal cell," from which only "a great love or a great task could release me," and hardly expects either from what remains in this life. But I already see so well how these limitations have fitted him for his peculiar work, that I can no longer quarrel with them; while from his eyes looks out the angel that must sooner or later break every chain. Leave him in his cell affirming absolute truth; protesting against humanity, if so he appears to do; the calm observer of the courses of things. Surely, "he keeps true to this thought, which is the great matter." He has already paid his debt to his time; how much more he will give we cannot know; but already I feel how invaluable is a cool mind, like his, amid the warring elements around us. As I look at him more by his own law, I understand him better; and as I understand him better, differences melt away. My inmost heart blesses the fate that gave me birth in the same clime and time, and that has drawn me into such a close bond with him as, it is my hopeful faith, will never be broken, but from sphere to sphere ever more hallowed. [   ]

What did you mean by saying I had imbibed much of his way of thought? I do indeed feel his life stealing gradually into mine; and I sometimes think that my work would have been more simple, and my unfolding to a temporal activity more rapid and easy, if we had never met. But when I look forward to eternal growth, I am always aware that I am far larger and deeper for him. His influence has been to me that of lofty assurance and sweet serenity. He says, I come to him as the European to the Hindoo, or the gay Trouvére to the Puritan in his steeple hat. Of course this implies that our meeting is partial. I present to him the many forms of nature and solicit with music; he melts them all into spirit and reproves performance with prayer. When I am with God alone, I adore in silence. With nature I am filled and grow only. With most men I bring words of now past life, and do actions suggested by the wants of their natures rather than my own. But he stops me from doing anything, and makes me think.

ELfr, from *Memoirs*, 2:67–69.
May be more than one letter. The recipient is probably William Henry Channing.
1. From Tennyson's "Ulysses":

> Most blameless is he, centred in the sphere
> Of common duties, decent not to fail
> In offices of tenderness, and pay
> Meet adoration to my household gods
> When I am gone. He works his work, I mine.
> [Tennyson, *Poems*, 2:90]

2. Though the name is omitted in *Memoirs*, it is undoubtedly Emerson.

388.   To Ralph Waldo Emerson

September, 1842
Concord

I am very idle now, though I do not wish to be, it cannot be helped. I write a great deal and talk, but there is no *force* in what I do. To Nature too I am no nearer. The woods and fields afford but superficial pleasure; and I have not that clear feeling of interpretation of her analogies, which so long has given me a thrill of delight in looking at these objects.

I do not read deeply either, and am not drawn into the secret of things, but only look on and do not feel myself powerfully while reading them. Pray for me that, while I patiently abide my time, I become not indolent and dull rather than submissive;—that after a season of energetic and intensely clear vision I become not stationary, living on the past as so many do. Perhaps this passive state will not continue long; for I have glimpses of beauty often times flitting before me, and all my emotions are tranquil and sweet. However I left off writing in my diary after about ten days,—for I found that what was written was good for nothing. I could not put into it my real life;—for that at present is so vague and mysterious to myself that I cannot take hold of it with sufficient firmness to describe it. Of the talks here with my friends I make notes; but they are made daily after occupying several hours in conversation; and, unless as many more had been given to the report, no true idea would be conveyed of what passed in these wonderful hours. Yet I deeply wish to keep some record of these days; for if well done, though not as beautiful and grand, yet they would be as significant of the highest New England life in this era, as Plato's marvellous Dialogues were of the life of Attica, in his time. For I do not believe that a life has been ever lived which without effort so nearly approached that of the accademic Grove. A conversation in Landor between Sir Philip Sidney and Lord Brooke is in the same style.[1] Nor are ours inferior in quality to that. But, alas, I cannot reproduce this life, while I am in it; and I shall never retain of my friendship with Waldo six years hence anything more than a faint shining reflex.

MsCfr in Emerson's hand (MH: Os 735Laa 1842.9).

1. Walter Savage Landor, *Imaginary Conversations of Literary Men and Statesmen* (London, 1824).

389. To Charles K. Newcomb

Septr 1842.

I believe I should have written to you, my always dear Charles, if you had asked it in your note to Mr Emerson, but there was something in the tone of your message that made me uncertain whether you wished it.[1] Perhaps I was mistaken, for your note was a hurried one. I have been waiting to see if you would not write to me when you got well.— Now I want very much to know whether you are entirely recovered, and whether you have been at "dear eternal Newport" and whether you want to see or hear from me.— I did not know of your illness till the danger was over, or I should have gone to Brook Farm to see if I could see you.— Write now to your friend

M. F.

Four days later at Brook Farm

I have your room here and think much of you. I have been every day to your pine wood, and wished I could hear there again of the life of Edith. I wish I could have a letter from you here, but there will not be time, after you receive this. So write to me at Cambridge. Should not you like to pass the winter there?

ALS (MH: fMS Am 1086 [10:140]). *Addressed:* Charles King Newcomb.

1. Newcomb, who had been ill the latter part of August, wrote to Emerson on 19 August (MH) saying that his health was so bad that he could not finish his "Dolon" manuscript until October. This is possibly the letter Fuller mentions.

390. To Caroline Sturgis

Concord 9th Septr 1842.

Dear Caroline,

Ellery left us on Saty morng intending to visit you at Naushon on Sunday.[1]

He said he should positively return Tuesday morning *at latest,* as there was reason to think Ellen might be here next day. It is Friday, and he has not come, nor can I conceive where he is. I fear something must have happened to him. I cannot think he would stay else. I suppose from letters that Ellen may arrive today, how she will feel, and how I shall feel, if he is not here; you may guess. Pray write to me instantly and take what measures you can that I may get your letter with all speed to tell me whether he came and when went away. He may be here to night, but if not, I shall not know what to think or to do for Ellen

MARGARET.

ALS (MHi). *Addressed:* Miss Caroline Sturgis, / at Mr Wm Swain's / Naushon / near New Bedford / Mass. *Endorsed:* Sept 1842.

1. Channing had thrown Fuller and the entire Emerson household into confusion by his trip to see Sturgis, an old flame who had invited him to visit her. As Fuller goes on to note, Channing was expected back in Concord on Tuesday the sixth, but he had not arrived by Friday the ninth. This delay created a delicate situation, for Ellen, who was coming from Cincinnati, was sure to be jealous of his attention to Sturgis. When Ellen arrived that evening, Margaret went out of her way to avoid answering her sister's questions about Channing's absence and spent an uncomfortable night until Ellery appeared the next morning. Fuller described the scene in her journal: "Mama [Ruth Haskins Emerson] & Lidian sympathized with me almost with tears, Waldo looked radiant, & H[enry] T[horeau] as if his tribe had won a victory. Well it was a pretty play, since it turned out no tragedy at last. Ellery told Ellen at once how it was, and she took it just as she ought" (Myerson, "Margaret Fuller's 1842 Journal," pp. 333–36).

391.   To Charles K. Newcomb

Monday, 10th,
Octr, 1842

Dear Charles,

I fear I have not one good word to say this fair morning, though the sun shines so encouragingly on the distant hills and gentle river and the trees are in their festive hues. I am not festive, though contented. When obliged to give myself to the prose of life, as I am on this occasion of being established in a new home I like to do the thing, wholly and quite,—to weave my web for the day solely from the grey yarn. So I have not that to say to you which I have had and shall have when you are my neighbor, as I truly hope you will be. Your mother seems pleased with the lodgings, and I think they will suit you and that you will find the position pleasant and advantageous for three or four months. I need not say how it will be a pleasure for me to have you there. I want to tell you about my new brother Ellery whom I truly love; He is a brother in the Spirit, a singular treasure.— But I shall see you soon. Take good care of yourself, my dear Charles. I should think the state of your health critical. You need judicious counsel as to regimen and bodily habits. Be wise if you love your friends among whom *eldest*, at least, ranks

M. F.

ALS (MH: fMS Am 1086 [10:141]). *Addressed:* Charles K. Newcomb.

392.   To Ralph Waldo Emerson

Sunday 16th Oct [1842]

Dear Waldo—

I can hardly believe that it is a month this day since I passed a true Sabbath in reading your journals and Ellery's book, and talking with you in the study. I have not felt separated from you yet.— It is not yet time for me to have my dwelling near you. I get, after a while, even *intoxicated* with your mind, and do not live enough in myself. Now dont screw up your lip to an ungracious pettiness, but hear the words of frank affection as they deserve "mente cordis"ⁿ Let no cold breath paralyze my hope that there will yet be a noble and profound understanding between us. We have gone so far, and yet so little way. I understand the leadings of your thought better and better, and I feel a conviction that I shall be worthy of thisⁿ friendship, that I shall be led day by day to purify, to harmonize my being, to enlarge my experiences, and clear the eye of intelligence till after long long patient waiting yourself shall claim a thousand years interview at least. You need notⁿ be terrified at this prophecy nor look about for the keys of your cell.— *I* shall never claim an hour I begin to understand where I am, and feel more and more unfit to be with any body. I shall no more be so ruled by the affectionate expansions of my heart but hopeⁿ is great, though my daily life must be pallid and narrow.

I must not try to say to you much that has passed in my mind which I should like you to know. I find no adequate expression for it.

I do not know whether it is owing to this feeling of your mind being too near me that I have not yet been able to finish the ragged rhymes I meant for you. I got along well enough till the point of division came, where I wanted to show that the permanent marriage cannot interfere with the soul's destiny, when lo! this future which has seemed so clear, vanished and left me without a word, yet unconvinced of your way of thinking. There lies the paper, and I expect the hour may yet come when I can make out my case, if so, it will be sent

Will you have the rhymes I gave Lidian copied and sent me by Ellery, that is, if she wishes to retain the original.[1] Dont think this request silly! I want to put them in my journal of that week, they interest me from their connection And will you send my little picture and all the papers you have of mine E. Hooper's and Caroline's letters &c[2]

Penknife and key were touching symbols for me to leave, how can L. wish to send them back?—[3] My love to her. I hoped she had had her share of nervous fever. To be sick and lose this weather of Paradise is sad. I have lost it well nigh as much amid my affairs. And yet not wholly for though shut up in the house, I have had the loveliest view from my window the same as from the window where I used to read the Italian poets, in young days. The thoughts of that time come back like an old familiar music at sight of the river and gentle hills; they are fair to me still. Heaven be praised it is the same cadence that I love best now, though then[n] less rich, less deep—

Apropos to the Italians, I am inclined to suspect H. T. of a grave joke upon my views, with his "dauntless *infamy.*"— There is also *abstraction* for *obstruction,* which one would have thought such hacknied Shakespeare might have avoided.— I *am a little* vexed, having hoped my notice might meet the eye of the poet.[4] Henry's verses read well, but meseems he has spoiled his "Rumors" &c by substituting

> And simple truth on every tongue

for

> All the poems are unsung,

or some such line which was the one that gave most character to the original and yet I admire the

> tread of high souled men.[5]

The Dirge is more and more beautiful, and others feel it no less than I.[6] S. Ward no less.— I like Parkers piece much; it is excellent in its way, the sneer is mild, almost courtly.[7]

Your essay I have read with delight, but it is true the passage about fate is weak; Seek a better. Why cannot the fate behind fate be brought out somehow?[8] Saadi I have read many times. As to my own piece every one praises the few Rhine ballads, none the Romaic.[9] If you could get me vouchers of interest for the Romaics, I should be encouraged to make a rosary of all the rest.— If any thing occurs to me I shall write for your Dial. I think now I should like to write my impressions of Dr Channing.[10] If you go away I should *rather* you would leave the *Record of the Months* to me than to any one else, allowing sixteen or twenty pages for it, but if you are here will give any thing I may have to your discretion.— The new Essays, come and read to me, if not to Boston, I pray.[11]

Alas! here I am at the end of my paper, and have told you nothing of my stay at Brook Farm, where I gave *conversations* on alternate evenings with the husking parties. But you will come to see me in my new home, and then I will tell you. My first visitor last Sunday was S.

Ward. My second next day W. Channing. The following day I expected *you,* and since you were not so kind as to come, observe with pleasure that your letter dates from that day. Adieu, dear friend, be good to me, think of me, and write to me. The days of toil and care are coming when I shall need your ray, mellow if distant. I owe to the protection of your roof, to the soothing influence of your neighborhood, and to the gentle beauty of the Concord woods, some weeks of health and peace which have revived my courage so unusually dulled last summer. To Lidians unfailing and generous kindness also I owe much. But you must be the better to me for my thanks

"Most welcome they who need him most."[12]

Love to Mamma and Lidian, and salute for me sweet Edith of the dewy eyes[13]

Richter is as you say.[14] I will send you a little notice of the book from my journal.

AL (MH: bMS Am 1280 [2367]). Published entire in Rusk, *Letters of RWE,* 3:89–90, and Wade, pp. 564–66. *Addressed:* R. W. Emerson / Concord / Mass. *Postmark:* Cambridge MS Oct 17. *Endorsed:* Margaret F. / Oct 1842.

"mente cordis"] "mentis cordis" ⟨?⟩
of this] of this⟨e⟩
You need not] ⟨Dont⟩ ↑ You need not ↓
my heart but hope] my ↑ heart ↓ but ⟨my⟩ hope
though then] though ↑ then ↓

1. In his reply of 19 October Emerson said that Lidian had copied the poem and that he was returning the Sturgis papers (Rusk, *Letters of RWE,* 3:92–93).

2. Ellen Sturgis Hooper, Caroline's sister, was a poet who contributed frequently to the *Dial.*

3. In his letter of 11 and 12? October, Emerson told Fuller of a "key & penknife which were discovered in your chamber" (Rusk, *Letters of RWE,* 3:92).

4. Several errors appeared in Fuller's review of Tennyson's *Poems* that was published in the October *Dial.* "I have to say," wrote Emerson to Fuller on 11 October, "that if your eyes were tormented by that fine 'various reading' of Tennyson of 'infamy' for 'infancy,' the faithful Henry T. must bear it." Emerson, who was out walking with Hawthorne when the proofsheets for the October *Dial* arrived, had left Thoreau to read the proofs. "I did not fail," concluded Emerson, "to bring you & Tennyson full before his eyes" (Rusk, *Letters of RWE,* 3:91).

5. Thoreau's "Rumors from an Aeolian Harp" (*Dial* 3 [1842] 3:200).

6. Ellery Channing's poem, "Dirge" (*Dial* 3 [1842]:256–58).

7. Theodore Parker wrote a vigorous defense of the Reverend John Pierpont, pastor of the Hollis Street Church in Boston, who had incensed his congregation by preaching against rum (*Dial* 3 [1842]:201–21).

8. Fuller had read Emerson's lecture "The Conservative," which he published in the *Dial* with the passage in question: "Here is the fact which men call Fate, and fate in dread degrees, fate behind fate, not to be disposed of by the consideration that the Conscience commands this or that, but necessitating the question, whether the faculties of man will play him true in resisting the facts of universal experience?" (*Dial* 3 [1842]:185).

9. Emerson published his poem "Saadi" in the October *Dial* (pp. 265–69). Fuller's "Romaic and Rhine Ballads" opened the same issue.

10. Emerson, not Fuller, finally wrote a tribute to Dr. Channing for the January 1843 *Dial* (p. 387). Fuller wrote out her "impressions," but they were not published until the *Memoirs* editors used them (*Memoirs*, 2:69–71).

11. In his letter Emerson had mentioned his tentative plans for "some lively chapters on the influences active in the last years on the intellect in America." What he finally wrote became lectures on New England that he gave first in Baltimore and then in other cities beginning on 10 January 1843 and continuing into 1844 (Rusk, *Letters of RWE*, 3:91; Charvat, "Emerson's Lecture Engagements," pp. 504–6).

12. From Emerson's "Saadi" (*Dial* 3 [1842]:266):

> And simple maids and noble youth
> Are welcome to the man of truth.
> Most welcome they, who need him most,
> They feed the spring which they exhaust.

13. Edith Emerson (1841–1929), third of Emerson's children, had been born the previous November. In 1865 she married William Hathaway Forbes (Benjamin Kendall Emerson, *The Ipswich Emersons* [Boston, 1900], p. 267; MVR 1929 49:495).

14. Emerson had confessed his weariness with Jean Paul Richter: "I find with all his manliness & insight outsight oversight & undersight I grow soon weary & nervous of reading the good Jean Paul for there is a perpetual emphasis perpetual superlative" (Rusk, *Letters of RWE*, 3:92). He probably read Eliza Buckminster Lee's *Life of Jean Paul Frederic Richter* (Boston, 1942), which Fuller reviewed in *Dial* 3 (1843):404–6.

393. To William H. Channing[?]

November 1842

When souls meet direct and all secret thoughts are laid open, we shall need no forbearance, no prevention, no care-taking of any kind. Love will be pure light, and each action simple,—too simple to be noble. But there will not be always so much to pardon in ourselves and others. Yesterday we had at my class a conversation on Faith. Deeply true things were said and felt. But to-day the virtue has gone out of me; I have accepted all, and yet there will come these hours of weariness,—weariness of human nature in myself and others. "Could ye not watch one hour?"[1] Not one faithfully through! [   ] To speak with open heart and "tongue affectionate and true,"—to enjoy real repose and the consciousness of a thorough mutual understanding in the presence of friends when we do meet, is what is needed. That being granted, I do believe I should not wish any surrender of time or thought from a human being. But I have always a sense that I cannot meet or be met *in haste;* as ——— said he could not look at the works of art in a chance half-hour, so cannot I thus rudely and hastily turn over the leaves of any mind. In peace, in stillness that permits the soul to flow, beneath the open sky, I would see those I love.

Dr. William Ellery Channing. Lithograph by D'Avignon, after Gambardella. National Portrait Gallery, Smithsonian Institution, Washington, D.C.

ELfr, from *Memoirs*, 2:71.
1. Matt. 26:40 and, in a different version, Mark 14:37.

394. To Elizabeth Hoar

Nov 1842

Both ye Conversations since you were here have been spirited.[1] Miss S. Burley has joined the class, and hers is a presence so positive as to be of great value to me[2]

MsCfr (MH: bMS Am 1280 [111, p. 108]). Published in part in *Memoirs*, 1:350; published entire in *JMN*, 11:478.
1. Among her topics for the Conversations was "Education" (George Curtis to Barbara Channing, 24 September 1842, MHi).
2. Susan Burley of Salem was known for her patronage of the arts. She had taken a special interest in Sophia Peabody and Nathaniel Hawthorne (Tharp, *Peabody Sisters*, p. 118).

395. To Anna Huidekoper Clarke

Novr 1842.

Dear Mrs. Clarke,

It seems a little too much to take your house, your time, your trouble and money too! for my chat, but, believing I understand the spirit in which your early missive was sent me, I accept it in the same, and sign myself yours with friendship

S. M. FULLER.

ALS (MH: bMS Am 1569.7 [471]). *Addressed:* Mrs James Clarke / Chestnut St.
Anna Huidekoper, daughter of Harm Jan Huidekoper of Meadeville, Pennsylvania, married James Freeman Clarke in 1839.

396. To Ralph Waldo Emerson

Nov 8th, 1842.

I suppose we poor private friends must not expect to hear from thee, dear Waldo, till it shall have been finally settled how many generations must live on "vegetables" before man can be[n] reinstated in his birthright and walk the market place, fair, strong, and pure as the Archangel Michael.— And then when that point has been sufficiently discussed come his scribblings for the instruction of a still unregenerate world, alas, alas! the poor privates are like to be "left sitting" as the Germans phrase it, for a long time.[1]

We live along here, a[n] moderate but not beggarly life, freed for the present from great questions or great wants, a pensioned sojourn in the outer porch, but where is heard music from the temple, not less sweet that it swells from a distance.

Should you write some notice of Dr C. for your *dial* if I did not? I have written, but the record seems best adapted for my particular use, and I know not whether I shall come to any thing more general. If you should not write more than you have, will you send me your one stroke on the nail head for me to look at.

ever your affectionate

MARGARET.

ALS (MH: bMS Am 1280 [2368]); MsC (MB: Ms. Am. 1450 [78]). Published in part in Higginson, *MFO*, p. 171. Published entire in Rusk, *Letters of RWE*, 3:95–96. Addressed: R. W. Emerson. Endorsed: Margaret Fuller.

can be] can ⟨finally⟩ be

here, a] here, ⟨b⟩ a

1. On 21 October Bronson Alcott returned from England, bringing with him Charles Lane (1810–70), his son William, and Henry Wright. Lane and Wright were disciples of J. P. Greaves, the English reformer. Emerson had used Alcott's letters as the basis for an article on the reformers (one of whose creeds was vegetarianism) in the October *Dial*. Lane and his son were spending the first few weeks at the Emerson home (Shepard, *Pedlar's Progress*, pp. 338–42; *Dial* 3 [1842]:227–41; Rusk, *Letters of RWE*, 3:93). Lane subsequently wrote for the *Dial* and persuaded Alcott's family to join him in creating Fruitlands, an experiment in communal, abstemious living, at Harvard, Massachusetts. Following a time of bitter tension between Mrs. Alcott and Lane, when he tried to separate Alcott from his family, Lane moved from Fruitlands to the nearby Shaker community on 14 January 1844 (Shepard, *Pedlar's Progress*, pp. 343–80; Myerson, *New England Transcendentalists and the "Dial,"* pp. 169–74; Edgell, "Bronson Alcott's 'Autobiographical Index,'" p. 714).

397. To Ralph Waldo Emerson

[I] [4?] December 1842

When you were here, you seemed to think I might perhaps have done something on the *Vita Nuova;* and the next day I opened the book, and considered how I could do it. But you shall not expect that, either, for your present occasion. When I first mentioned it to you, it was only as a piece of Sunday work, which I thought of doing for you alone; and because it has never seemed to me you entered enough into the genius of the Italian to apprehend the mind, which has seemed so great to me, and a star unlike, if not higher than all the others in our sky. Else, I should have given you the original, rather than any version of mine. I intended to translate the poems, with which it is interspersed, into plain prose. Milnes and Longfellow have tried each their power at doing it in verse, and have done better, probably, than I could, yet not well.[1] But this would not satisfy me for the public. Besides, the translating Dante is a piece of literary presumption, and challenges a criticism to which I am not sure that I am, as the Germans say, *gewachsen.*[2] Italian, as well as German, I learned by myself, unassisted, except as to the pronunciation. I have never been brought into connection with minds trained to any severity in these kinds of elegant culture. I have used all the means within my reach, but my not going abroad is an insuperable defect in the technical part of my education. I was easily capable of attaining excellence, perhaps mastery, in the use of some implements. Now I know, at least, *what I do not know,* and I get along by never voluntarily going beyond my depth, and, when called on to do it, stating my incompetency. At moments when I feel tempted to regret that I could not follow out the plan I had marked for myself, and develop powers which are not usual here, I reflect, that if I had attained high finish and an easy range in these respects, I should not have been thrown back on my own resources, or known them as I do. But Lord Brougham should not translate Greek orations, nor a maid-of-all-work attempt such a piece of delicate handling as to translate the *Vita Nuova.*[3]

[II] [   ] a wonderful performer, and one in whom the execution is subordinate to the music, he has soul, freedom, and a fine, masterly hand, though he is only twenty one. We made a party one eveg, E. and E. S. and A. Caroline Rakemann and myself, a pretty party, *on* the whole.—[4] I have had pleasant meeting with Caroline; perhaps we shall not be so much companions now, but dear friends.— Aunt Mary Rotch has been in town. I had good talk with her. Passing a day with Miss Burley I found in two of her nieces the most charming young people I have seen, so natural, beaming with sweetness, and archness and intelligence.[5] Give my love to Lidian and Mamma, and tell me about Edith— Say to my dear Elizabeth that I meant no "grave censure" on her silence, but only to say I wanted a letter, but that I will not plague her at all any more. That she must not do that writing for me when she is so busy, I had rather wait a year; it was a very trifling reason I had for wanting it soon. I will write to her when I can. Do forgive me for scrawling so, writing tires me, and I want to finish before I go into town to hear "conversation by A B Alcott in which Messrs Lane and Wright will participate"!—[6] When are you going away? dont forget to tell me this, and let me have Paracelsus and Ernest when you can.—[7] Ever, ever yours

M. F.

I: ELfr, from *Memoirs*, 1:240–41; II: ALfrS (MH: bMS Am 1280 [2382]).

On 12 December Emerson acknowledged Fuller's "generous pacquet which came by Thoreau" (Rusk, Letters of RWE, 3:102). He went on to respond to Fuller's comments on Dante; thus the Memoirs fragment clearly was written before 12 December. The manuscript fragment can be dated from Fuller's reference to Alcott, Lane, and Wright, who gave a Conversation on 4 December. Because the manuscript has no address on the back, it may have been part of a "pacquet" of material sent by Thoreau.

1. A few months later Emerson wrote Fuller, saying that he had done a prose translation and that Ellery Channing has "turned my prose sonnets & canzoni into verse or ten or more of them so that if he continues we shall after some correcting & filing get that which you were to do for me" (Rusk, *Letters of RWE*, 3:183–84). Written about 1292, *La Vita Nuova* is an autobiographical description of Dante's first encounters with and love for Beatrice. Emerson's version has since been published (*Dante's "Vita Nuova" Translated by Ralph Waldo Emerson*, ed. J. Chesley Matthews [Chapel Hill, N.C., 1960]).

2. *Gewachsen:* to be up to it.

3. Henry Peter Brougham (1778–1868) was a founder of the *Edinburgh Review*. A prominent abolitionist, he was instrumental in making the slave trade a felony.

4. Probably Ellery and Ellen Fuller Channing, Sam and Anna Ward, and Caroline Sturgis.

5. Susan Burley with her nieces, Elizabeth and Susan Howes.

6. On 3 December Alcott advertised for "his friends and others interested in Human Culture, to favor him with their company at Hall No. 4 Marlboro Chapel on Sunday Evening, December 4th. Messrs Lane and Wright, recently from England, will be present and participate in the Conversation" (*Boston Daily Advertiser*). A mob gathered and forced the Conversation to be shifted to Ritchie Hall (Shepard, *Pedlar's Progress*, p. 351).

7. Emerson had been reading Robert Browning's *Paracelsus* (London, 1835) and Capel Lofft the younger's *Ernest; or, Political Regeneration* (London, 1839).

398. To George T. Davis

Cambridge
17th Decr 1842.

Dear George,

I have thought of you many times since we parted on that dreary night in that dreary street. I did not like to bid you good bye so, and next day, when I found I had unexpectedly an hour at noon, regretted that I could not send for you to come and see me if you would.— Yesterday was one of my very sick days, and I had time to think and thought of you so much, that I must write and ask you to write to me

I am not fond of dwelling on the past, and prefer pressing onward to the things that are before. But objects round me now irresistably recal the days when we were so much together. The house where I live stands in the orchard of the old Dana house, and is shaded by trees on which I looked from my window. The view is the same, the river so slow and mild, the gentle hills, the sunset over Mt. Auburn, I love to look on it. My father would often try to check my pride, or as he deemed it my *arrogance* of youthful hope and pride by a picture of the ills that might come on me,—and all have come of which he spoke, sickness, poverty, the failure of ties and all my cherished plans, but none of these changes have had the effect he prophesied. I feel the same heart within my breast, I prize the same objects, though more deeply, and I may say more wisely. For the same persons I am still interested, nor have I been deceived in any of them, there is not one I have ever loved who did not possess the groundwork of character, and has not in some degree justified my election, for all of them as for myself, I am emboldened to an immortal hope. The best of what I could say to you on this subject I have expressed in some papers which I have prepared as I agreed with you I would and shall give you when you come to town. You must then bring your children as you promised and show me. I love to know these new lives in which my friends bloom again.— I feel that the darkest hue on my own lot is that I have neither children, nor yet am the parent of beautiful works by which the thought of my life might be represented to another generation. Yet even this is not dark to me, though it sometimes makes me pensive.— I have not lived my own life, neither loved my own love, my strength, my sympathies have been given to others, their lives are my aims. If here I could call nothing my own, it has led me to penetrate deeper into the thought which pervades all. I have not been led to limit my thoughts to a span, nor fix my affections with undue order on some one set of objects. So all things are equalized at last.— I cannot help regretting sometimes that I can do so little for any one, so little for my nearest and dearest to soothe their pains, or remove obstacles from their path. Yet is *that little* not often to be met with. I can say from the depth of my heart, never cease to hope and trust if you deserve you will at last be satisfied. I can understand each mind in its own way, for I see men in their several natures; and not by any rule taken from my own character and experience. This those who love me know, and you do, I am sure, though you said, as we parted, that the sympathy of friendship was superficial, if it did not answer with warmth to some things you said, especially of *ambition,* you will see the reason when you come. Write to me at once if you can, and let me know how the green fields look beneath December snows. Always affectionately your

COUSIN M.

I was surprised to hear from James you had not read Tennyson.— Do read him at once. He has solved his own problems.

MsC (MH: fMS Am 1086 [9:91a]).

George Davis, a lawyer and newspaper publisher in Greenfield, Massachusetts, was Fuller's distant cousin. In the late 1820s she was in love with Davis, who apparently did not take her feelings seriously.

399. To Frederic H. Hedge

Cambridge.
17th Decr 1842.

My dear Henry

I wish your printed missive had been accompanied by a few lines from your "kylevise pen," (by the way I use this word without surely knowing what it means, I only fancy from the look on't that it suits my purpose) however I will not fail to answer, since you have been brought near me by what I did get. It is no easy task to speak of our lost friend at this time.[1] I vainly attempted to write something for the Dial. I found I could not observe that moderation and truth which would be my only homage without seeming cold and ungrateful. I fancied from my own experience that only verse was fit for such times, and that the limitations, the summing up, the prose portrait must wait some ten years yet. But I like yours, though I think it gives the idea of a *greater* man than he was. (of his purity and high intent none can speak too highly) I like especially what you say of him as a believer and a fore-sayer.[2] Sometime I will show you what I wrote in my journal at the time of his death there are coincidences between our statements that will please you, I think.— Neither you nor any have spoken of the *lovely* side of his character, perhaps because it was rarely seen, perhaps that it had nothing to do with his public[n] kind of

Frederic Henry Hedge. From the collection of Joel Myerson;
courtesy of the Harvard University Archives.

panegyric. Ingham who saw him last summer at Lennox, when he was enjoying the beauty of the country, has painted a picture of him which, though somewhat inefficient and waxen, gives that side of him.[3]

I am interested in what you say of those who are "in advance of their age p. 13, and should like to hear more from you on that subject. A large proportion of the poets and great religious minds are surely in the class you speak of as "untimely births."[4]

I think of you very often since our meeting last autumn, to me it seemed that our minds met more nearly and that we were brought into truer relations than for a long time before. Of many things I see and hear and think. I wish you were here that I might speak to you. Lately I saw an engraving from the German Artist Lessing which brought you to mind; the subject is from Uhland's poem that you have liked so well The Castle by the Sea.[5] It is called the Royal Couple and represents the father and mother of the beautiful princess after her death. Schadow sat for the king, and such a lion aspect of regal wo, I would not even have imagined. The king gazes before him, the lines between his eyebrows have an iron look, he seems worthy to face the worst, to feel, to bear it all, a true monarch. The Queen is only a woman and without beauty, but of the same illustrious line. She leans[n] on her husband, her eyes are bent on the ground but the proportions of her nature seem no less large and severe. It is the finest conception I have seen by any of these artists.

We are doing little hereabouts in the [   ] line. No new crochet started of late that I know of, people seem a little more simple and humble, but it may be only a temporary lull of the winds.— Mrs Ripley I have not seen for sometime, but hear of her as making collections of lichens, and am glad she is led out into the woods, rather than plodding through some book by the fire. I mean to go and see her soon. Mr Emerson is preparing to lecture in some of the more Southern Cities.[6] I see him little to my sorrow, out here at Cambridge, I am out of his way. Mr Alcott and his new allies make some little stir. Lane has good abilities a depth of experience within himself and seemingly a more gentle and reverent spirit than is common to reformers.— I continue my weekly meetings in Boston: they are uncommonly pleasant this winter. Our subject is constancy "Were man but constant, he were perfect" give me some hints about this.[7]

I read little, for in these middle heights of life contemporary spirits call to us in crowds, and do not let us listen much to the past. I have, however been much pleased of late with the life of Lord Herbert of Cherbury.[8] He had a strong and bold wing in thought, and in character a union of purity boldness and variety that has not many times been seen on this earthball. I admire his view of life as shown in his Latin poems.[9] And then the answer of the lover to his mistress who fears about the future life

> Let then no doubt, Celinda, touch,
> Much less your fairest mind invade
> Were not our souls immortal made,
> Our equal loves can make them such.[10]

Is it not noble?— Well one comes very soon to the end of a[n] poor sheet of paper. Please my friend, fill one for me as soon as may be, and tell all you can of yourself. With friendly remembrances to Lucy yours affecy

M. F.

Did you receive Schelling's lecture?"[11]

ALS (MH: fMS Am 1086 [10:104]). *Addressed:* Rev. F. H. Hedge / Bangor / Maine. *Postmark:* Cambridge Ms Dec 21.

Frederic Henry Hedge, then the Unitarian minister in Bangor, Maine, had been Fuller's early and valued friend when he introduced her to German literature and language in the 1830s.

his public] his ↑ public ↓
She leans] She l⟨?⟩eans
of a] of ⟨one⟩ ↑ a ↓

1. Hedge had delivered a memorial sermon on Dr. Channing at Bangor on 17 November (*A Sermon on the Character and Ministry of the Late Rev. William Ellery Channing, D.D.* [Bangor, 1842]).

2. Hedge described two distinguishing qualities in Dr. Channing: he was "a *Believer*, a man distinguished before all his contemporaries, by the clearness and intensity of his faith," and he was "a *prophet*." "Not a fore-seer," said Hedge, "but a fore-sayer of new things, according to the strict etymology of the word" (Hedge, *Sermon*, pp. 4, 11, 12).

3. Charles Cromwell Ingham (1796–1863), a painter working in New York City, was known for his portraits of eminent people (*DAB*).

4. "[Dr. Channing] was not in advance of his age, in the sense in which many others are in advance of their age. They are not the most effective or the most useful, who occupy this ground. They are untimely births, which come to nothing, like blossoms which have burst forth before the winter is past" (Hedge, *Sermon*, p. 13).

5. At the home of Cornelius Felton, Harvard's professor of Greek, Fuller read with enthusiasm Atanazy Raczyniski's *Geschichte der neueren deutschen Kunst* (Berlin, 1836–41) (Margaret Fuller journal [1842], MH). There she saw Karl Friedrich Lessing's (1808–80) engraving *Das trauernde Königspaar* (1830), which had immediately made him famous. Lessing was a member of the Dusseldorf Academy, founded by Friedrich Wilhelm von Schadow (1788–1862), who was known for his paintings on biblical scenes and subjects (Geraldine Norman, *Nineteenth-Century Painters and Painting: A Dictionary* [Berkeley, 1977], pp. 133, 157–58). Ludwig Uhland wrote "Das Schloss am Meere" in 1805. Hedge's translation of the poem appeared in the July *Dial*, 3 (1842):74–75.

6. Emerson delivered two lectures in his "New England" series in Baltimore (10 and

17 January), then gave the full five-lecture series in Philadelphia from 23 January through 1 February. Moving to New York, he repeated the series with some additions from 7 February through 7 March (Charvat, "Emerson's Lecture Engagements," pp. 504–5).

7. From *Two Gentlemen of Verona*, V.iv.110–12:

> O heaven, were man
> But constant, he were perfect; that one error
> Fills him with faults; makes him run through
> all th' sins.

8. Fuller probably had read Horace Walpole's edition of *The Life of Edward Lord Herbert of Cherbury Written by Himself* (Strawberry-Hill, 1764). Edward Herbert (1583–1648), first baron Herbert of Cherbury, was a philosopher, diplomat, and poet whose thought ran parallel to that of the Platonists and whose work anticipated that of the deists.

9. Fuller refers to two of Lord Herbert's Latin poems, "De vita humana philosophica disquisitio" and "De vita coelesti, ex iisdem principiis conjectura." She freely translated the poems in "The Two Herberts" (*Present* 1 [1844]:301–12), an essay written in imitation of Landor's imaginary conversations (Edward Herbert, *The Poems English and Latin of Edward, Lord Herbert of Cherbury*, ed. G. C. Moore Smith [Oxford, 1923], pp. 99–118).

10. From "An Ode upon a Question Moved, Whether Love Should Continue for Ever," ll. 121–24.

11. Friedrich Wilhelm von Schelling (1775–1854), the German philosopher, had moved to Berlin from Munich, where he had taught for over three decades. Charles Stearns Wheeler, who was in Germany, sent Emerson a long letter commenting on German literary and philosophical news and enclosed Schelling's first lecture to his Berlin students. Emerson asked Hedge to translate the lecture, but first gave it to Fuller to read. Apparently she sent it on to Hedge, for his translation appeared in the January 1843 *Dial* (*OCGL*; Rusk, *Letters of RWE*, 3:97–99; *Dial* 3 [1843]:398–404).

400.   To Ralph Waldo Emerson[?]

[I] 26 December 1842

I have been reading the lives of Lord Herbert of Cherbury, and of Sir Kenelm Digby.[1] These splendid, chivalrous, and thoughtful Englishmen are meat which my soul loveth, even as much as my Italians. What I demand of men,—that they could act out all their thoughts,—these have. They are lives;—and of such I do not care if they had as many faults as there are days in the year,—there is the energy to redeem them. Do you not admire Lord Herbert's two poems on life, and the conjectures concerning celestial life? I keep reading them. [   ]

[II] Ellery is here, but he is too much harassed by anxiety for companionship I can do nothing so will not take the possible tragedy to heart.[2] I am inclined to say with Mephistopheles, "*He is not the first!*"[3]

Ay, surely, it is the enigma of my time that no genius shall bear both flower and fruit; may as well trouble myself for a thousand as one. So I am not troubled.

I: ELfr, from *Memoirs*, 1:294–95; II: MsCfr (MH: bMS Am 1280 [111, pp. 555–56]). Published in part in *JMN*, 11:486.

May be two separate letters, for fragment II, in Emerson's journal, has only the day and year.

1. Kenelm Digby (1603–65) wrote on scientific topics and was one of the first members of the Royal Society. He also served as a naval officer and as a diplomat.

2. Ellery Channing lived with Margaret and Mrs. Fuller from September 1842 to April 1843.

3. From *Faust*, pt. 1, "Truber Tag." In answer to Faust's rage over Margaret's ruin, Mephistopheles cynically answers, "Sie ist die Erste nicht!" (She is not the first!) (Johann Wolfgang von Goethe, *Gedenkausgabe der Werke, Briefe und Gespräche*, ed. Ernst Beutler [Zurich, 1950], 5:280).

401. To James F. Clarke[?]

1843

I have been happy in the sight of your pure design, of the sweetness and serenity of your mind. In the inner sanctuary we met. But I shall say a few blunt words, such as were frequent in the days of intimacy, and, if they are needless, you will let them fall to the ground. Youth is past, with its passionate joys and griefs, its restlessness, its vague desires. You have chosen your path, you have rounded out your lot, your duties are before you. *Now* beware the mediocrity that threatens middle age; its limitation of thought and interest, its dulness of fancy, its too external life, and mental thinness. Remember the limitations that threaten every professional man, only to be guarded against by great earnestness and watchfulness. So take care of yourself, and let not the intellect more than the spirit be quenched.

ELfr, from *Memoirs*, 1:81.

402. To [?]

1843

I believe I told you about one new man, a Philistine at Brook Farm. He reproved me, as such people are wont, for my little faith. At the end of the first meeting in the hall, he seemed to me perfectly ham-

Brook Farm. Oil by Josiah Wolcott. Courtesy of the Massachusetts Historical Society.

112

pered in his old ways and technics, and I thought he would not open his mind to the views of others for years, if ever. After I wrote, we had a second meeting, by request, on personal relations; at the end of which, he came to me, and expressed delight, and feeling of new light and life, in terms whose modesty might have done honor to the wisest.

ELfr, from *Memoirs*, 1:313–14.

403. To Elizabeth Hoar

16th Jany [1843]

Dear Lizzie,

I will see Nancy K. in the course of the week and inform her of Lidian's proposal.[1] Meanwhile, keep in thy mind the school; she may prefer that, and yet I do not know, for she wanted much the other time to go to Mr E's on count o' influences, and with the same compensation as Louisa receives would make more money than at the school, it seems.

I have inquired further into the reports about Mr C. and find there is no certain ground for the assertion that he had acted dishonorably; it was said his character was bad in other respects, but this would surprize and grieve me far less. I feel somewhat relieved on this score, and very glad at any rate that E. is gone.[2]

I have had a "sweet pretty" letter from Waldo, whose playful grace seems to say that this journey will do him good.[3] Heaven bless him!— It seems he will stay away rather long, but it does not to me matter so much. I could not see him at any rate. I think I shall write to him every week.

Mr Alcott[n] and Mr Lane made me a visit of some hours the other day, and I could tell you several little traits of it that would please your ready sense, but we are not near enough and letters too short. I have thought of writing some words to Mr L. apropos to something that was said, if I do, it will be enclosed here for you to send. I like him much, what I have seen of him so far, and should find profit in talking with him, for he speaks nobly, and is also precise and full of resource. When he speaks I attend not only to the thing, but to all the words, thus I am not tired, as with most talkers.

113

Of Jane I see a good deal lately: we have sweet communion. She seems to learn much from the day as it passes.— I am in town two days in the week. My conversations are quite good now. Those days I usually dine at some pleasant place, but am, mostly, too tired to enjoy it. There are concerts, but I do not care so much for music this winter, perhaps that I hear the music of the spheres, more distinctly —perhaps that the heart has folded its wings, and does not follow the ardent flight— It signifies not, I do little. My time is frittered away in writing letters to dear friends like thee: but who will forgive me when nothing else is done that I have given time in this way?—surely *not the dear friends*!!— I have plagues about me, but they dont touch me now, and I thank nightly the benignant spirit for the unaccustomed serenity in which it enfolds me.— Ellery is very wretched, almost hopeless now, and once I could not have helped taking on me all h[is] griefs, and through him the griefs of all his class, but now I drink only the wormwood of the minute, and that has always equal parts, a drop of sweet to a drop of bitter.

But I shall never be callous, my Elizabeth, never unable to understand "homesickness." Am not I too one of the band who know not where to lay their heads.[4] Am I "wise enough" to hear such things? Perhaps not, but "happy enough" surely, for that Power which daily makes me understand the value of the little wheat amid the field of tares,[5] and shows me how the kingdom of heaven is sown on earth like a grain of mustard seed[6] is good enough to me and bids me call unhappiness happy, and yet,—ⁿI do not express myself—why should I, you know it.

I have written to Mr Lane, but shall send it by post. I have tonight a letter from Waldo at Washington he was having a good time There is copied into the Boston Transcript a laudatory annunciation of his lectures in Phila from the Phila paper.[7]

I forgot to tell about the Farrars. Mr F. has been very unwell, she much depressed.

At the last conversation Anna Ward declared her conviction that wedlock was not eternal infinite is the word ratherⁿ that souls could not be together beyond a certain point; they were then alone with God.— She is reading Petrarch with me: she feels very truly the beauty and dignity of his nature.

17th

I dreamt last night that I was at Concord and little Waldo was playing near usⁿ and talking in his beautiful tones, but they all called him Charles and when I asked about it said "His name is Charles now.

ALS (Collection of Nelson C. White). MsCfr (MH: bMS Am 1280 [111, pp. 150, 154–55]). Published in part in *Memoirs*, 1:309, and *JMN*, 11:485. *Addressed:* Miss Elizabeth Hoar / Concord / Mass. *Postmark:* Cambridge Ms Jan 18.

Mr Alcott] Mr ⟨Wright⟩ ↑ Alcott ↓
happy, and yet,—] happy, ⟨to me⟩ ↑ and yet, ↓ —
not eternal infinite is the word rather] not eternal ↑ infinite is the word rather ↓
near us] near ⟨i⟩us

1. Probably Mrs. Fuller's cousin Nancy Weiser Kuhn.
2. Alfred Cumming and his wife, Elizabeth Randall Cumming.
3. Emerson wrote on 7 January and again on the thirteenth. The tone of Fuller's letter suggests that she refers to his of the seventh, in which he wrote, "Elizabeth H & I held good talk concerning you my dear friend just before I left home & agreed to set our saint very high, if we differed a little in the naming of our sentiment" (Rusk, *Letters of RWE*, 3:117). Later in this letter, Fuller acknowledges the second Emerson letter.
4. "The foxes have holes, and the birds of the air have nests; but the Son of man hath not where to lay his head" (Matt. 8:20 and Luke 9:58).
5. Fuller refers to the parable of the wheat and tares in Matt. 13:24–30.
6. The familiar parable occurs three times in the gospels: Matt. 13:31–32, Mark 4:30–32, and Luke 13:18–19.
17. The *Boston Daily Evening Transcript* for 13 January quoted from the *Philadelphia Gazette*, which concluded that "we do not always find the good we seek, but our disappointment in the object is sometimes overpaid by the excellence of the unexpected discovery."

404. To Nathaniel Hawthorne

Cambridge 16th Jany
1843.

Dear Mr Hawthorne,

You must not think I have any black design against your domestic peace— Neither am I the agent of any secret tribunal[n] of the dagger and Cord. Nor am I commissioned by the malice of some baffled lover to make you wretched[1]

Yet it may look so, when you find me once again, in defiance of my failure last summer, despite your letter of full exposition, once more attempting to mix a foreign element in your well compounded cup.

But, indeed, Oh serenest and most resolute man, these propositions are none of mine. How can I help it if gentle souls, ill at ease elsewhere, wish to rest with you upon the margin of that sleepy stream? How can I help it, if they choose me for an interpreter, when their reason is the undoubted, not to be doubted truth that I can bear hearing the cold cruel word No, better than any soul now living. Better surely than our friend and youngest brother Charles Newcomb in behalf of whom I now "take up the pen"

Nathaniel Hawthorne. Oil by Charles Osgood. Courtesy of the Essex Institute, Salem, Massachusetts.

Charles is desirous, very, if all circumstances should be with him as at present, to come to Concord next summer, work with you on your farm, if you have employment for him, be received as a boarder beneath your roof, if such arrangement would be pleasant for you and Sophia.

I told him that, when you wrote declining to receive Ellery, you said you should not wish to have any man but Mr Bradford.[2] Yet knowing your regard for Charles, we have thought it possible you might think again.

Charles is in very delicate health. He needs work, needs influences both cheering and tranquillizing. He would like to be with you and in Concord, but his heart is not set upon the plan and he is prepared for a denial. If you do not want him, simply say so, and trouble not to state the reasons; we shall divine them.— In fact I am not annoying you with a proposition, being employed only to sound your dispositions, but as I know no diplomacy and can move only in a straight-forward direction, you have the present blunt epistle and are only requested to imagine all has been done in the indirect, delicate style of old European policy, and answer accordingly.[3]

I should like much to hear something about yourselves, whether ther[e] is writing, or drawing or modelling in what room[n] you pass the short, dark days, and long bright evenings of Jany, what the Genius loci says whether through voice of ghost, or rat, or winter wind, or kettle singing symphony to the happy duet, and whether, by any chance, you sometimes give a thought to your friend[4]

MARGARET.

ALS (NN-B). *Addressed:* Mr / Nathaniel Hawthorne / Concord / Mass. *Endorsed:* Margaret Fuller. *Postmark:* Cambridge Ms / Jan 18.

secret tribunal] secret⟨ly⟩ tribunal
modelling in what room] modelling ⟨where⟩ ↑ in what room ↓

1. Fuller had written the recently married Hawthorne in 1841, proposing that Ellery and Ellen Channing board with the Hawthornes at the Manse. Though Hawthorne politely but firmly rejected that idea, Fuller here tries again on behalf of Charles Newcomb (Julian Hawthorne, *Nathaniel Hawthorne and His Wife* [Boston, 1884], 1:252–53).

2. George Partridge Bradford graduated from Harvard in 1825 and from the Divinity School in 1828, though he was never ordained. He became a teacher and spent some time at Brook Farm (Harvard archives).

3. Not surprisingly, Hawthorne again refused to accept a boarder, hinting that there was a reason why Newcomb would not be welcome. He may have anticipated Sophia's first pregnancy, which did occur in the early summer of 1843 (Nathaniel Hawthorne to Margaret Fuller, 1 February 1843, MH).

4. Hawthorne replied that he was writing, "being a monthly contributor to three or four periodicals," and skating like a "schoolboy." He neglected to mention Sophia's work, saying merely that "I keep her as tranquil as a summer-sunset." She was, however, copying a painting of a bas-relief of Endymion (Tharp, *Peabody Sisters*, p. 161).

405. To Elizabeth Hoar

Cambridge
30th Jany 1843.

My dear Elizabeth,

Nancy Kuhn has decided that she will not leave home, unless she can get a school, will you then let me know as soon as may be the result about those in Concord, as if there is not one there for her, I want to write to some other places.

If she could go to C. do they not give the board as well as money? In some places they give four dollars a week and board.

Since I have begun upon dollars I will ask your congratulations, (for I know you dont disdain the prose side of my life,) on my having paid up all my first quarter's bills for housekeeping out of Mother's quota, and what I had left from the foregoing year, so I have only nine months' bread, fire light and shelter[n] to provide. I could not but congratulate myself that I persisted against all the people's persuasion, in doing all I could the winter previous, though it *did* hurt me, for otherwise I should have been in debt now, and I look on that position with a horror worthy any old dutch burgomaster.

I also must inform you how completely my little objects are attained. The little household is so well arranged that all goes on as smooth as a wheel turns round. Mother really enjoys her tranquil home, now she has got over the first fret and fatigue. She has just enough active exertion for her strength, she reads and thinks she is patient and trustful for the absent, disposed to make the best of the present. *At last,* she relies on me and believes that I shall carry through what I undertake without killing myself. She has learnt not to be over anxious when I suffer, so I am not obliged to repress my feelings when it is best to yield to them.

On Richard's account I daily rejoice to be here. Our relation is, indeed, grateful to me; it is such as I always wished for with one of my kin.

Ellery has harassing cares, but, since I cannot aid, I do not dwell upon them, and I am able to prevent Mother from doing it, too, which sometimes seems to me an absolute miracle, and it is worth them all, to see with what sweetness and resolute patience Ellen bears daily trials. I never saw a being so improved in a short space I truly respect her.

I still have some tedious affairs to wind up which hang upon me, day by day; they are uncongenial, but I only mind it at the moment when I am obliged to.— I am in better health these last three weeks, than I have been in the winter for seven years. It is good for my health that I have not quite so much to do as my purse requires, and though I dont well see how I shall make up the deficit, I avail myself of what benefit there is in the circumstances.

I have told you all this, because you said you should be "glad of any shade of comfort to me or mine," and I wan[t] you to know how much sweet lovely leisure I enjoy in my sunshiny room, undisturbed by fears of pain to others, and that I am truly grateful for being enabled to fulfil obligations, which to some may seem humble, but to me are sacred.

Did you know Belinda had heard four times from E. Cumming, that she is well and taking great pleasure in her journey.

I have no letter from Waldo since I wrote and long for one, but he is well, I know, he wrote to Cary. I see Jane every week now, for I give a lesson in her happy little parlor to a girl in whom she takes an interest She has been ill with ague, but is now almost well again. Her life, as usual is full of lovely details, of quiet thought and aspiration.

Farewell, dear E. Are you not coming here by and by, your affece

M.

Mr Farrar is far worse I think than ever. Mrs F. depressed and unwell; it is a desolate picture.

ALS (MHarF). *Addressed:* Miss Elizabeth Hoar / Concord / Mass.
fire light and shelter] fire⟨and⟩light ↑ and shelter ↓

406. To Mary Rotch

Cambridge
5th Feby 1843.

Dear Aunt Mary
and Miss Gifford,

The wind howling without, as it drives the snowflakes thickly against the windows, makes still more sweet the warm seclusion of the well lighted chamber, and yet by its distant sounds suggests the thought of distant friends. Your little note, Aunt Mary, I was pleased to see and the rather that it spoke of my friend J. C. so truly.[1] He is as you say, a meek and faithful servant of the Spirit. To him it [   ] There is nothing, I trow, in the most detailed beliefs as to the

119

outward facts of revelations, which *need* interfere with a reception of their spiritual[n] sense and it is only that men are so partially developed here that they can hardly be at once "myriad minded" and simple, philosophical and poetical. But to be too reverent a believer in truth and love to doubt that these may maniwise be sought by many men, to wish to enlarge our tolerance and hope in proportion with those of the creative Spirit is much and this J. C. has done.

You ask has William Channing received your letter. I doubt not he has, if it went to that address.[2] But, I believe a silence has fallen upon him (and such [   ] great acceptance of the majority;—the clergy wisely tolerate him, go to his lectures and meet him at friends houses.[3]

This influence widens, and it ought for his outlook is wide; it will not deepen, unless his fount of inward knowledge should deepen. He is still, I hear, too polemical in his tone. Truth needs no such weapons. However those who use them do disturb the waters till, perchance, an angel may be tempted down to still, and better—to purify them.

Mr Emerson is absent on a lecturing tour to Phila, Baltimore and N.Y.— He finds few persons of deep living force, as is indeed not to be expected now. This is the era of experiment of difusing, that of assertion, of concentration will succeed. But he has seen Lucretia Mott, and is pleased with her.[4] Are there no other persons now of note among the Friends? I suppose you know about them still, and have wished much to talk with you. I hear of *George White* in N.Y. but he seems to be polemical like Mr Parker, and denounces a "hireling ministry" instead of superseding them by pouring in upon the world the tide of truth.

I have wished to talk with you of these things and others, and I beg you to make that catarrh grow better and to stay here for more than a day. I grieve you are never here at my class meetings They are sometimes quite good now, yet I dare not offer them as any inducement, because if you were present only at one, it might not prove one of worth. The winter has been to me a very happy one in mine own mind, giving new clues and showing many passages already partially trod of the great labyrinth lined like the others with the accumulated crystals of ages reflecting the purest light in blazes of glory— These are sad hours in which I see our friends Mr and Mrs Farrar: it is truly a desolate house. Farewell write, if you do not come to yours affecy

S. M. FULLER.

ALS (MH: fMS Am 1086 [9:92]); MsCfr (MH: fMS Am 1086 [Works, 1:27–29]). *Addressed:* Miss Mary Rotch / New Bedford / Mass. *Postmark:* Cambridge Ms. Feb 6.

their spiritual] their ⟨part⟩ spiritual

1. James Freeman Clarke.

2. Channing was at this time in New York City (Frothingham, *Memoir of William Henry Channing*, p. 185).

3. In the missing portion Fuller apparently began to describe the troubles Theodore Parker was then having. The Boston Association of Ministers had taken offense at both *Discourse of Matters Pertaining to Religion* and Parker's defense of John Pierpont in the *Dial*. On 23 January 1843 they called him to a meeting and berated him for his "deistical" book and for slandering the Hollis Street Council of ministers. The tense meeting was characterized by Nathaniel Frothingham's declaration that "he could have no ministerial intercourse with [Parker]—though he still hoped to have a friendly and social intercourse" (John Weiss, *Life and Correspondence of Theodore Parker* [New York, 1864], 1:188–93). For several years afterward, few ministers would exchange pulpits with Parker for fear of damage to their reputations (ibid., pp. 248–64).

4. Lucretia Coffin Mott (1793–1880) was a Hicksite Quaker, an abolitionist, and a feminist. She and her husband, James Mott, were living in Philadelphia (*Notable American Women, 1607–1950*, ed. Edward T. James [Cambridge, Mass., 1971]).

407. To Ralph Waldo Emerson

7 February 1843

I saw the letter of your new friend, and liked it much; only, at this distance, one could not be sure whether it was the nucleus or the train of a comet, that lightened afar.[1] The daemons are not busy enough at the births of most men. They do not give them individuality deep enough for truth to take root in. Such shallow natures cannot resist a strong head; its influence goes right through them. It is not stopped and fermented long enough. But I do not understand this hint of hesitation, because you have many friends already. We need not economize, we need not hoard these immortal treasures. Love and thought are not diminished by diffusion. In the widow's cruse is oil enough to furnish light for all the world.[2]

ELfr, from *Memoirs*, 1:284.

1. Probably William Aspinwall Tappan (1819–1905), who later married Caroline Sturgis. Emerson met Tappan, the son of Lewis Tappan, the abolitionist, during the first week of February in New York (MVR 1905 87:49; Rusk, *Letters of RWE*, 3:143).

2. The prophet Elijah begged food from the poor widow of Zarephath: "For thus saith the Lord God of Israel, The barrel of meal shall not waste, neither shall the cruse of oil fail, until the day that the Lord sendeth rain upon the earth" (1 Kings 17:14).

408. To Mary Rotch

Cambridge 16th Feby 1843.

I shall, with great satisfaction, dear Aunt Mary, visit you as you propose, only do not disappoint me by not coming now you have put it into my head. Possibly I shall not be with you during the Saty eveg, as, if there is a concert at the Academy, I shall not be willing to miss hearing Beethoven, but if there is no concert I will and certainly all Sunday.[1] If you wish me to stay at the Tremont, as thinking we shall thus see one another more, I will, but it is not needful that you should make such an arrangement *for my convenience,* as there are friends' houses to which I have a standing invitation for the sleeping hours, even when I do not give the waking, such disinterested kindness is at times to be found. Shall I not hear from you the day previous, whether you will be there.

I saw Mrs Farrar on Sunday and gave her your note. Mr F. was a little better that day, but today I hear he is, since then, worse than he has ever been. He is visibly altered; it is very sorrowful to see him.

I will not write more, for I am unwell and fatigued this last day or two, and hope so soon to see you.

Maria was much gratified by your remembrance.[2] With love to Miss Gifford always affectionately yours

S. M. F.

If there *is* a good Concert could not you go. Beethoven is the missionary angel of our age. Or should you be too tired from the journey?

I want to read one or two good books by Friends, could not you lend me such? Is Sewall's History good to read?[3]

ALS (MH: fMS Am 1086 [9:93]); MsCfr (MH: fMS Am 1086 [Works, 1:29–31]). *Addressed:* Miss Mary Rotch / New Bedford / Mass. *Postmark:* Cambridge Ms. Feb 17.

    1. The *Boston Daily Advertiser* for this date announced a concert at the Boston Academy of Music for Saturday, 18 February. The concert was to include Beethoven's Second Symphony.

    2. Maria Rotch was Mary Rotch's niece, the daughter of Francis and Ann Waln Rotch.

    3. William Sewel, *The History of the Rise, Increase, and Progress of the Christian People Called Quakers* (London, 1722). Sewel (1654–1720) was an English Quaker who was born and raised in Amsterdam. A student of languages and of the history of his sect, he originally published his work in Dutch in 1717. Emerson owned his brother Charles's 1832 edition of Sewel's work (*DNB*; Harding, *Emerson's Library*).

409. To Henry W. Longfellow

Cambridge 3d May
1843.

Will Mr Longfellow oblige Miss Fuller by lending her for a short time Des Knaben Wunderhorn?[1]

AL (MH: bMS Am 1340.2 [4208]). *Addressed:* Mr Longfellow / Cambridge.

1. Achim von Arnim and his brother-in-law Clemens Brentano compiled *Des Knaben Wunderhorn: Alte Deutsche Lieder* (Berlin, 1806). The popular collection of more than 700 German folksongs was a major contribution to German Romanticism (*OCGL*).

410. To Sarah Ann Clarke

Cambridge
May 8th [18]43.

Dear Sarah,

I shall certainly go under these circumstances and would, on no account, give up Niagara, though, I fear Cary will not go, if she is to have no guardianship, but ours.[1] Mr S, perhaps, may not prize that as it deserves.

I very much hope you will not go before the 29th, that was the earliest date I had planned for, but will try to be ready. I, too, am constantly unwell, dull, headachs putting me back in every thing I undertake. A change of air and scene I surely need, and hope to bear travelling well. Headach tonight makes me unwilling to add a word more except yours ever affecy

M. F.

ALS (MHi). *Addressed:* Miss Sarah Clarke / Newton, / Mass. *Postmark:* Cambridge Ms May 9.

1. Fuller and Sarah Clarke did go to Niagara Falls and then on to Chicago and the Midwest, but Caroline Sturgis did not accompany them beyond Niagara.

411. To Ralph Waldo Emerson

9th May. [1843]—

Dear friend,

I am trying to write as hard as these odious east winds will let me.[1] I rise in the morning and feel as happy as the birds and then about eleven comes one of these tormentors, and makes my head ache and spoils the day. But if I get ready to print, as I think will be the case by the middle of next week, I wish to be sure of the first place, because I wish to go away quite free and not be followed by proof sheets to Niagara!

We shall go the last week in this month or the first of June, and I think I shall go to Chicago and the Lakes, and be absent some weeks. The Eastern girls are as bad as the East winds only in[n] a different way, one *will* come and the other *wont*. Anne thinks they will come tomorrow. I cant tell, but sigh about Lidian a doleful Ach, with each sunset that they are not here yet.[2]

S. W's child is named Lydia because his mother in the flesh bears that name.[3] Had it been a son it would have been named Jacob Barker! Why is not the advent of a daughter as "sacred" a fact as that of a son.[n] I do believe, O Waldo, most unteachable of men, that you are at heart a sinner on this point. I entreat you to seek light in prayer upon it.

I have read a shallow book Howitt's Germany, shallow, but with items not to be found elsewhere.[4] I have a really good book Die Seherin von Prevorst.—[5] However I am tired now of books and pens and thought no less, and shall be glad when I take wing for an idle outdoors life, mere sight and emotion. Ever your

M.

Can you send me the vol[n] on Philosophical Necessity giving an acct of the St Simonians &c.[6]

I hope you are getting time for your chapter.[7]

ALS (MH: bMS Am 1280 [2365]). *Addressed:* R. W. Emerson / Concord. *Endorsed:* M. Fuller / 1842. Published in Rusk, *Letters of RWE*, 3:170.

only in] only ↑ in ↓

as that of a son.] as ↑ that of ↓ a ⟨?⟩ son.

the vol] the ⟨book⟩ ↑ vol ↓

1. Fuller was writing her essay "The Great Lawsuit. Man *versus* Men. Woman *versus* Women," which appeared in the July *Dial* 4 (1843):1–47.

2. Fuller is answering Emerson's letter of 20 April, in which he told of Lidian's interest in Abby Stevens, a young woman from Maine. On 7 June Emerson reported that Lidian liked Abby and that they were sending for her twin, Anne (Rusk, *Letters of RWE*, 3:167, 179).

3. In his letter of 29 April, Emerson asked why the Wards' second child was named Lydia. As Fuller says, Lydia Gray Ward (who was born on 24 April) was named after Sam's mother. Emerson had said, "Though no son, yet a sacred event" (Rusk, *Letters of RWE*, 3:170; Charles Henry Jones, *Genealogy of the Rodman Family* [Philadelphia, 1886], p. 127).

4. William Howitt, *The Rural and Domestic Life of Germany* (London, 1842). An American edition was published in Philadelphia in 1843.

5. Justinus Kerner, *Die Seherin von Prevorst* (Stuttgart and Tübingen, 1829), was an account of the psychic case of Friederike Hauffe (*OCGL*). Fuller later gave an expansive account of the book in *Summer on the Lakes, in 1843* (Boston, 1844), pp. 126–64.

6. Fuller probably was asking for Pierre Leroux's *De l'humanité, de son principe, et de son avenir* (Paris, 1840), which Emerson apparently was reading and which Orestes Brownson had reviewed at length in *Boston Quarterly Review* 5 (1842):257–322. Pierre Leroux (1797–1871) was a journalist, philosopher, and political thinker. Claude-Henri

de Rouvroy, comte de Saint-Simon (1760–1825), was the founder of French socialism. His work focused on class conflict and historical necessity.

7. In his letter of 20 April, Emerson told Fuller that the imminent arrival of Carlyle's *Past and Present* meant that he was to be distracted just as "I was getting meditative on a chapter which I greatly wish to write" (Rusk, *Letters of RWE*, 3:167). Exactly what his topic was is unclear, though in his journal for 17 April he wrote four pages on Lane and Alcott, material that later appeared in his essay "Nominalist and Realist" (*JMN*, 8:386–87).

412. To Charles K. Newcomb

22d May [18]43.

Dear Charles,

I hoped to have seen you before I went, but have had much too much to do, and fear I must go without. Did I hope that such words would avail, I would urge you to take care of yourself, especially not to exhaust the bodily frame by sitting up late at night. When I return we shall meet I hope at Brook farm.

I shall not have time to write to your mother as I expected. Remember me to her with affece regard, and, when convenient, please send her this little sum which I owe her.

This book I thought you would like to receive from my hand unless you have it already. Should the mind prompt to write to me, and I wish it may, address me at Chicago, care William Clarke.[1]

Always your friend

M. F.

ALS (MH: fMS Am 1086 [10:142]). *Addressed:* Charles King Newcomb, / Brook Farm.

1. William Hull Clarke, James and Sarah Clarke's brother, moved to Chicago in 1835. He was an assistant engineer for the Chicago Board of Public Works (William W. Johnson, *Clarke-Clark Genealogy* [North Greenfield, Wis., 1884], p. 85).

413. To Elizabeth Hoar

Niagara 30th May
[18]43

My dear Lizzie,

I must write you a little note from here, (though it must be only a little note, for the time is too precious to spend on writing) because I should not have got here at all, but for your sweetness at the very last.— And then the parasol!! Just as I was mournfully reflecting on the trouble the affectionate Mrs Greeley[1] had had, and the trouble Lizzie had had *for nothing,* and how well I deserved to have my head ache all the way, there was your face at the window looking, indeed, like Unas and Sisters of Mercy.[2] For very different is the order of Mercy from that of Charity, in its modern acceptation at least. The quality of Mercy is not strained not winnowed and double sifted like Charity for "discovering objects."[3] But droppeth like the gentle dew from heaven, alike on the careful and the careless, the forgetters and rememberers of parasols.[4]

But your face, though it looked sweetly was flushed, and I really want to hear that you did not hurt yourself, for you must have darted down there like lightning. Write to me how you are, and also of Jane's wedding, you alone will tell me of it.[5] And a little of Ellen and Ellery. Just one long full letter to Chicago, care William Clarke or Clarke and Co. and I shall write to you at least one letter full either of trees, and rivers or out a' the way men and women "according to taste" as the cooking book hath it.

Now I will not write much except to tell you, that I *do* feel like going now. The reason I did not was, as I supposed, that I had had no rest. However I was able to take it on the journey. The first day in the cars, we were silent, and I enjoyed sitting idle all the day, and just letting all that had passed filter itself clear. At Albany we had a long good night. Next day and night, though we travelled through the 24 hours, there were couches in the cars and I could lie down as much as I liked. We slept through the night, though we were waked very often for a few minutes. It was pleasant that night, the ceaseless, steady motion, the gentle dripping of the rain, snatches of low talk among the passengers, but just seen by the one lamp on some mysterious subject, which speedily mingled with a dream, then occasionally to hear "We are passing Genesee river" and the like and make pictures of these unseen places. The whole night has to me the effect of phantasmagoria, as I look back.

We reached Buffalo too late for the cars, which was a good thing, though it did not seem so at the time, as it gave us time to rest before coming here. We are not going in the Illinois after all, and A. Clarke goes on without us, for Mrs C. was too ill to come.[6] So, if there had been a clear understanding all round we might have staid to Jane's marriage. Well; it was not fated so. And we have at least a whole week here, of which nothing at present from your friend

M.

ALS (NRU).

1. Mary Young Cheney (1811–72), daughter of Silas and Mary Cheney, married Horace Greeley on 5 July 1836, after they met at a Grahamite boardinghouse. Fuller had an often strained friendship with the intense Mary Greeley (*Greeley Family*, p. 671).

2. Fuller refers to Edmund Spenser's *Faerie Queene*, bk. 1, canto 10, where Una introduces the Red Cross Knight to the three sisters Faith, Hope, and Charity. Charity in turn introduces him to Mercy.

3. Shakespeare, *The Merchant of Venice*, IV.i.184.

4. Fuller slightly misquotes *The Merchant of Venice*, IV.1.185, then modifies Matt. 5:45, where the rain falls "on the just and on the unjust."

5. Jane Tuckerman married John Gallison King on 25 May.

6. Abraham Fuller Clarke (James's brother) and his mother, Rebecca Hull Clarke.

414. To Sarah Shaw

Niagara, 30th May [18]43.

Dear Sarah,

The inclosure you sent me before I went was three times what I should have thought of, if indeed I had put any precise value on the time I gave you. Had we met I should have had some little talk about it for though I love you well enough to like to receive from you, I would have you suit what you do to your own convenience.

However as I could not see you, I thought best to appropriate the small fortune you sent, and you will be glad to know[n] that it puts me entirely at my ease about my journey. I shall not be obliged to hurry home or trouble myself too much about details to keep within a certain sum. And I doubt not I shall thus owe to you you health, happiness and thought.

On my side I shall expect you after my return to let me examine for you any translations you may have made or do any thing else I can for you about *the book.*

I shall always look on you with a tenderer regard for the ready and dear sympathy you showe[d] with those pages, to me full of prophetic meanings. It is a sweet remembrance to have read it with one who never showed cavil, frivolity[n] or dullness, but a pure and feeling sense of what is[n] holy, and of the beautiful atmosphere that enfolds the whole. May you be happy, dear Sarah, that is, may you continue to grow as you have these years that I have known you!

And thus a sweet farewell from your friend

M. F.

ALS (MH: bMS Am 1417 [185]). *Addressed:* Mrs Sarah Shaw / West Roxbury / Mass.
glad to know] glad to ⟨know⟩ know
cavil, frivolity] cavil, fr⟨vo⟩ivolity
what is] what ↑ is ↓

415. To Ralph Waldo Emerson

1 June 1843
Niagara

I send you a token, made by the hands of some Seneca Indian lady. If you use it for a watch-pocket, hang it, when you travel, at the head of your bed, and you may dream of Niagara. If you use it for a purse, you can put in it alms for poets and artists, and the subscription-money you receive for Mr. Carlyle's book.[1] His book, as it happened, you gave me as a birthday gift, and you may take this as one to you; for, on yours, was W.'s birthday, J.'s wedding-day, and the day of ————'s death, and we set out on this journey.[2] Perhaps there is something about it on the purse. The "number five which nature loves" is repeated on it.

Carlyle's book I have, in some sense, read. It is witty, full of pictures, as usual. I would have gone through with it, if only for the sketch of Samson, and two or three bits of fun which happen to please me.[3] No doubt it may be of use to rouse the unthinking to a sense of those great dangers and sorrows. But how open is he to his own assault. He rails himself out of breath at the short-sighted, and yet sees scarce a step before him. There is no valuable doctrine in his book, except the Goethean, *Do to-day the nearest duty.*[4] Many are ready for that, could they but find the way. This he does not show. His proposed measures say nothing. Educate the people. That cannot be done by books, or voluntary effort, under these paralyzing circumstances. Emigration! According to his own estimate of the increases of population, relief that way can have very slight effect. He ends as he began; as he did in Chartism.[5] Everything is very bad. You are fools and hypocrites, or you would make it better. I cannot but sympathize with him about hero-worship; for I, too, have had my fits of rage at the stupid irreverence of little minds, which also is made a parade of by the pedantic and the worldly. Yet it is a good sign. Democracy is the way to the new aristocracy, as irreligion to religion. By and by, if there are great men, they will not be brilliant exceptions, redeemers, but favorable samples of their kind.

Mr. C's tone is no better than before. He is not loving, nor large; but he seems more healthy and gay.

We have had bad weather here, bitterly cold. The place is what I expected: it is too great and beautiful to agitate or surprise: it satisfies: it does not excite thought, but fully occupies. All is calm; even the rapids do not hurry, as we see them in smaller streams. The sound, the sight, fill the senses and the mind.

At Buffalo, some ladies called on us, who extremely regretted they could not witness our emotions, on first seeing Niagara. "Many," they said, "burst into tears; but with those of most sensibility, the hands become cold as ice, and they would not mind if buckets of cold water were thrown over them!"

ELfr, from *Memoirs*, 1:261–63.

1. Emerson arranged for Carlyle's *Past and Present* to be published in a Boston edition of 1,500 copies to sell for seventy-five cents each. Unfortunately, a New York publisher pirated the book and sold it for twelve and a half cents. Still, in October, Emerson sent Carlyle £25 in royalties on all of the American editions of his books (Joseph Slater, ed., *The Correspondence of Emerson and Carlyle* [New York, 1964], pp. 343, 345–61). When Emerson sent Fuller a copy is not clear, for in his letter of 24 May he says he is sending Theodor Mundt's *Geschichte der Literatur der Gegenwart* (Berlin, 1842) (Rusk, *Letters of RWE*, 3:176).

2. Both Emerson and William Henry Channing were born on 25 May; Jane Tuckerman married on that day in 1843, and Maria Randall died on 25 May 1842.

3. The monk Samson, who becomes abbot of St. Edmundsbury in bk. 2, is a version of Carlyle's hero.

4. Goethe's maxim, made popular among Fuller's friends by Carlyle in *Sartor Resartus*.

5. Carlyle's analysis of the Chartist movement appeared in his *Chartism* (London, 1840).

416. To Ralph Waldo Emerson

Chicago, 16th June
43.

Your letter, dear friend, was the first I received and most welcome. I stand rather forlorn on these bustling piers. I put a good face on it, but, though I believe I shall yet draw some music from the stream of sound, I cannot vibrate with it yet. In this thoroughfare scarce better thoughts come than at the corner of two busy streets.

The dissipation of thought and feeling is less painful than in the eastern cities in this that it is at least for *material* realities. The men are all at work for money and to develope the resources of the soil, the women belong to the men. They do not ape fashions, talk jargon or burn out life as a tallow candle for a tawdry show. Their energy is real, though its objects are not invested with a poetic dignity

It does not seem half so unpleasant to see them really *at it*, as it did coming along to hear the talk of the emigrants from the East, so wholly for what *they could get* It did not please to think that the nation was to be built up from such materials as teemed in the steam-boats, or crowded the landings. At one of the latter I selected from the to-bacco chewing, sharp, yet sensual looking crowd, (and it was, they said, the entire male[n] population that was out to stare at the steam-boat.) one man that looked more clean and intellectual than the rest, and was told he was a famous Land-Shark.

Here I am interested in those who have a mixture of Indian blood. With one lady I may become well acquainted as she is to travel with us. Her melancholy eyes, slow graceful utterance, and delicate feeling of what she has seen attract me. She is married here and wears our dress, but her family retain the dress and habits of their race. Through her I hope to make other acquaintance that may please me

Next week we are going into the country to explore the neighbor-hood of Fox and Rock rivers. We are going in regular western style, to travel in a wagon, and stay with the farmers. Then I shall see the West to better advantage than I have as yet.

We are going to stay with one family, the mother of which had what they call a "claim fight." Some desperadoes laid claim to her property which is large they were supposed to belong to the band who lately have been broken up by an exertion of Lynch law. She built shanties in the different parts, she and her three daughters each took one to defend it. They showed such bravery that the foe retreated.

Then there is an Irish gentleman who owns a large property there. He was married to the daughter of an Irish[n] earl, his son, a boy who inherits the her[n] fortune he has left in Europe, and since the death of his wife lives alone on the Rock River; he has invited us to stay at his house, and the scenery there is said to be most beauti[ful.][1]

I hear too of a Hungarian count who has a large tract of land in Wisconsin. He has removed thither with all his tenantry several hun-dred persons[n] they say. He comes to market at Milwaukie, they call him there the Count; they do not seem to know his name.[n] We are to stay at Milwaukie and I shall inquire all about him I should like to know how he has modified his life from the feudal lord to the broth-erly landlord. I should think he must be a good and resolute man to carry out such a scheme successfully.

I want to see some emigrant with worthy aims using all his gifts and knowledge to some purpose honorable to the land; instead of lower-ing themselves to the requisitions of the moment as so many of them do.

Niagara and the great lakes, seen for the most part under lowering skies with few fitful gleams of light, have left on my mind rather the impression of a vast and solemn vision than of a reality. I got quite tired at last of seeing so much water in all ways and forms. Yet am glad I have had it and just so. I got so familiar that I might have been tempted to address even[n] the British fall with the easy impertinence of the Yankee visitor "I wonder how many years you've been aroaring[n] at this rate. I wonder if all you've been pouring could be ciphered[n] on a slate." I shall be very willing to go inland and ford shallow streams However the lake voyage *is* very fine. You stop often to wood for hours, and can then escape into the woods We did at the Manitou islands and saw real old monarch trees. And though I want now to get out of sight of the water for a while I cant forbear going to walk on the narrow shore of Lake Michigan. There is almost always a strong breeze and real billows tumbling in with a wild gray expanse and steamboats fire winged cleaving the distance. It is grand too to take a walk which might be extended with scarce a variation of feature for hundreds of miles.

Write again, for I dont know when I shall return certainly not till August— Mention the Christian name[n] of Mr Wms and I will try to see him on my way back.[2] I shall stay a day or two in Buffalo with an old friend.[3] Love to your Mother and Lidian. I am relieved to hear the Kennebecker proved true at last.[4] I have thought of it many times.

Your ever affectionate

MARGARET.

direct your next letter here too. I shall return here before going to Mackinaw.

ALS (MH: bMS Am 1280 [2369]); MsC (MB: Ms. Am. 1450 [167]). Published in part in Higginson, *MFO*, pp. 196–97, and Rusk, *Letters of RWE*, 3:177–78. *Addressed:* R. W. Emerson / Concord / Mass. *Postmark:* Chicago Ill. Jun 17. *Endorsed:* Margaret Fuller / June 1843.

entire male] entire ↑ male ↓
an Irish] an ⟨Englis⟩ ↑ Irish ↓
the her] the ↑ her ↓
hundred persons] hundred ↑ persons ↓
his name.] his ⟨other⟩ name.
address even] address ↑ even ↓
been aroaring] been ↑ a ↓ roaring
be ciphered] be cip⟨p⟩hered
Christian name] Christian ⟨way⟩ name

1. Fuller met Alexander Charters (b. 1800), who was originally from Belfast and had settled at Dixon, Illinois. In 1827 Charters married Ellen Boomer (d. 1832) of Belfast. They had one son, James B. Charters (*Biographical Encyclopedia of Illinois of the Nineteenth Century* [Philadelphia, 1875], p. 187).

2. In his letter of 7 June, Emerson asked Fuller to see "a young man in Buffalo of

the Name of Williams a lawyer, who once kept school here." Probably he was Charles H. S. Williams, Sr. (Rusk, *Letters of RWE*, 3:180; MVR 311:72).

3. Albert Haller Tracy, a lawyer in Buffalo, had been in the U.S. Congress with her father.

4. Abby Stevens.

417. To Richard F. Fuller

Milwaukee, 29th July, 1843.

My dear Richard,

I should have written to you long since, but that I expected to receive a letter from you. No formal engagement was made, 'tis true but I thought you would feel the wish to communicate to me somewhat of yourself during the summer. It has been a painful surprize to me that Mother should never once write. I have felt very anxious about her health, and about yours, but a letter received from Ellen, a day or two since, implies, though it does not say that you are none of you ill. She tells me, too, you are gone to Groton where I hope you will live as you did last summer, and regain the natural temper of body and mind of which Cambridge, with its artificial and mechanical disciplines, threatens to deprive you.

I see by the list of those to whom the Bowdoin prizes were awarded that the essay to which you devoted so much time and study did not gain one. This failure I know could not fail to be dispiriting at the moment, but I trust you recovered from it in the manly spirit you thought you should. You will not suspect me who am your true and manly friend, of any insincere soothing when I say that the award of Cambridge is no test of what the world's will be. Seeing Carey's name at the head of the list, and knowing what he is from those well capable to judge, I cannot regret that you should fail before a tribunal so sensible to his merits.[1] I feel that your abilities are excellent, your ambition deeper and purer than is usual at your age or any other, and I have no doubt of your eventual success with yourself, and with the world, if you do not unsettle your health on the way.

Daily I thought of you during my visit to the Rock River territory. It is only five years since the poor Indians have been dispossessed of this region of sumptuous loveliness, such as can hardly be paralleled in this world. No wonder they poured out their blood freely before they would go.[2] On one island, belonging to Mr Hinshaw, a gentleman with whom we staid, are still to be found their "caches" for secreting provisions, the wooden troughs in which they pounded their

132

corn, the marks of their tomahawks upon felled trees. When he first came he found the body of an Indian woman, in a canoe, elevated on high poles, with all her ornaments on. This island is a spot where nature seems to have exhausted her invention in crowding it with all kinds of growths, from the most rich trees down to the most delicate plants. It divides the river which there sweeps along in clear and glittering current betwixt noble parks, richest green lawns, pictured rocks, crowned with old hemlocks, or smooth bluffs three hundred feet high, the most beautiful of all. Two of these, the Eagle's nest, and the Deer's walk, [still][n] the habitual resort of the grand and beautiful creatures from which they are named, were the scene of some of the happiest hours of my life.[n] I had no idea from verbal description of the beauty of these bluffs, nor can I hope to give any to others. They lie so magnificently bathed in sunlight; they touch the heavens with so sharp and fair a line!— This is one of the finest parts of the river but it seems beautiful enough to fill any heart and eye all along its course, and nowhere broken or injured by the hand of man.— And there, I thought, if we two could live and you have a farm which would not be a twentieth part[n] the labor of a N England farm, and would pay twenty times as much for the labor, and have our books and our pens, and a little boat on the river, how happy we might be for four or five years, at least *as* happy as fate permits mortals to be. For we, I think, Richard, are really congenial, and if I could hope permanent peace on the earth, I might hope it with you.

You will be glad to hear that I feel overpaid for coming here. Much is my life enriched by the images of the great Niagara, of the vast lakes, the heavenly sweetness of the prairie scenes, and above all by the lovely region where I would so gladly have lived. My health too is materially benefitted. I hope to come back better fitted for toil and care, as well as with the beauteous memories to sustain me in them— Let me find you well and bright, too, do not let me be met by sorrow— I have recd a letter from Mother since I began this Where it has been lingering I cant conceive; it bears date 29th June. Affectionately always your sister

MARGARET.

ALS (MH: fMS Am 1086 [9:96]); MsCfr (MH: fMS Am 1086 [Works, 2:675–83]). Published in part in *WNC*, pp. 366–67. *Addressed:* Richard F. Fuller / Student Harvard University / Cambridge / Mass. *Postmark:* Milwaukee Jul 31.

still] *Added from the copy.*

were the scene of some of the happiest hours of my life.] ↑ were the scene of some of the happiest hours of my life. ↓

be a twentieth part] be ↑ a twentieth part ↓

1. The Bowdoin prize for the junior class went to George Blankern Cary (1824–46), son of George and Helen Paine Cary of Boston. The best writer in the class, Cary had been Alcott's pupil at the Temple School (*The Class of 1844, Harvard College* [Cambridge, Mass., 1869], pp. 25, 30).

2. The Sac and Fox tribes had ceded yet another portion of their land to the United States in 1837 (after previous cessions in 1804 and 1832). Their bloodiest resistance occurred in 1832, when Chief Black Hawk tried to stop the white encroachment into the Indian land (William T. Hagan, *The Sac and Fox Indians* [Norman, Okla., 1958]).

418. To Samuel G. Ward

Milwaukie,
3d August, 1843.

My dear Sam,

I have let a longer interval than I intended pass between my letters, but first I waited for yours, and then, I thought I would postpone writing till after my journey in Wisconsin, from which I returned last night. It has been pleasant, but I saw nothing like the Rock River Edens. We passed one day in the neighborhood of a chain of lakes, where there was fine fishing for the gentlemen; they fished from sunrise to sunset while we rode about, hunting the picturesque, in charge of our host, a native Kentuckian, a mixture of the boy, the hunter and chivalrous gentleman very agreeable in brief companionship. He knows no less than forty of these lakes, and, from one high point, thirteen can be seen at once. They are clear as you described Chrystal Lake, and with beautifully wooded sloping banks, sometimes rich with oaks, sometimes more wild with the tamarack. In the afternoon we saw at a distance on the banks of the Silver or Nepossa Lake, an encampment of Indians. A poor remnant of the tribe that used to inhabit these regions have returned, driven back, it is said, by the Pawnees, perhaps, *drawn* back rather by invincible homesickness. The farm of our host had once been the beautiful site of one of the largest Indian villages, and lying among the long grass the other day he saw one of them standing on[n] the brow of the hill, with folded arms,[n] surveying the old home, over whose soil the tent poles are still scattered. "I was," said he, "*somewhat* moved by the melancholy of his look, and kept still, observing him, when at last I did move, he started, snorted out an angry *hui*, turned on his heel, and stalked away."

They have been in Milwaukie since we were here,[n] the poorer sort highly painted, dancing before the stores and taverns to get whiskey and food, the grandee strolling about, sullenly observing every thing. One was a noble Roman figure; he had a very large red blanket, with a purple[n] rim, falling from his shoulders to the ground, which he wore with great grace and dignity he was the finest looking Indian by far I have seen.— In this encampment there were not more than thirty or forty; we got out and went to the encampment, and just as we got there a violent thunder storm came on, during which we had to take refuge under their tents, too low to stand upright in and too small for more than three or four to get in together. Their grave and graceful courtesy, near us as they were, prevented even the dirt, though that was *as* great as I expected, from being offensive. The kettles were boiling over fires in the open air,[n] which the rain could not put out. Their horses much excited by the thunder were careening wildly around among[n] the trees, one theatrical looking old Indian stood gazing up to the heavens, while the rain poured and the thunder crashed[n] there could not be a finer scene. The first object we saw on arriving crouching[n] at the mouth of a tent was a family groupe, the foremost member of which, a beautiful looking, wild-eyed boy, perfectly naked, except a large gold bracelet on one arm was the foremost member.[n] We compared him with the South Sea Island king who considered the cocked hat presented him by the Europeans as a full court dress.

Next day we visited some Swedes, established on the bank of Pine Lake. It is surprizing what numbers of Swedes, Danes, and Norwegians are here in Wisconsin, and still arriving in great numbers. But the sight of these we visited today made my heart ache. They were a young couple of elegant and cultivated persons who came out here as soon as they were married with golden dreams no doubt of a life of mutual love, and rural freedom and money enough to have secured at least some share of *comfort* in the hard life to which the circumstances of these regions compel, had not the husband, Colonel Schneider injured his foot on the passage. Since he has been here, near[n] a year now, he has scarcely been able to use it, and it has constantly grown worse, so that he has not been able to superintend his work people, and they have been imposed upon in every way, so that now they feel too poor to be willing to go to a city for medical attendance and the new physician here threatens amputation Their first child is dead: it lies[n] on the point that juts into the lake; the mother raised with her own hands the pile that marks the spot. She has gone through all the hardships that women do here; they have not marred her beauty yet but only left a shadow in the rich dark eyes. But his expression touched me still more, as he sat so disabled with his books and papers round him and obliged to see his wife exert herself in the way she must even to attend on him. It was a pretty picture for the log cabin; he had such a handsome *storied* face, with his dog at his feet, his guitar in the corner, and his little purple cap on his brown locks; she looked like some Italian lady he had persuaded to run away with him for love. He seemed dignified and calm as if he would not waste time on useless regrets and if he ever gets well, they may be happy yet if not in Wisconsin.

—Well! I must come to a close, dear Anna, I am *very* sorry you dont get strong.—[n] I am wonderfully the gainer in strength and spirits for my summer.— Will you write, Sam, once more and direct to Chicago, and they will forward me the letter. Yours, though brief, have been a great pleasure to me.

MARGARET.

ALS (MH: bMS Am 1465 [922]). *Addressed:* S. G. Ward Esq / Boston / Mass. *Postmark:* Milwaukie Wn.T. Aug 7.

standing on] standing ⟨lately⟩ on
folded arms,] folded ⟨ha⟩arms,
Milwaukie since we were here,] Milwaukie ↑ since we were here ↓,
a purple] a ⟨darker⟩ ↑ purple ↓
fires in the open air,] fires, ↑ in the open air ↓
around among] around ⟨gay⟩ ↑ among ↓
while the rain poured and the thunder crashed] ↑ while the rain poured and the thunder crashed ↓
arriving crouching] arriving ⟨crouched in one tent, was a family group⟩ crouching
arm was the foremost member.] arm ↑ was the foremost member ↓.
near] ⟨?⟩near
it lies] ⟨she⟩ it lies
get strong.—] get str⟨e⟩ong.—

419. To Ralph Waldo Emerson

Chicago, 4th August, 1843.

Just after writing to you, my dear friend, was received yours, and presently after that, the Dial, which I read quite through with an enjoyment it needs to be so far off to appreciate. Ellery's poem, "The Earth" gave me singular pleasure. His "letters" too look better yet in print. I hope he will continue and print the whole while the Dial yet lives. It was pity to break Mr Lane's piece. He needs to fall his whole length to show his weight. There are fine touches of his peculiar dignity in it as "So that there is still an occupation left for a few small actors on this stage" &c The letter from Fruitlands made me laugh till I cried it contrasted so whimsically with all I had been seeing and feeling in this region, where strong instincts and imperative necessities come upon you like the swoop of the hawk. "Gifts" is charming. "Notes from the journal of a Scholar" I had seen before, it is good to have it in my own possession. Why have I never seen that voyage to Jamaica, how excellent, though so slight a thing for its life and health and spirit. There are not many such leaves in those volumes, I trow. One or two questions I had to ask, but you will have no chance to answer them till we meet. I shall not be able to do any thing for the October number and am glad to see you are well furnished.[1]

Hints on A and A, I enjoyed reading again with Sarah; their strength and sense make me proud. Imagine my satisfaction at finding the verses To Rhea, in so high a state of preservation.[2] I was a simpleton to distress my self, as I really did several beautiful prairie hours, lest they were lost. I might have known his were no carelessly scattered Sybilline leaves, but carefully[n] rolled papyri.

Since I wrote I have passed several days travelling in the interior of Wisconsin; it was a pretty journey, though not to compare with my delightful pilgrimage in Illinois. Then apart from the superiority in beauty of that region we travelled in a way that left us perfectly free to idle as much as we pleased, to gather every flower and to traverse every wood we fancied. We were then in a strong vehicle called a lumber[n] waggon which defied all the jolts and wrenches incident to woodpaths, mudholes, and the fording of creeks; we were driven by a friend, who drove admirably, who had the true spirit that animates daily life, who knew the habits of all the fowl,[n] and fish, and growing things, and all the warlike legends of the country, and could recite them not in a pedantical, but a poetical manner. Thus our whole journey had the gayity of adventure, with the repose of intimate communion. Now we were in a nice carriage, fit for nothing but roads, and which *would* break even on those with a regular driver, too careful of his horses to go off a footpace &c &c However we had[n] much pleasure and saw many pretty things, of which I must tell you at my leisure. Our time was chiefly passed in the neighborhood of a chain of lakes, fine pieces of water, with the wide sloping park-like banks, so common in this country.

We visited an encampment of Indians, and some Swedes that interested me much. I have made slight mention of these in my letter to

Sam and Anna. The tide of emigration now sets strong for Wisconsin and is almost wholly a continental population, hundreds of Swedes, Norwegians, Germans, Dutch are constantly arriving. There are many in Illinois, but far more in Wisconsin, a few fortunately rich, for they have a weary apprenticeship to serve, before they can use and enjoy the lands it is so easy to buy. These foreign women, however, I rejoice to see do not suffer as our Eastern women do; they have, for the most part, been brought up to work in the open air and have better constitutions, but all the Eastern women say "oh it is well for the men, who enjoy their hunting and fishing, but for us, we have every thing to bear and no time or health to enjoy or learn."— Farewell, I hope I may hear from you again once more, but hardly expect it. Yours always

MARGARET.

I have missed by an accident a good chance to go to Sault St Marie, but have reason to hope another.

As this goes by private hand I send yr Mundt; the book is good for nothing except to set the last watermark of literary gossip but there is a short acct of Frederica Bremer and other Swedish writers that would be worth translating for the Dial, just now when interest is excited on the subject.[3]

ALS (MH: bMS Am 1280 [2370]). Published in part in Higginson, *MFO*, pp. 166, 193–94, and Rusk, *Letters of RWE*, 3:194–95. *Addressed:* R. W. Emerson / Concord / Mass. *Endorsed:* Margaret Fuller / Aug. 1843.

but carefully] but ⟨ro⟩carefully
a lumber] a lum⟨p⟩ber
the fowl,] the fo⟨?⟩wl,
we had] we ⟨?⟩had

1. Fuller mentions several contributions to the July *Dial:* Ellery Channing's "The Earth" (p. 64) and "The Youth of the Poet and the Painter" (pp. 48–58); Charles Lane's "Social Tendencies" (pp. 65–86); "Fruitlands," a joint "communication" from Alcott and Lane (pp. 135–36); Emerson's "Gifts" (pp. 93–95); Charles C. Emerson's "Notes from the Journal of a Scholar. No. II" (pp. 88–92); and Benjamin P. Hunt's "Voyage to Jamaica" (pp. 116–33).

2. More contributions to the July issue of the *Dial:* Sam Ward's "Notes on Art and Architecture" (pp. 107–15) and Emerson's poem "To Rhea" (pp. 104–6).

3. Theodor Mundt, *Geschichte der Literatur der Gegenwart*, which Emerson had received from Stearns Wheeler. Emerson wrote on Mundt in the October issue of the *Dial.* He ignored Fuller's suggestion about Frederika Bremer, however, and translated instead Mundt's comments on Hölderlin (pp. 265–66). Mundt (1808–61) was a journalist, novelist, and teacher (*OCGL*); Bremer (1801–65) was a Swedish novelist later known for her feminist point of view. In 1842 Mary Howitt, an English author, had translated Bremer's *The Neighbours*, the book that aroused the interest that Fuller mentions.

420. To Albert H. Tracy

Chicago
7th August [18]43.

My dear friend, Mr Tracy,

When I saw you in Buffalo, and told you I should return to the East in about six weeks you thought you might be at home then and could provide me with an escort to Boston. But I have delayed my return, am likely to delay it still longer.

Now I write to ask whether if I come on between the 25th August and 15th Septr you are likely to be at home then.

I wish to have some prospect before me, in case of my leaving Mackinaw where I shall stay the last days, without an escort.

I am very desirous to go down the North River[1] on my way home, as I have not seen it for some years.

I hope circumstances will favor my seeing you a little at Buffalo. I have never forgotten the time you passed at our house, and always wished, since my mind grew up, that it might renew acquaintance with yours.

An answer will reach me if directed Care Clarke and Co., *Chicago, Illinois* with great regard yours

S. M. FULLER.

ALS (MHarF). *Addressed:* Hon Albert H. Tracy / Western Hotel / Buffalo. *Endorsed:* Miss S. M. Fuller / Aug 8—

1. The Hudson River.

421. To Mary Rotch

Chicago 9th August 43

I have hoped, from time to time, dear Aunt Mary, that I should receive a few lines apprizing me how you were this summer, but a letter from Mrs F. lately comes to tell me, that you are not better, but, at least while at Saratoga, worse.[1] So writing is, of course, fatiguing and I must not expect letters any more. To that I would make up my mind, if I could hear that you were well again. I fear, if your malady disturbs you at night as much as it did, it must wear on your strength very much, and it seems in itself dangerous. However, it is good to think that your composure is always such that disease can only do its legitimate work, and not mire two ways, the body with its pains, and the body through the mind with thoughts and fears of pains.

I should have written to you long ago, except that I found little to communicate this summer, and little inclination to communicate that little, so what letters I have sent have been chiefly meant to beg some from my friends. I have had homesickness sometimes here, as do children for the house where they are little indulged when in the boarding school where they are only tolerated. This has been in the towns, when I have felt the want of companionship, because the dissipation of fatigue, or expecting soon to move again has prevented my employing myself for myself, and yet there was nothing well worth looking at without— When in the country I have enjoyed myself highly and my health has improved day by day. The characters of persons are brought out, by the little wants and adventures of country life as you see it in this region, so that each one awakens a healthful interest and the same persons who if I saw them at these hotels, would not have a word to say that could fix the attention, become most pleasing companions, for their topics are before them and they take the hint. You feel so grateful too for the hospitality of the log cabin, such gratitude as the hospitality of the rich, however generous, cannot inspire, for these wait on you with domestics and money, and give of their superfluity only, but here the master gives you his bed, his horse, his lamp, his grain from the field, his all, in short, and you see that he enjoys doing so thoroughly, and takes no thought for the morrow, so that you seem in fields full of lilies perfumed with pure kindness, and feel, verily, that Solomon in all his glory could not have entertained you so much to the purpose.[2]

Travelling, too, through the wide green wood, and praires, gives a feeling both of luxury and repose that the sight of highly cultivated country never can. There seems to be room enough, for labor to pause, and man to fold his arms and gaze, forgetting poverty and care,[n] and the thousand walls and fences that in the cultivated region must not only be built, but daily repaired both for mind and body. Nature seems to have poured forth her riches so without calculation, merely to mark the fulness of her joy, to swell in larger strains the hymn "The one Spirit doeth all things well, for its life is love"

I will not ask you to write to me now for I should not receive the letter, probably as I shall be at home in Sept early, or the middle of the month, if things turn out as I expect. Probably, too, I shall reserve a visit to Butternuts for a future summer.[3] I have been so much a[n] rover and when once on the road shall wish to hasten home. I should like to know how Maria is and her mother and intend to write, to Miss Gifford my love, as always. I hope your health may permit of your both coming to town after my return and that we may meet and talk as we did last winter.[n] If I should continue so well, conversation will become to me, too, a recreation, not fatigue. With affectionate good wishes dear Aunt Mary yours

S. M. FULLER.

ALS (MH: fMS Am 1086 [9:94]); MsCfr (MH: fMS Am 1086 [Works, 1:31–35]); MsCfr (MH: bMS Am 1280 [111, pp. 133–35]). Published in part in *WNC*, pp. 367–69, and *JMN*, 11:481–82. *Addressed:* Miss Mary Rotch / New Bedford / Mass. *Postmark:* Boston Ms Aug 15.

poverty and care,] poverty and ca⟨s⟩re,
much a] much ⟨an⟩ a
did last winter.] did ⟨then⟩ ↑ last winter ↓ .

1. In her letter of 25 July (MH), Eliza Farrar said that Mary Rotch had gone to Saratoga, become worse, and "found out the meaning of *Chronic* it means *for ever*."
2. Matt. 6:28–29 and Luke 12:27.
3. The home of Eliza Farrar's brother, Francis Rotch, in Morris, New York.

422. To William H. Channing

Chicago, 16 August 43.

As I am going in the boat as far as Mackinaw with a party for N. York, I will send you a few lines by them,—for a post-office letter it seems I have not materials of worth.

Ever since I have been here, I have been unwilling to utter the hasty impressions of my mind. It has seemed they might balance and correct one another till something of wisdom resulted. But that time is not yet come.

When I have been in the country, its beauty has filled me with rapture, but among *men* oh, how lonely! If it is my fault that I have met with so little congenial, it has not been for want of good will. I have earnestly wished to see things as they are, and to appreciate the great influences which are at work here at their just value. But they seem to me to tend so exclusively to bring the riches out of the earth; should that task ever have a long period *exclusively to itself?*— I have now seen a good range of character, both in country and in town,[n] and it has been a cause of true grief to me, dear William, that I could do nothing in aid of your purposes, simply for this reason, that I have had no intercourse with any one, with whom I should naturally introduce a mention of objects such as your periodical is intended to pursue.[1] Always it has been that I should hear from them accounts of the state of the country, in politics or agriculture, or their domestic affairs, or hunting stories. Of me, none asked a question. Like Mr Es lonely poet

What she has, nobody wants[2]

I have not been led to express one thought of my mind with warmth and freedom since I have been here, and all I have ever learnt or been is useless as regards others in the relations in which I meet them as a traveler or visitor. I dare say it might not be so, if I lived here, and had quiet tasks of my own. Then I should meet people, only as natural affinity brought us together, and gradually it would be seen that whatever is truly human in one must be of consequence to what is truly human in another, and that the same ether animates the lives of all. But now, it is as I tell you, for, if I have formed one or two ties, it is merely from community of sentiment and taste, some natural sympathy of organization.

My friend, I am deeply homesick, yet where is that home?— If not on earth, why should we look to heaven. I would fain truly live wherever I must abide, but[?] with full energy on my lot, whatever it is. He who alone knoweth will affirm that I have tried to work whole hearted, from an earnest faith. Yet my hand is often languid, and my heart is slow.— I must be gone, I feel, but whither?— I know not, if I cannot make this plot of ground yield me corn and roses, famine must be my lot forever and ever surely.

If the first number of[n] your periodical is sent out here, and has due chance to get read, this people will take it, if it has anything for them that suits their needs; and otherwise it is not desirable they should. I hope to be of some use in this way. When the first number is issued, send me as many as you can spare at Cambridge. I expect to be at home by the 20th or 25th Septr and I have seen enough now to know of some persons to whom it *may* be of use to send them I believe[n] my stay here may have been useful, in opening a path for some of my family but as this is not quite decided, I will not write you about it yet.

I stay at Mackinaw a fortnight till after the payment of the tribes and then home, stopping a day or two at Buffalo.[3] I hope to pass down the North River which I have not seen for some years, and through your city, but do not expect to stop there.

Farewell.

AL (MB: Ms. Am. 1450 [51]). Published in part in Higginson, *MFO*, p. 311. *Addressed:* William H. Channing / New York City. *Endorsed:* Aug 1843—

in town,] *The remainder of this sentence has been canceled by a later hand.*
If the first number of] If ↑ the first number of ↓
believe] *The paragraph to this point has been canceled by a later hand.*

1. On 15 September Channing began to publish his new journal, *Present* (Frothingham, *Memoir of William Henry Channing*, p. 204; Clarence L. Gohdes, *The Periodicals of American Transcendentalism* [Durham, N.C., 1931], pp. 83–100).
2. A modification of Emerson's "Woodnotes, I" l. 22 (*Dial* 1 [1840]:242).
3. Fuller described the annual payments to the Chippewa and Ottawa tribes in chap. 6 of *Summer on the Lakes*.

423. To Ralph Waldo Emerson

Chicago, 17th August 43.

I must write to you this evening, my friend, as a solace, though that is a way you do not like to love or be loved

O what can be so forlorn in its forlorn parts as this travelling? the ceaseless packing and unpacking, the heartless, uncongenial intercourses, the cheerless hotel, the many hours when you are too tired and your feelings too much dissipated to settle to any pursuit, yet you either have nothing to look at or are weary of looking.

This is my last evening in Chicago, (*the place of onions*, is the interpretation of the Indian[n] name, and I can attest there is some quality here fitted to draw tears and so can two or three infants that are screaming in the gallery at this instant) I have just done packing Sarah is quite unwell, and nobody comes in to claim my vacant hour. But there are two of them (the hours c'est à dire)[n] yet before bed time, probably there will be some leave-takings.

But I shall scarce leave friends behind me though, perhaps, no foes. I have[n] not reached forth the hand, neither has it been offered to me. I am silenced by these people, they are so all life and no thought, any thing that might fall from my lips would seem an impertinence I move about silently and look at them unnoticed

Truly there is no place for me to live, I mean as regards being with men. I like not the petty intellectualities, cant, and bloodless theory there at home, but this merely instinctive existence, to those who live it so "first rate" "off hand" and "go ahead," pleases me no better

The country ah! that is another thing in these wide plains, with their endless flowering treasures one could breathe a breath, free as rapture, over these smooth green hills could stray no more burthened than the deer. But I have not been there all the time. You say, (for I have received your letter this afternoon,) that I did not write you of Rock River, but I had written of it to others who, I thought would show you the letters, and I dont like to write circulars. There were fair days, grand sights, worth coming all this way and paying all this time for. But of details that must wait now till we meet.

At Milwaukie too I had an eye full, every day. From the lighthouse to look out over the lake, to see the thunder clouds gathering, reflected in that vast mirror, and the huge steamers looming up was very fine. Or to follow the margin of the lake beneath the tall bluff whose crumb[ling] soil changed almost daily its bold and picturesque juts, to watch the color on the lake various as the prism with[n] the varying depths lying in strata, an immense pallette, emerald, sapphire, amethyst Or along the smiling river with its many ravines, there grow the most twisted old arbor vitae trees that ever were seen, and the waterfall—but I have not room to describe!

Here at Chicago every thing is flat as Holland. The place is made for trade, and used as such, let us be glad of any thing that fulfils its destiny— Not without sadness even here have I taken my last drive over the prairie, my last walk along the shore, goodbye is always sad; we know we have not taken from the places, from the persons all they were capable to give

I have received your letter and I thank you for all its news.— Who are "the children of the Tunic"? have I lost some hieroglyphic key to the home dialect already.[1] And what is that about "laurels and myrtles,"[2] I have seen no such plants here; "red, red roses" grow amid the oaks, but they are not without thorns and their perfume is transient they do not bear gathering

How could I fail in answering your last to speak of the translations of Dante and their paraphrase.[3] I am impatient to see these leaves. Where there is a will, there is a way *surely*. I go to Mackinaw tomorrow to pass a fortnight and then back to Massachusetts, probably to be there by the middle of September. The Dial you sent came safe and though another had been sent I was glad of it, for the first was worn and soiled, though by use of only a few hands. In hope of a meeting ere long, (it is just a year ago today that I went to Concord to pass a pleasant tranquil month) your friend

MARGARET.

ALS (MH: bMS Am 1280 [2371]). Published in Rusk, *Letters of RWE*, 3:200–201; published in part in Miller, pp. 112–13. *Addressed:* R. W. Emerson / Concord / Mass. *Postmark:* Boston MS Sep 8. *Endorsed:* Margaret Fuller / Chicago / Sep 8 1843.

the Indian] the ↑ Indian ↓
(the hours c'est à dire)] ↑ (the hours c'est à dire) ↓
I have] ⟨But⟩ I have
prism with] prism ⟨at⟩ ↑ with ↓

1. In his letter of 7 August Emerson wrote: "Mrs S. W. Ripley too has written me again of the children of the Tunic," a reference to the tunic that the men at Brook Farm wore in place of a conventional coat (Rusk, *Letters of RWE*, 3:196; Lindsay Swift, *Brook Farm; Its Members, Scholars, and Visitors* [New York, 1900], p. 65).

2. Again Emerson resorted to circumlocution: "S. Larned at Plymouth had a laurel & myrtle leaf of a report which some west wind blew to him" (Rusk, *Letters of RWE*, 3:198).

3. On July 11 Emerson described the joint translation of Dante's *Vita Nuova* that he and Ellery Channing made (Rusk, *Letters of RWE*, 3:183).

424. To Richard F. Fuller

[7? September 1843]

Dear Richard,

I think best from your account to give you an order for twenty dollars instead of fifteen. You had better begin and keep an exact account. You ought to know what your expenses will be this year that you may judge as to the next. I suppose you have some safe lock up place in your room, and can wear the key when you go out, otherwise it is not safe to keep money in a college room.

As to the mending, be sure you never wear[n] things ragged. Mother may not be able to do it for you this fortnight, though we expect her now every day till she comes.

You dont mention whether you have Eugene's direction from George Kuhn, be sure you do when you write to me. I had a letter from E. the day after you were here by which I found with great regret he had not had one from me this summer, it is hard for him to be thus deprived of news[n] and for me to seem negligent when I have written. He is, however, too considerate to complain. He speaks very affecy both of you and Arthur. I shall show you the letter when I come.

Much love to Arthur, I was glad to get his letter and shall write to him soon, if I do not see him.

I have taken a house in Cambridge, for a year, which Mrs Farrar thinks every way desirable. It is on the hill, next Dr Wesselhoefts.[1] I have not room to tell you why, but this has seemed to me the best way. I do not do it, expecting any thing in the way of pecuniary assistance from you or Arthur. We will manage in all respects as may be best for

145

you. Notwithstanding your fears of being disturbed in your studies, I think you will find it both pleasant and profitable to have your mother and me there.

Ellery is gone away for two or three days. He liked you.

We go on in our even way, woods, and fields, and books,—books and fields and woods. The soft lustres of autumn mellow on us gradually. Last Sunday was a day illustrious for its beauty, and Mr Ward spent it here.

Well, dear R. I have no more time tonight I write so much, again, that my letters tire me, and I want to write to Aunt Abi. I thought best to send this letter by post, as you may want the *order*. If you or Arthur would like to write me a note, carry it to Mrs Farrar on Tuesday eveg next, she will have an oppory to send. Always affecly Your sister

M.

Have you heard from Lloyd? Arthurs mentioned having been unwell—how is he now?

Get a little account book for this year, and keep all in order— Dont count last term's expenses.

ALS (MH: fMS Am 1086 [9:101]); MsC (MH: fMS Am 1086 [Works, 2:705–11]). *Addressed:* R. F. Fuller. / Student Harvard University / Cambridge / Mass. *Postmark:* Concord MS Sep 8.

never wear] never ⟨go with⟩ wear
deprived of news] deprived ↑ of news ↓

1. Dr. Robert Wesselhoeft, a homeopathic physician from Germany, later established a successful hydropathic spa in Brattleboro, Vermont. The Wesselhoefts lived next to the Fullers in Cambridge (*CVR*; Louise Hall Tharp, *The Appletons of Beacon Hill* [Boston, 1973], p. 253; MVR 122:59).

425. To Maria Rotch

Cambridge, 20th Septr 43.

I doubt, dear Maria, whether you have remembered my promise of writing as I have though not, indeed, to keep it. It was again and again in my mind during the many changes of place of the summer, but as I really had no time for more than one letter I kept postponing that *one* till I could say I would visit you in your own home on my return. This I truly wished to do, and always thought I should till the last days and those were so crowded that then I laid aside the pen entirely.— But, as to the visit, I thought, never mind perhaps I can come on next summer as far as Buffalo, make a visit to a dear friend there, see Niagara in warmer weather, the North River by daylight and Maria at Butternuts and thus repair all that went amiss in this present expedition. So soon as I get home, the letter shall be written and tell her this.

But here the news salutes me that you are going away from your pretty home and quite out of my reach. I am sorry now that I did not come to see you if it were only for a day.

But I am very glad to hear you are to go. A year or two later indeed would have been better in some ways for you, for you might then have been more fully prepared both to learn and to enjoy. But you will have the benefit of all your brother has learned and is ready to see, and in your father an excellent guide.[1]

If you do not see sights and society to as much advantage as you might a little later, yet in details of various kinds, such as practise of eye and hand in the arts, and learning to speak and write modern languages, you are quite old enough, just at the right time to make the best use of every advantage.

Here at Cambridge I shall see you and get, I hope, a good full account of your summer. Also shall you not have with you your drawings and show me what you have done? If you have some one you should like to give me, it would be pleasant to me to keep it in my room as a memento of the past. I suppose you have sketched from nature this summer and may have something to show me from your neighborhood which now I shall not see.

Sarah Clarke has made many sketches from the magnificent and lovely scenes we have visited.[2] She has, in this way, quite a good journal of our summer. I have made scarce any record of it with *my* instrument, the pen, for the days were so full of new impressions that there was not time left to tell of them but all that was seen is fresh in memory and, if you are interested, you may easily hear something of the newest new world before going on to the Old.

To me Europe lost[n] its interest as I looked upon these dawnings of a vast future. But you have time enough for both, time to learn the past and use it for the present. May your fine opportunities be made fruitful to you! If you remain in the same mind as when we were last together, you will not misspend the moments in a continual fever of shallow excitement like the vulgar crowd of travelers, and are not in danger of the languid obtuseness and narrow tastes which send many a fine lady back to us better drest, perhaps, but, as a companion, still more tiresome than she went.

Well now adieu, my dear Maria, I write, having not easily the half hour to spare because it is my last chance and I have the vanity to think you will like to receive my letter, even in these busy days. With much regard to your parents and Frank your friend

S. MARGARET FULLER.

To your Mother I would send especial love. I can scarcely expect her leisure here will permit me to see her even *as* well as last spring

ALS (MH: fMS Am 1086 [9:97]). *Addressed:* Miss Maria Rotch / Care Francis Rotch Esq. / Butternuts / New York. *Postmark:* Boston MS Sept 24.

Europe lost] Europe ⟨?⟩ lost

1. The Rotches were on their way to Europe. Maria's brother was Francis Morgan Rotch (1822–63). During this trip, Maria's mother kept a journal, parts of which have been published in Bullard, *Rotches*, pp. 264–86.

2. Fuller later used Clarke's sketches in *Summer on the Lakes.*

426.   To Henry D. Thoreau

25th Septr 43

Dear Henry,

You are not, I know, deeply interested in the chapter of little etiquettes, yet I think out of kindness you will be willing to read a text therein and act conformably in my behalf— As I read the text on the subject of Visits or Visitations, our hosts martyr themselves every way for us, their guests, while we are with them, in time, temper, and purse, but we are expected to get to them and get away from them as we can.[1]

Thus I ought to have paid for the carriage which came to take me away, though I went in another. But I did not see the man when I got down to the landing.— I do not know what is the due, but E. Hoar told me the enclosed was enough, will you pay it for me wherever it belongs and pardon the carelessness that gives you this trouble?

Immediately after my return I passed two days at Concord, a visit all too short, yet pleasant. The cottages of the Irish laborers look pretty just now but their railroad looks foreign to Concord.[2]

Mr Emerson has written a fine poem, you will see it in the Dial.[3]

Ellery will not go to the West, at least not this year. He regrets your absence, you, he says, are the man to be with in the woods.

I remember my visit to Staten Island with great pleasure, and find your histories and the grand pictures you showed me are very full in

148

my mind. I have not yet dreamt of the fort, but I intend to some leisure night.

With best regards to Mr and Mrs Emerson, whose hospitality I hold in grateful remembrance, yours

S. M. FULLER.

ALS (ICarbS). MsCfr in F. B. Sanborn's hand (MB: Ms. Am. 1450 [181]). Published in *New England Quarterly* 33 (1960):372–73, and *Companion to Thoreau's Correspondence,* ed., Kenneth W. Cameron (Hartford, Conn., 1964), pp. 182–83. *Addressed:* Mr Henry Thoreau / Care W. Emerson Esq / 61 Wall St / N. York. *Endorsed:* S. M. Fuller.

1. Emerson's brother William was a lawyer in New York City. He and his wife, Susan Haven Emerson, lived on Staten Island. On 6 May 1843 Henry Thoreau left Concord to become the tutor for William Emerson's children. He lived with them until mid-December, when he returned to Concord (Harding, *Days of Henry Thoreau,* pp. 147–56). Fuller visited the Emersons when she left Buffalo.

2. During her absence, the railroad connection between Boston and Concord had opened. Waldo Emerson, too, was struck by the multiplication of workers' shanties around Concord: "the villages of shanties at the water's edge & in the most sequestered nooks of the town and the number of laborers men & women whom now one encounters singly in the forest paths." Despite the changes, he was remarkably cheerful about the work, not least because it kept the Irishmen busy and out of trouble: "Fear haunts the building railroad but it will be American power & beauty, when it is done. . . . Though deplored by all the humanity of the neighborhood & though all Concord cries shame! on the contractors, [it] is a better police than the Sheriff & his deputies to let off the peccant humours" (Rusk, *Letters of RWE,* 3:256; *JMN,* 9:7, 23).

3. Probably Waldo Emerson's "Ode to Beauty," *Dial* 4 (1843):257–59.

427. To Albert H. Tracy

Cambridge, 26th Septr 43

Dear friend,

It was truly a disappointment not to see you on my return. I had made up my mind to take up the links in a broken chain, and it was not easy to give up the hope. Nor can I flatter myself with much hope of repairing my present loss. For eight years I have not been able to stray far, being too much wanted in one place, and too probably this may be the case for the coming eight years.

The cause too of your[n] absence seems more sorrowful [*illegible*] feel that I have the impression you have had much to suffer in the illness or departure of those dear to you. But I do not know well the events of your life, since you were with us, nor indeed before either. Some things I have heard of you as a public man, but do not know your course even in that way. I only know you as when your eye rested for a period upon us, so friendly and intelligent. Its beam saluted me with the same influence after long separation, and I am now desirous to know more of the life where the light is kindled.

Now, my dear friend, since you express an unchanged interest in me, and we are not likely to meet, could you not write to me at length of what I wish to know? I shall wish much to hear how your little boy is, and will ask you to write me of that at any rate. But, if you go abroad, and are separated from accustomed duties, you may have time for more. They tell me you are indolent and I can well conceive you may seem so in a state of flurry and bustle such as we live in. But I suppose you do whatever you think worth doing, will not it seem so to give me an account of your life and its relations at least in outline, and enable me to know better one whom I have always loved?

I regretted much not seeing Mrs Tracy, in fact I got no idea of your life, except from seeing the outside of a large hotel. I wish to know the names of your children.[1] One of them I saw when you came to our house at Jamaica Plains, but do not recollect his name.[2] At that time I did not take the same interest. I was sick and, as I supposed, dying, after years of manifold sadness and obscure struggle, I did not prize any friend much, for in none had I found help and soothing; and was even reluctant to see any whom I had known in earlier life, for I thought they could see in me only a sinking flame, and, not knowing the causes, only wonder and blame that it had cast so little light around.

Now my health is almost restored, if not to its native tone, yet to one that enables me to walk forward with some energy. Some objects have been attained, others willingly given up, and I am much better able to meet out ward perplexities without violation of inward peace.

So now I am interested in all that is interesting, and I wish that you may feel desire to meet this frame of mind.

You called me your dear child, I know not with what depth of feeling, but the expression was grateful to me, from you. With one of the large knowledge of men and things and the delicacy of feeling that I believe you to possess I could enjoy the repose that belongs to such a relation and if you should not incline, as I hope you may, to answer to my wish should silence as well as distance continue to separate us, I will still think of you in the same way and remain affectionately yours

MARGARET F.

Mother desires her love to you. Please address me here at Cambridge I have a box in this post office.

ALS (MHarF). *Addressed:* Hon Albert H. Tracy / Buffalo / New York. *Endorsed:* Miss S. M. Fuller / Sept 26, 1843—

of your] of ⟨ou⟩your

1. Tracy married Harriet Foote Norton, daughter of Ebenezer Norton. The Tracys had two sons: Albert Haller (b. 1834) and Francis Walsingham (b. 1839) (Evert E. Tracy, *Tracy Genealogy* [Albany, N.Y., 1898], p. 109).

2. For Fuller's description of the visit, see letter 269.

428. To Henry James, Sr.

West Roxbury
Octr 13th 43

Dear Mr James

With much regret, as far as ourselves are concerned, we hear that you will choose Europe rather than Boston this winter! Mr Emerson writes "so passes this friendly figure from the group soon as we go to think how to draw the bonds closer."[1] For us, we must regret, for who knows where another year may find us. The rail-road threatens to drive Mr E. from his beloved fens; my local habitation is always precarious. But, for yourself, no doubt it is well—the student (of books) should see Europe; on its own theatre he better understands the life whence the literature sprang.

Mr Emerson adds that you would like to do something for me abroad. By an acquaintance who sailed from here the 1st, I sent the only commission I had for the present. But I have often favors to ask[n] and questions to spear at the traveller, and if you will let me know where your course is likely to be and your address, you may probably hear from me.

From you I shall, no doubt hear, through my friend, if not directly, what you learn, what you think.

In this part of the country, where fortunes are so tranquil, winning and thoughtful, I am enjoying the recollection of the past summer, and N. England, in these splendid October days, seems to me as good a place as any in the world. Though while traversing the ample fields of the West, it seemed a[n] poor shady little nook. Perhaps you too will find its limitations and the pure waters of its stony soil agreeable after the historic glories of Europe. I wish it may be so.

With regards to Mrs James, whom I should like to see again,[2] yours

S. MARGARET FULLER.

Should you meet Tennyson I should like much some good account of him.

ALS (NN-B). *Addressed:* Mr James.

Henry James, Sr. (1811–82), father of Henry the novelist and William the philosopher, was a Swedenborgian who admired Emerson.

favors to ask] favors ↑ to ask ↓
it seemed a] it seemed ⟨to⟩ a

1. Emerson thus described James to Fuller on 10 October, when he wrote to suggest that she give James any commission she might have that he could fulfill in Europe (Rusk, *Letters of RWE*, 3:211-12).

2. James's wife was Mary Robertson Walsh (1810–82) (Ralph Barton Perry, *The Thought and Character of William James* [Boston, 1935], 1:xxxv).

429. To Ralph Waldo Emerson

[ca. 16] Oct 1843

Will not Lidian come to our Conversations this Winter if I get a class the subject Health

MsCfr (MH: bMS Am 1280 [111, p. 108]). Published in *JMN*, 11:478.

430. To Marianne Mackintosh Clarke

Sunday Oct 23d 43.

Dear Mrs Clarke,

We trouble you with a large parcel of letters, but Mother was not able to procure other things that she wished to send.

In your distant sphere you may perhaps chance to meet those who might desire and be benefitted by a periodical such as this whose prospectus I inclose. Its promise, though large, will I am sure, from the character of the editor, be borne out by its performance.[1]

On another score I am led, by the kind regard you have shown our house, to request your interest. It is not unusual for people in the southern climates to send their children to the north two or three years for the advantages of education. Should you know of such cases would you bear in mind my sister Ellen? She now teaches a little school, but would prefer, and it would be much better for her to have two or three little girls in the house with her. She is very fond of children and has been uncommonly successful both in the care and instruction of them. I think her influence would be found refining and strengthening on any minds given to her charge. She would receive children at a very reasonable rate.

You mentioned to Mother your cousins, the Misses Burdett and I wish they would come and see her.[2] During the seven months of the year that I give lessons, my engagements are too many for me to be as good a companion to her as I could wish, and it is uncertain whether Ellen will be with us any part of the winter. I wish Mother might find some pleasant society in the neighborhood, for she is very delicate now, and it is frequently too great an exertion to see her distant friends.

With best wishes for your safe and speedy passage to your distant home

S. MARGARETT FULLER.

ALS (MHarF). *Addressed:* Mrs Marianne Clarke / Cambridge.

1. Undoubtedly William Henry Channing's *Present*.

2. Marianne Clarke's uncle was James Burditt, a Boston bookseller. His daughters were Mary (1804–1900) and Cordelia (1810?–82) (Suffolk Probate, no. 115132; MVR 507:448, 339:228). The Clarkes were probably returning to New Orleans.

431. To William H. Channing

Cambridge, Octr 27th 43.

My best friend,

Why did you not wish me to come and hear you last night. It was a great satisfaction to me to hear your statement; it was grand and simple, no preaching no poetry, but the habitual tone of thought, electric with the feelings of many years. It seemed to me a truly human, manly address which it required no individual sympathy or preparation to understand but that all present must inevitably be put in possession of your point of view. Though you went over so much ground you did clear justice to each position.[n]

After hearing I wanted to meet you again, for many thoughts had risen in my mind, during the discourse But when we cannot gratify these wishes to express ourselves it is probably as well. If we are prevented from gathering and giving away the flower, it withers indeed, unenjoyed, but leaves a seed on the stem. My thoughts generally seem too slight or too much in need of more to be written down, so I like to speak them, but if they lie in the mind, they attract *the more* they want. Some degree of expression is necessary for growth, but it should be little in proportion to the full life

153

As fire lays open, and the plough awakes a virgin soil, successions of seeds are called into development, which the powers of nature had generated in different moods and left there in the cold dark, perhaps for ages quite forgotten. So shall it be with a mind that works lonely, unsolicited, unutterable, the destined hour of tillage shall find it rich.

I will rejoice in every gladsome spring day, eloquent with blooms, or autumn with its harvests, but the silent fields of stubble or snow shall be no less prized.

Your mind has acted with beneficent force on mine and roused it now from a repose which it has long enough enjoyed. Let me try a little to note some results of my reflections.

The third thought which is to link together each conflicting two is of course the secret of the universe It is sought alike by the fondest dream of love, the purest pain of thought. The Philosopher exacts, the poet expects it, the child believes it is already here. It is the beloved Son in whom both God and Man will be well pleased.[1] In no destiny whether of individual or world will this thought be grasped, the chain be clasped till one entire revolution in its orbit[n] has been fulfilled. Yet every time the orb turns on its axis it realizes its presence, and each night is followed by a morning, though that again yields to darkness.

Faith and hope are gradually transmuted into knowledge, but very slowly is this mass of matter leavened by the divine wisdom. Yet [the t]hird thought is gradually taking possession [of u]s; when we have at last become thoroughly [posse]ssed by, we may in turn possess it.

[Ti]ll then our lives, can only foreshow, our thoughts only [foresee]; to one another we can only predict what [sh]all make of several parts a unison. Only through [eter]nity can time be illustrated

[C]an we not wait very patiently, if sometimes [s]adly, steering the bark over the waste of waters and thus becoming ourselves that which we seek?

We have different ways of steering the ship. Yours is to seek conclusions, which as you often hasten to you must afterwards modify, mine to give myself up to experiences which often steep me in ideal passion, so that the desired goal is forgotten in the rich present. Yet I think I am learning how to use the *present,* and were my calendar published, it might lead to association too. An association if not of efforts, yet of destinies. In such an one I live with several, feeling that each one by acting out his own casts light upon a mutual destiny, illustrates the thought of a master mind. It is a constellation, not a phalanx to which I belong.

[   ] No doubt if I could I should be childish enough to clear them all away. I thought when you were talking about a home and I saw how weary you m[ust] be of the throng of influences and decisions that if [any?] energy of mine could avail, I would throw [   ] all other objects and get you and though I k[now?] you could not stay in it a minute,[n] for the "children of the future" cannot now rest in a[ny but] the holiest nook, they must be out in the aven[ue] righting the wrongs which must then again be righted. But a little sleep would do you goo[d] and all of them want it. E. Hoar was wishi[ng] for home last night, "and yet, she says, when I see any of the birds building their nests I am not sure they ought to take the time yet I want my nest, if it were only to fly from" But I told her the birds ought now to be conten[t] if they can hang to the boughs by their tails, and by a queer coincidence she had seen ere of that no longer to be esteemed fabulous kind the day before in a museum.— Yet though I answer like Mephistopheles to the desires of those sweet souls "You are not the first"—and coolly deprecate their peculiar claims to happiness. Ye[t] I know well that the instruments need a place and a gentle hand by which they may be tuned, and should I ever rise to ministry, will ask for the keeping of some star, and there in their sleeping if not their waking hours will I conduct them to prune and purify their ruffled plumage.

Yet for you I would do better if I could, I would [   ]

ALfr (MB: Ms. Am. 1450 [166]). Published in part in Higginson, *MFO*, pp. 110, 285–86.

position.] *The opening paragraph has been canceled by a later hand.*
revolution in its orbit] revolution ↑ in its orbit ↓
minute,] *The paragraph to this point has been canceled by a later hand. The first two manuscript lines are unrecovered.*

1. Fuller's modification of the gospel declaration: "This is my beloved Son, in whom I am well pleased" (Matt. 3:17, 17:5; Mark 1:11; Luke 3:22).

432. To Albert H. Tracy

Cambridge 6th Novr 1843.

I cannot forbear, my dear friend, to thank you for your compliance with my request; it was such as I love, frank and full, and yet not so full as I could have wished. I could have wished that you had freely given two hours and two sheets instead of one, then[n] you would not have clipped or compressed the narrative in any part.

I am too grateful for what has been given, and too much afraid of entrapping the "indolent" man i e the man not easily acted upon by common motives! into a continued correspondence against his will, not to be timid in asking for more, yet I will say, should there ever be a time when you incline to write out the train of reasoning which made the crisis in your youth and decided to[n] the change of profession, let me have that leaf also and add it as appendix to what I now possess.

In an English book I read last year, by Capel Lofft, which, under the somewhat oldmaidish title of *Self-Formation*, contains free and accurate descriptions of mental life, are indicated with a good deal of skill those sharp turns of fate or character when, after preparation of unknown length beneath the soil, an unexpected plant springs up and shadows all the remaining scene.[1] With him these seed, though they throve vigorously seemed not native to the soil, and with you there seem to be many signs that medicine rather than law would have suited you. The physician may be so mild, so reflective, so close in his observation of facts, so patient and clear-eyed in inferring laws.

I do not know why you seem so sure that I had some ideal picture in my mind rather than a portrait of you. Perhaps from some recollection of what I was when you were with us, and yet it seems to me that I avowed to you very little of what was in my mind. Yet so keen an observer may have seen that mine was an ardent and onward-looking spirit, and more occupied with its visions than with the actual world around. Still though both from constitution and a premature and excessive culture in the thoughts of Europe, which I have had slowly to undo or transmute to live in my own place and with my own people, idealist enough in that young day[n] my relation to you and the feelings you inspired were strictly real. A girl, such as I was, with a head full of Hamlet, and Rousseau, and the ballads of chivalry, is not inclined to idealize lawyers and members of Congress and *father's friends*; the impression you made on me *was* from *your* nature, not mine, and such as I then felt, and have since supposed you to be I find you in your own outline.

When I have thought of you, I have felt these very things, that your life might be outwardly common-place, because you were clear-sighted and there would be no straining or effort in parts. I supposed the common day, the common light would suffice to this clear vision. I did not think you needed the embellishments of fancy, or the ardors of temperament. But I have felt that there was no limitation on you to prevent your comprehending anything that might be set before you, and this, in the same sense and degree, I have thought of none other.

If you knew me now, I feel confident that you would think I was not deficient in justness of perception, that[n] life had been a good schoolmaster to me, and had only left enough of the native glow for heart and intellect to warm themselves at on frosty days. I think you would feel that I understood you well, and that I should be inclined to say much to you. Let me then flatter myself with the hope that this may be, and, even if I should not come to you in fact, I shall be led by the thought of meeting sometimes mentally to address you.

Intimacies with persons make no figure in your history, and yet, apart from your brothers, you must have had friendships. Yet if they had been important in unfolding the life, been connections not only of pleasure and esteem, but a bearing of one nature on the other, I think you would have mentioned them.

I was deeply interested in what you say of what the children are to you. How you evade your prevoyance there I do not know, but it is[n] what they are meant to be to us, to renew life in its simplicity, a passionless happiness. I suppose none can enter fully into these feelings, can perfectly know how "very good" is this "new creation" without being really a parent, but I have loved one little boy so long and so well, that I have some idea of what that second life may be. He is dead now and though it is some time since he left us, my thoughts still rest on the remembrance of his looks and words and little ways that seem fraught with such a world of meaning, as they do on nothing else, and I often wonder that the sun can shine upon his grave.[2]

I am glad that yours are boys; men are much wanted in this country and till there have been some nobler men, women cannot have so fair a chance as I wish them. The next generation I trust may not like this[n] be exhausted by a premature excitement of the intellect and may have a wider path to walk in and to as noble a goal.

Farewell, my dear friend, surely in your heart you know it is not fancy but knowledge that permits me thus to address you. Mother desires her affectionate remembrance,— yours—

MARGARET F.

ALS (NNC-B). *Addressed:* Hon Albert H Tracy / Buffalo / New York. *Endorsed:* Miss S. M. Fuller / Nov 6 1843.

one, then] one ⟨to the letter⟩, then
decided to] decided ↑ to ↓
idealist enough in that young day] ↑ idealist enough in that young day ↓
perception, that] perception, ⟨and would think⟩ that
it is] it ⟨was⟩ ↑ is ↓
not like this] not ↑ like this ↓

1. Capel Lofft the younger, *Self-Formation* (London, 1837).
2. Waldo Emerson.

433. To William Emerson

Cambridge Novr 8th, 1843.

To Mr Emerson,

Dear Sir,

I have postponed writing to you till I could speak definitively as to Miss Sheafe's going out to Arthur, and it is only this morng that I am able so to do.[1]

My letter to you did not reach you so soon as it ought, in consequence of my trusting to a friend who sends by Harnden's express. I waited several days and receiving no answer in that quarter, applied in another, and secured the services of a young lady, a Miss Bassett[n] said to be every way qualified, on condition Arthur would accede to her terms, somewhat different from those he had proposed.— I wrote to him on the subject; she went home and made every preparation to start at a moment's warning in case he should accept her proposal.

Meantime I found from Mr May of the Normal school,[2] that he had written to A. that the person he most wished to engage while here, and who could not then go with him was now willing to go, if he still wished it.

Amid all these uncertainties I have been waiting to hear from him, and the result is that he has accepted Miss Bassett's proposition; she came here from the country last night and is gone this morng.

Arthur, I believe, depends on me to notify the other ladies of his choice. Miss Sheafe's letter he had not recd when he wrote but he asked me to do whatever was necessary here.— I trust Miss S. has not made any arrangements that may inconvenience her, as the matter was lying in so conditional a state, and that you may be glad to retain her with you, as Mrs Emerson, I hear with pain, is still very ill.[3]

I have requested A. if he hears of any other position likely to suit Miss S. to inform her, for I was interested about her from what Mrs E. told me, and thought as she had a will to go to the West, if she once had a foothold, she would find the means to do well there. But I believe she has never yet taught, and on Arthur's account, I am glad he has secured the aid of a teacher who has had some experience, for it is all important to him in this new emprize, where he has invested not only his time and hopes, but the little money he possesses.

Would you do me the favor when you write to Concord to send me a message, letting me know whether Miss Sheafe finds herself disappointed, and whether she still wishes a place, in case any such should present itself. I should like to know her precise qualifications; people in want of aid sometimes apply to me.

I hope to hear how Mrs Emerson is from the same quarter: can it be fever that lasts so long?

With great regard yours

S. MARGARET FULLER.

ALS (NjP). *Addressed:* William Emerson Esq / 61 Wall St / New York City. *Endorsed:* S. M. Fuller / Nov 8 / 43 / Recd 9th.

lady, a Miss Bassett] lady, ↑a Miss Bassett↓

1. Margaret Sheafe, a cousin of William Emerson's wife, Susan Haven Emerson, was the daughter of Jacob and Mary Haven Sheafe. The William Emersons' nursemaid on Staten Island, Margaret later married a John Taylor (Clarence Winthrop Bowen, *The History of Woodstock, Connecticut: Genealogies of Woodstock Families* [Norwood, Mass., 1935], 6:733–34; Alphonse J. Sheafe, "Some Guilford, Connecticut, Settlers, and Their Relationship, or the Sheafe Family in England and New England," NEHGS, p. 34; Rusk, *Letters of RWE,* 3:110). Arthur Fuller had become schoolmaster at Belvidere, Illinois.

2. At the urging of Horace Mann, a school for women was established at Lexington in 1839, then moved to Newton. The second supervisor at the school was Bronson Alcott's brother-in-law, the Reverend Samuel J. May (1797–1871), who was noted for his work in reform and education movements (George B. Emerson, *Education in Massachusetts: Early Legislation and History* [Boston, 1869], p. 491; Charles Hudson, *History of the Town of Lexington* [Boston, 1868], p. 372; *DAB*).

3. Susan Emerson had been ill since mid-September, when Fuller visited the family (Rusk, *Letters of RWE,* 3:207–8).

434. To Ralph Waldo Emerson

Cambridge 12th Novr 1843.

Thy letter, o best Waldo, displays the wanted glorious inconsistency, beginning as a hymn in praise of indolence, and ending with demands of work.— It was a good idea to send me the other plays. I will bring in Taylor's and Coleridge's too, and make an olla, where Stirling will figure to more advantage than he would alone.[1] Some leaves are written of my record of the West out of which I hope to make a little book.— It is for this I want back Triformis, intending to make a chapter at Chicago.[2] I shall bring in with brief criticisms of books read there, a kind of letter box, where I shall put a part of one of S. Ward's letters, one of Ellery's and apropos to that July moon beneath whose influences I received it, a letter containing Triformis. So delay not to send it back, for when I have once concocted any such little plan, I am in a fever till I get it arranged, and you are almost as bad about keeping things as myself, and till I get the paper, I feel as if I never should see it again.

Dont expect any thing from the book about the West. I cant bear to be thus disappointing you all the time. No lives of Goethe, no romances.—ⁿ *My* power of work is quite external. I can give lessons or do errands while there are minutes in the day, but I cannot think a thought, or write a line except under certain conditions. To have you in the world, doing something yourself, and ready to be pleased if I do any thing, I like—but dont expect. I cannot promise any thing. Often and long I am without any real energy.—

Yet I hope to write your piece about Strafford, for I have thought it out in some measure, and I mean to do it soon, while I am reading the books in the Collegeⁿ library about the West, the old travellers I am reading. I like now to go over the ground with them and shall not continue my own little experiences till I have done with theirs.

I must scold you about that little translation on these grounds.[3]

When I had the care of the Dial, I put in what those connected with me liked, even when it did not well please myself, on this principle that I considered a magazine was meant to suit more than one class of minds. As I should like to have writings from you, Mr Ripley, Mr Parker &c so I should like to have writings recommendedⁿ by each of you. I thought it less important that everything in it should be excellent, than that it should represent with some fidelity the state of mind among us as the name of Dial said was its intent.

So I did not regard your contempt for the long prosa on Transcendentalism, Progress &cⁿ any more than Parker's disgust at Henry Thoreau's pieces.[4]

You go on a different principle; you would have every thing in it good according to your taste, which is in my opinion, though admirable as far as it goes, far too narrow in its range. This is *your* principle; very well! I acquiese, just as in ourⁿ intercourse I do not expect you to do what I consider justice to many things I prize. So if I offered you anything for your Dial and you yourself did not like it, I am willing you should reject it.

But if you are going to take any other person's judgment, beside your own, why should you not take mine? Why do you set some other person to read and judge that which pleases *me*, which you know I should have put into the book?

I said I would scold you, however I do not mean to, but simply state how discourteous this act seems to me. It is good to catch sight of such a fact as this now and then; we balance it against his fine speeches and get the average of his view better than else his sweet smiles might let us.

I do not care for your *not liking* the piece, because when you wrote in your journal that I cared for talent as well as genius I accepted the words, written in dispraise, as praise.⁵ I wish my tastes and sympathies still more expansive than they are, instead of more severe. Here we differ. I know it, and am prepared for consequences, but this setting some other person to read and judge is quite another thing.

Now I have begun on the chapter of adjustments, let me tell you a little thing about E. Hoar, who hates to have things left out of order. When at Brook Farm I wrote you about E. that she would not stay there because of some little scruple, I supposed about annoying her sister and added it on to her old account. I was vexed at the time because I thought I could have been the means of her having a good time, and I like to have her enjoy herself, and get pictures and materials for thought. Since, it turns out that it was my rude impetuous conduct that made it difficult for her to stay and not little scruples of her own.

Will Lidian be present at my first Conversation? It will be next Thursday 16thⁿ eleven oclock morng at Miss Peabody's. I shall then expound certain thoughts, that have interested me during the summer. I fear I shall have but a small class this winter and am sorry for various reasons. But there is no persuading people to be interested in one always or long even.

How is little Edith, she was unwell when last I heard. Dear friend yours ever

MARGARET.

Write word that you will certainly stay here when you come to lecture and when that will be.⁶ I want to look forward to a meeting. Please let Ellen have the parcel Tuesday *morng.*

ALS (MH: bMS Am 1280 [2372]). Published in part in Higginson, *MFO*, pp. 166–67; Rusk, *Letters of RWE*, 3:220–21; and Miller, pp. 114–16. *Addressed:* R W. Emerson / Concord Mass. *Endorsed:* Margaret Fuller / Nov. 1843.

no romances. —] ⟨?⟩ no romances. —
the College] the ↑ College ↓
writings recommended] writings ⟨f⟩ recommended
Progress &c] Progress ↑ &c ↓
in our] in ⟨yo⟩ our
Thursday 16th] Thursday ↑ 16th ↓

1. In his letter of 5 November, Emerson had urged Fuller to write the "autobiographic chapters once begun under this roof." With the letter he sent copies of William Henry Smith's *Athelwold* (London, 1842), J. W. Marston's *Patrician's Daughter* (London, 1841), and Henry Wadsworth Longfellow's *Spanish Student* (Cambridge, 1843). She reviewed them, with John Sterling's *Strafford* and Henry Taylor's *Philip Van Artevelde*, in *Dial* 4 (1844):307–49 (Rusk, *Letters of RWE*, 3:220–22).

2. She published without attribution James Clarke's poem "Triformis" in *Summer on the Lakes*, pp. 71–72. Clarke had sent her the poem in July while she was on her trip (*Letters of JFC*, pp. 142–44).

3. Fuller had sent her translation of a French piece to Emerson for the *Dial*. Not liking it, he solicited the opinions of Thoreau and Ellery Channing, both of whom agreed that it should not be published (Rusk, *Letters of RWE*, 3:222).

4. The prosa was written by Jonathan Ashley Saxton, "Prophecy—Transcendentalism—Progress," *Dial* 2 (1841):83–121. Parker recorded his disgust with Thoreau in a journal entry of 10 August 1840: "In our walk E[merson] expressed to me his admiration of Thoreau, & his foolish article on *'Aulus Persius Flaccus'* in the Dial. He said it was full of life. But alas the life is Emersons, not Thoreau's & so it had been lived before. However he says T is but a boy. I hope he will writte for the newspapers more & less for the Dial" (Carol Elizabeth Johnston, "The Journals of Theodore Parker: July–December 1840," Ph.D. dissertation, University of South Carolina, 1980, p. 35).

5. In September 1839 Emerson wrote of Fuller and Henry Hedge in his journal: "[They] must have talent in their associates & so they find that, they forgive many defects. They do not require simplicity. I require genius &, if I find that, I do not need talent: and talent without genius gives me no pleasure" (*JMN*, 7:236).

6. Apparently Emerson did not lecture in her area that season until 17 January 1844, when he spoke at the Cambridge Lyceum (Charvat, "Emerson's Lecture Engagements," p. 505).

435. To Abigail Allyn Francis

Cambridge, Tuesday
5th Decr 1843.

Dear Mrs Francis,

I have not been able earlier to return an answer to your note and plan for the young ladies and am, just at present, too much engaged to do so in person.

I will take a class of six, though I should for every reason prefer its being larger. But I could not give to so small a class, on any terms they would be likely to accept, two days from the week. For my health is so unstable, and I am so much obliged to guard against fatigue, that to teach two half days would, with me, be giving two whole days. And to pass an entire day with one class would not do for me; it would tire me, and my interest would flag.

A single meeting in the week will, I think, enable me to accomplish the objects you propose, as I can easily plan out for the pupils studies and exercises that will occupy them in the interim. To this purpose I can give every Tuesday afternoon from two till half past four or five as their wants demand.

Should there be engagements that I do not know of to interfere with this day, I could assign another, but this is the one that suits me best.

My terms in Boston have been sixteen dollars from each member of the class for twenty four lessons of an hour and a quarter each. To the proposed class I appropriate double the time, and it will be much more care than one in a single branch would be. I shall ask twenty five dollars each for twenty four lessons, (which under the proposed arrangement would be a course of six months instruction,) if the class be of less than ten, but if it is of that number twenty dollars each.— These terms, perhaps, are higher than is usual in Cambridge or the country any where, but they are the lowest I have ever offered, for I should much prefer having a class at home to one in Boston.

Should these terms and the arrangement suit you and others concerned, I should like to have the class assemble here next Tuesday afternoon at 2. pm. I shall need to talk with them, know what their dispositions are and studies have been, before arranging a plan for them.

If you have time, and wish to see me on this subject, dear Mrs Francis, I shall be at home tomorrow, and then again on Saturday. I will expect to hear something definite by the end of the week, as I have another plan, in case this should fall through, and the winter days, the days of work, are wasting away already.

With much regard yours

S. M. FULLER.

ALS (MB: Ch. B. 4. 57). *Addressed:* To / Mrs Francis / Cambridge.

Abigail Allyn (1796–1860) of Duxbury married Convers Francis in 1822 (MVR 139: 62; *CC* 18 May 1822).

436. To Ralph Waldo Emerson

12 December 1843

When Goethe received a letter from Zelter, with a handsome superscription, he said, "Lay that aside; it is Zelter's true hand-writing. Every man has a daemon, who is busy to confuse and limit his life. No way is the action of this power more clearly shown, than in the handwriting. On this occasion, the evil influences have been evaded; the mood, the hand, the pen and paper have conspired to let our friend write truly himself."[1]

You may perceive, I quote from memory, as the sentences are anything but Goethean; but I think often of this little passage. With me, for weeks and months, the daemon works his will. Nothing succeeds with me. I fall ill, or am otherwise interrupted. At these times, whether of frost, or sultry weather, I would gladly neither plant nor reap,—wait for the better times, which sometimes come, when I forget that sickness is ever possible; when all interruptions are upborne like straws on the full stream of my life, and the words that accompany it are as much in harmony as sedges murmuring near the bank. Not all, yet not unlike. But it often happens, that something presents itself, and must be done, in the bad time; nothing presents itself in the good: so I, like the others, seem worse and poorer than I am.

ELfr, from *Memoirs*, 1:224.

1. Fuller knew a similar episode in Eckermann's *Gespräche mit Goethe:* "It is from Zelter [said Goethe]. Pen and paper were favorable on this occasion; so that the writing is happily expressive of his noble character" (Johann Peter Eckermann, *Conversations with Goethe*, trans. Margaret Fuller [Boston, 1839], p. 287).

437. To Anna Barker Ward

Cambridge 26th Dec
43

My sweet Anna,

I would not have you count me among those upon whom gentle cares are thrown away. I treasure them all every movement of pure love and faith in my direction or any other. When I remember how much of this elixir I have already detected amid the bitter waters of life, I feel that I should always greet my friends, nay all men, with smiles.

It is melancholy to me that an interview should, through me, be polluted with sadness, which my pillow would always bring counsels wise enough to remove— It is, indeed, inevitable that I should suffer a good deal of sadness. My wiser mind, my steadfast convictions disown it. I do never doubt the music of the universe amid seeming death or discord. But my spirits get tired out, and my mind refuses to sustain me at times. I suffer extremely now from a lack of vital energy. At twenty I had already lavished more of this on inward conflict than suffices to sustain many mortals through their three-score and ten years, and though I was endowed by nature with a larger share than almost any one, yet so many years of forced exertions and complex cares under almost constant bodily suffering have taken almost all the rest, so that I have scarcely enough now to serve me day by day. Add to this a powerful imagination, which, at the first glimpse, embraces all the dangers of a plan looming up in the future, and, at the least touch of an old wound, retraces and concentres into a moment of perception the long scene of strife and pain where it was made, and I cannot expect to rise entirely above childishness, till I am translated either into a sphere or into a body, better fitted for free and mature existence.

Let not such apparitions, however, make much impression on you. Believe that I always know I have no more than my share[n] of the tragedy of life, and am sure the time will come when from all tragedy must be reaped due harvests of prayer and praise.

It was even a relief to me to find, after you were gone, that Mother had such real cause for fresh sadness. I never blame her, if mere solitude and thought bring it. She is a widow a mother, separated from several of her children, without the cheering consciousness that they are well, happy, or like to be what old age needs, a sure support, or figures of hope. They all, in various ways, deserve her tenderness, and this must often be a cause of painful thought. Add that she has a disease of the heart always preying upon her. She tries all she can to be cheerful, but sewing which it is needful for her to do to aid us, is bad for the spirits as a steady employment. Do what I can, I am not much of a companion for her. I cannot talk a great deal, or read aloud, if I did, I should not have strength for indispensable duties. Those who should have filled that place and who did fill it well, are absent. Thus, do what I can, I can but fill a gap to keep[n] the coldest wind away, while my heart whispers that I was born to fill the atmosphere around me with light and glow in which all things should bud[n] and leave out and cheer my soul with promise.

This is the ugly side. There are many others and much more often before me, but this will come up in turn. Then I feel as if "I could lie down like a tired child" &c but presently I return to "Hold on in courage of soul"[1] &c &c Who that is mortal does not know these *and so forths.* Who that has turned them once to due profit does not know that the tree born to lift its head into pure air, and rejoice in opulent existence, like Henry here before me, will yet bless with many a blossom the struggles of its root to establish itself in the cold dark earth. It is hardly worth speaking about, we know it all so well, only tears seem to belie our convictions.

Mother had just heard of the death of her only brother.[2] Thirty six years ago the boy left the little farm-house home, without the consent of his parents. He knew they would not give it, if asked, and he was sure that, in some distant Eldorado, he could do more and be happier than in the narrow path marked out for him at home. He and my mother were the flower of the family, sweet-tempered, generous, gay and handsome; they were very dear to one another and to their parents, who were only consoled for the rashness of Peter, by the fortunate marriage of Peggy. This was the only piece of good fortune that ever did befal them, during his life-time my father upheld the house and supplied the place of the wandering son. For a time this last did well, he often sent money to his parents, and sisters; "when he had made *a little more,* he would return, and see the brook, and the old orchard and climb Mount Eros, with his sisters." Then news came that he was married, could not come yet. Then longer and longer gaps in correspondence, for many months, at last for years, they would not know where he was, what doing?— My father once, while at Washington, went into Virginia and found him, but pride made him very reserved. He had gone out without a blessing, and he had not gained what he thought would excuse it, he said he would not return till he had. Then his father died, and it was in one respect too late. So it went on and on, he never came, his aged mother could not forget her only son, nor wish to see him the less, because she at last ascertained that his hair was white, his health broken down, and his fortunes, too. He was intreated to return, and he longed to, wife and children were all dead, and he had no other ties, but he could not bear to come back thus, old, sad, and poor to lift the latch again of the door from which he had stolen by night in presumptuous youth.— It was he, of whom I spoke in the morning at breakfast, to whom I sent by post a letter and inclosure which were never received. A letter had come to mother from him, during her absence; it moved me greatly. He had *never* asked any aid from here, nor did he now, unless we were rich and able. I saw that his spirits were broken, his health declining, but the tone of the letter showed a mind whose pride and delicacy could not be destroyed while fibres of life were left. I wrote him a letter I thought adapt[ed] to move him to further trust, and sent him the same sum he sent mother from the first fruits of his labors, and out of which she bought her first white gown. Poor man! he never received it, and strangers, probably, furnished the last white robe for him. He has been dead some months, but no one near him took an interest to inform his family, and they have only just heard of it in answer to a letter of inquiry.

Oh these long sad tales of ineffectual lives; these are what move me deeply. It *is* sad when a man lays down the burden of life frustrated in every purpose, learning only the lesson Man was made to mourn, but not *why?* Happy the prodigal son who *returns!*

Farewell, my dear Anna. I thank Sam for his letter; it gave me great pleasure May life ever be as fruitful to you both as now, and amid all its changes may there be granted you the solace of mutual tenderness and an ennobling sympathy! Your friend

MARGARET.

ALS (MH: bMS Am 1465 [26]). *Addressed:* S. G Ward Esq for / Mrs Ward. / Boston, / Mass. *Endorsed:* Margaret.

more than my share] more ↑ than my share ↓
to keep] to ⟨stop⟩ keep
should bud] should bu⟨t⟩d

1. Shelley, "On Death" (*The Complete Poetical Works of Percy Bysshe Shelley*, ed. Neville Rogers [Oxford, 1972], 1:112–13):

> O man! hold thee on in courage of soul
>   Through the stormy shades of thy worldly way,
> And the billows of cloud that around thee roll
>   Shall sleep in the light of a wondrous day,
> Where hell and heaven shall leave thee free
> To the universe of destiny.

2. Aside from the information in this letter, nothing is known of this uncle save the fact that he lived in Washington, D.C., in 1818 (Margarett C. Fuller to Timothy Fuller, 31 January 1818, MH).

438. To [?]

[1844]

The tax on my mind is such, and I am so unwell, that I can scarcely keep up the spring of my spirits, and sometimes fear that I cannot go through with the engagements of the winter. But I have never stopped yet in fulfilling what I have undertaken, and hope I shall not be compelled to now. How farcical seems the preparation needed to gain a few moments' life; yet just so, the plant works all the year round for a few days' flower.

ELfr, from *Memoirs*, 2:119.

439.   To Sarah Shaw

Cambridge 10th Jany 44.

My well beloved Sarah,

I was very sorry that I could not, when at West Roxbury the other day, come to see you and the new little friend, but I had not strength or time to walk so far, and no fiery-footed steeds offered themselves to convey me.[1]

I feel especially interested in the young stranger, as it is the first that has been given you since we were acquainted. It will share (if as I believe the child represents the state of the parent preceding its birth) some of the thoughts and feelings we have had in common.

Thus I wish to look upon it. However, if a meeting be delayed, it will look more like itself than it can at present.

I hope you will be well[n] enough to hear the 7th Symphony, if it is given again.[2] I have thought of you every time. It does not move me quite so deeply as the 5th, but has a sufficient greatness of its own. There are a succession of soaring passages towards the end of the third movement, that need not be surpassed in this world or any other.

Farewell, my dear Sarah, write me a line, when you are able. If I had a rose I would send it you.

Affectionately Your friend

M. F.

ALS (MH: bMS Am 1417 [175]). *Addressed:* Mrs Sarah Shaw / West Roxbury.

be well] be ⟨left⟩ well

1. Fuller refers to the Shaws' fourth child, Josephine (1843–1905), who was born on 16 December. In 1863 she married Charles Russell Lowell (*Sturgis of Yarmouth*, p. 52).

2. On Saturday, 6 January, the Boston Academy of Music concert concluded with Beethoven's Second Symphony (*Boston Daily Evening Transcript*, 5 January 1844).

440.   To Mary Rotch

Cambridge Jan 21st 44.

My dear Aunt Mary
and Miss Gifford,

I am anxious to get a letter telling me how you fare this winter in the cottage. Your neighbors who come this way do not give very favorable accounts of your looks, Aunt Mary, and if you are well enough, I should like to see a few of those prim, well-shaped characters from your own hand, otherwise perhaps Miss Gifford would write and tell me exactly how you are.— Is there no chance of your coming to Boston all this winter?— I had hoped to see you for a few hours, at least— Mrs Farrar tells me[n] that she has urged upon you to consult Dr Wesselhoeft at least once. My own opinion of him, as sagacious and a close observer of constitutions and symptoms, is high, and perhaps this is the best, certainly the rarest part of the physician's art. If your present medical attendant do not succeed in relieving you, I should think it well worth your while to consult Dr W.— *I* cannot follow his advice, wh was that given me by all to encounter no fatigue &c, but *you* could take his prescription and act upon it.

I wrote you one letter while at the West. I know not whether it was ever received; it was sent by a private opportunity one of "those traps to catch the unwary" as they have been called. It was no great loss, if lost; I did not feel like writing letters, while travelling; it took all my strength and mind to keep moving, and receive so many new impressions. Surely I never had so clear an idea before of the capacity to bless of mere Earth, merely the beautiful Earth, when[n] fresh from the original breath of the creative spirit. To have this impression one must see large tracts of wild country where the traces of man's inventions are too few and slight to break the harmony of the first design.— It will not be so long even where I have been now; in three or four years those vast flowery plains will be broken up for tillage, those shapely groves converted into logs and boards. I wished I could have kept on now for two or three years while yet the first spell rested on the scene. But I feel much refreshed even by this brief intimacy with nature in an aspect of large and unbroken lineaments.

I came home with a treasure of bright pictures and suggestions, and seemingly well. But my strength which had been sustained by a free careless life in the open air has yielded to the chills of winter and a very little work with an ease that is not encouraging. However, I have had the Influenza, and that has been almost as bad as fever to every body. *Now* I am pretty well, but much writing does not agree with me.

I wore your black dress at Niagara and many other places where I was very happy and it was always an added pleasure thus to be led to think of you.— I wish, dear Aunt Mary, you were near enough for me to go in and see you now and then. I know that, sick or well, you are always serene and sufficient to yourself, and that you have a most affectionate friend always by your side, but now you are so much shut up, it might[n] animate existence agreeably to hear some things I might have to tell.— The Boston people are eager as usual after this and that, music and Fourier conventions,—[1]lectures excite less interest now; there are such hordes of dullards in that field; it is almost as bad as the church.— Do you remember my friend Mr Lane of "unleavened bread" memory? He has gone to try living with the Shakers.[2] I trust he will thus try out his total abstinence experiment so completely as to give it up. You take "The Present," I suppose, but cannot expect you will be pleased by William's tendency to pledges and plans. I wish you could have heard him speak at the Convention though. The spiritual beauty of his aspect and eloquence melted all hearts.

Well, a few lines in return shall be given, shall they not to yours affecy

MARGARET F.

ALS (MH: fMS Am 1086 [9:115]); MsC (MH: fMS Am 1086 [Works, 1:37–41]); MsCfr (MH: bMS Am 1280 [111, pp. 132–33]). Published in part in *WNC*, pp. 370–71, and *JMN*, 11:481. *Addressed:* Miss Mary Rotch / New Bedford / Mass. *Postmark:* Cambridge MS Jan 22.

tells me] tells ⟨y⟩me
Earth, when] Earth, ↑ when ↓
it might] it ↑ might ↓

1. William Henry Channing and several of his friends held a Convention of the Friends of Social Reform in Boston the last week in December and the first in January. In an essay on the convention in the *Dial*, Elizabeth Peabody called it "the first publication of Fourierism in this region" (*Present* 1 [1843]:207; *Dial* 4 [1844]:473).

2. On 14 January 1844, Lane and his son left Fruitlands to stay at the Shaker village at Harvard, Massachusetts (Edgell, "Bronson Alcott's 'Autobiographical Index,'" 714).

441. To Maria Rotch

Cambridge, 22d Jany, 1844.

My dear Maria,

I have this morning received and read twice with much pleasure your letter, and have determined, if possible, to write in turn this same day. I have thought of it before, oftener than weekly, but this winter has brought more than usually frequent demands upon my pen, and so I have postponed writing to you and two and three other friends now abroad, for it seemed that letters to go so far ought to be of some length and fulness, too. But yours is so good it really leaves me in your debt, and I will try to give you something, if not an equivalent, in return.

And first a few words as to your letter. I am not surprized that you do not feel much charmed by the English in general; if we may judge from what we see of them now, and the tone of their literature, they are now as a people greatly degenerate from their old nobility of blood and temper, and as much encrusted in mere externals as any in the civilized world. Nothing can be more characteristic of this than the general want of beauty you speak of, but I think you *will* see among the aristocracy some specimens of beauty that shall exhibit the original type. Their artists (though I do not like their mode of treatment) evidently have some such before them.

When you travel in the country,[n] you will probably find many signs to contradict, as well as many to confirm what you see in the society of London.

I feel some regret that you cannot, where you are, pursue some study, because you will not, probably, remain so long stationary again, and much as you may and will learn from mere observation, it is pity to suspend for so long a time the power of voluntary application in which you had so much improved I am extremely sorry you could not have passed one more winter in study before going, however your advantages are, as it is, so great, we must not repine at what is wanting. I trust that both in France and Italy you will take some lessons while there in the languages of the countries. If you can write exercises and dictus with a good master while hearing the language spoken round you, you will make more progress in a month, as to the mere use of it, than you could here in a year. The advantages of positive[n] study as to forming the taste and judgment can never be superseded, but the mere mechanical part of any branch of knowledge cannot be too quickly mastered.

I am very glad you keep hold of your drawing and coloring;—through this tendency, if faithful you may obtain[n] insight to many of the most valuable possessions, of the mind. I advise you to read some books connected with your pursuit, such as the lectures of artists upon art, for instance Flaxman, Sir J. Reynolds, Fuseli and of colorists, Field which I had here last winter is an interesting book.[1] Eastlake, I think I have heard has written a good one. Before you go into Italy I would read Lanzi or some good history of painting. De Quincy's lives of Raphael and M. Angelo. Forsyth's and Bell's Italy would be useful to you in the way of suggestion.[2]

I cannot wonder at what you say of the effect produced on your mind by the great religious edifices. We who must do without these great permanent prayers, the religious desire of nations and ages chronicled in stone, need be doubly intent and pure to erect in the heart the temple not made with hands.[3]

But I must hasten, if I mean to answer any of your questions. It would highly gratify you, I am sure, if you could know what a solace your letter[s] have been to your friend Anna. All her young companions are very attentive, still the long confinement of her sick chamber is dreary, and you are both the favorite of all and have most to tell. You have no doubt heard ere this of her father's death; it was fortunate it happened when it did, else Belinda would have fallen a sacrifice.[4] She is now slowly recovering from her long fatigue and really terrible exertions. Anna's state seems very doubtful; she continues weak, with little appetite, her hip troubles her as much as ever, when she tries to walk or stand. Should she recover, however, I think she and her sister might be happier and freer than ever before, for their father, though he loved them, was not fitted to make those round him happy none can be who indulge vindictive[n] feelings and lose sight[n] of gentle sympathies Mother has passed several weeks with them; she was with their father when he died. He resigned himself to death very tranquilly, and his great sufferings ceased before the last hours.

Of our family, Mother is not very well, partly in consequence of such calls on her feelings. If she or any of them were here they would send love to you, but I am this day alone. The poor plants have suffered much this winter from the cold, however I have by my side the Cyclamen, of poetical renown in blossom.

Sister Ellen is in Boston now; her health is better, I think, than it has been for years. Ellery was here last week, he is a woodcutter,[n] now he cannot be a gardener, he seems gay in his new vocation and is happy at evening with his pen. He is very soon to make a visit to the Wards. They are pretty well, Rakemann has been staying there, and we have had much pleasant time with the music, and small parties of friends to hear it. I grieve to tell you how the mighty are fallen, Ellery eats meat, Mr Lane has gone to live with the Shakers. He does not write to me now I have several new correspondents since him, and, if you were here, perhaps you would hear some compositions read which would strike you as truly *original*. Richard I think you would find improved in as much as he is more attentive to his dress and less blunt in his manners without losing the valuable part of his "*independence*" He visits a little in Boston now however his chief devotion is still to the Muses and I must say his progress is very great. His present plan is to give a year to general studies and choose law afterward as his profession. Sarah Hodges seems as gentle as ever and more lively; she belongs to a class of Cambridge girls who come to me once a week.[5] I wish I had had it when you were here; it would have been pleasanter for you. But as for your improvement, I shall always think that was sufficient for the time, for I believed there were marks of an expansion of your powers, not the less obvious that it was gradual. I am gratified at the conviction you express of this, may every year of your life bring you a similar happy consciousness! My health is not so good as in the summer I am weak and suffer somewhat. I am more dissipated than when you were with me and more so than I like to be. The concerts I still take great pleasure in The 7th Symphony of Beethoven we have this winter and it is very great. In Vieux Temps I found great delight![6] his violin playing was different from any I have ever heard, so intellectual, calm and masterly.— Your *room* we kept[n] for sometime as a spare room and it accommodated several fair ladies, and some reverend, (or revered) men. At present I occupy it, and there often think of you.— Its chief ornament at present is a most beautiful drawing by Mr Ward which he gave me Christmas day. I have also some Indian things mementoes of my Western experiences an Indian cradle &c.

The little Wesselhoefts are in full voice and vigor. They are never sick, of course. The Dr has undertaken to cure for me a hang nail (or ag-nail as he calls it,) by a course of eight powders! To little Minna I have taken quite a fancy and might make a pet of her, if I had time to make a pet of any one.[7]

Now, my dear Maria, I know not whether I have written all you would like to hear I fancy you get from other quarters news of your young friends.— Write to me whenever you can make it convenient, and I will answer when and as I can. The freedom and flow of your letter gave me true pleasure, no less what you say of conquering your reserve. I never wish to see in you those demonstrative manners which are unnatural to you and would be uncongenial with your character, but, so far as this reserve is a mere husk or frosty covering which prevents your doing justice to your feelings or affording pleasure to those you love by free, simple utterance of your thoughts, I would gladly see it disappear. I please myself, however, that you have friends who have the good sense to prefer that nothing should be forced. With remembrances to your parents and Frank Farewell for this time from your [affec]tionate friend

S. M. FULLER

ALS (MH: fMS Am 1086 [9:100]). *Addressed:* Miss Maria Rotch, / Care Mrs. Rotch / 8 Sidemouth St / London / England. *Postmarks:* 4 Eg 4 / Fe 19 / 1844 and O /19 Fe 19 / 1844.

travel in the country,] travel ↑ in the country ↓ ,
of positive] of ↑ positive ↓
may obtain] may ⟨lay⟩ obtain
who indulge vindictive] who indulge⟨s⟩ vindictive
lose sight] lose<s> sight
he is a woodcutter,] he is ↑ a ↓ woodcutter,
we kept] we ⟨had⟩ ↑ kept ↓

1. John Flaxman, *Lectures on Sculpture* (London, 1829); Joshua Reynolds, *Discourses on Painting and the Fine Arts* (London, 1825) or his *Discourses of Sir Joshua Reynolds* (London, 1842); Henry Fuseli, *Lectures on Painting* (London, 1801); George Field, *Chromatography* (London, 1835).

2. Charles Lock Eastlake had not at this time written on art, but he had edited Franz Theodor Kugler's *Handbook of the History of Painting, from the Age of Constantine the Great to the Present Time* (London, 1842); Luigi Antonio Lanzi was an Italian archaeologist who wrote *The History of Painting in Italy* (London, 1828); Antoine Chrysostome Quatremère de Quincy wrote *Histoire de la vie et des ouvrages de Raphaël* (Paris, 1824) and *Histoire de la vie et des ouvrages Michel-Ange Bonarroti* (Paris, 1835); Joseph Forsyth, *Remarks on Antiquities, Arts, and Letters, During an Excursion in Italy, in the Years 1802 and 1803* (London, 1813); John Bell, *Observations on Italy* (Edinburgh, 1825).

3. The false witnesses in Mark 14:58: "We heard him say, I will destroy this temple that is made with hands, and within three days I will build another made without hands."

4. Hannah Adams Randall (1824–62), whose father, John Randall, Sr., died on 27 December. Belinda is Belinda Randall, who is mentioned in many earlier letters (Randall, *Poems*, pp. 41–42).

5. Sarah Hodges (1825–1910), daughter of the Reverend Richard and Elizabeth Donnison Hodges of Cambridge, married the Reverend Joshua Augustus Swan (1823–71) in 1851 (*Hodges Family*, pp. 44, 52; MVR marriages 55:45; Harvard archives; *Boston Globe*, 18 October 1910).

6. Henri Vieuxtemps (1820–81), a Belgian violinist and composer, made the first of his three American tours in 1843. The very popular performer gave concerts in Boston on 19, 22, and 23 December 1843 (*The New Grove Dictionary of Music and Musicians*, ed. Stanley Sadie [London, 1982]).

7. Minna Wesselhoeft (1835–1913), daughter of Dr. Robert and Ferdinande Hecker Wesselhoeft, later completed the translation of *Günderode* begun by Fuller (MVR 1913 26:27).

442. To Orestes A. Brownson

Cambridge 28th Jany 44.

Dear Sir,

Mr Brisbane offered to lend me a volume of Fourier now in your hands.[1] Will you, when you have done with it, have the kindness to leave it with Miss Peabody directed to me? I am at her bookroom every Thursday morning.

With respect yours

S. M. FULLER.

ALS (InNd-archives). *Addressed:* Mr Brownson.

Orestes Brownson (1803–76), a minister, reformer, and writer, founded the *Boston Quarterly Review* in 1838 but then merged it with the *Democratic Review.* In 1844 he started *Brownson's Quarterly Review* and converted to Catholicism (*DAB*).

1. Albert Brisbane had recently published a major book on Fourier, *Association: or a Concise Exposition of the Practical Part of Fourier's Social Science* (New York, 1843). Which Fourier book Fuller wanted is unknown, but undoubtedly the recent convention on Association led her to read his work. In her journal for 1844 (MHi) she says she read Fourier's *Nouveau Monde industriel et sociétaire* (Paris, 1829) in September.

443. To Ralph Waldo Emerson

Cambridge 28th Jany 1844.

Dearest Waldo,

I know you are not a "marker of days" nor do in any way encourage those useless pains which waste the strength needed for our nobler purposes, yet it seems to me this season can never pass without opening anew the deep wound.[1] I do not find myself at all consoled for the loss of that beautiful form which seemed to me the realization of hope more than any other. I miss him when I go to your home, I miss him when I think of you there; you seem to me lonely as if he filled to you a place which no other ever could in any degree. And I cannot wish that any should. He seemed, as every human being ought,[n] a thought fresh, original; no other can occupy the same place. Little Edith has been injured in my affections by being compared with him. She may have the same breath in her, and I should like to love her in the same way, but I do not like to have her put in his place or likened to him; that only makes me feel that she is not the same and do her injustice. I hope you will have another son, for I perceive that men do not feel themselves represented to the next generation by *daughters,* but I hope, if you do, there will be no comparisons made, that Waldo will always be to us your eldest b[o]rn, and have his own niche in our thoughts, and have no image intruded too near him.

I think, too, that by such delicacy, and not[n] substituting in any way what is inferior or at any rate different, we shall best be entitled to see the end of the poem, for I fully expect to know more of what he used to suggest in my mind.— I think of him a great deal and feel at this distance of time[n] that there was no fancy, no exaggeration in the feelings he excited. His beauty was real, was substantial I have all his looks before me now. I have just been reading a note of yours which he brought me in the red room, and I see him just as he looked that day, a messenger of good tidings, an angel.

I wish, if you are willing, I may have a copy of your poem about him, even if it is not finished[2] I will confine it as strictly to myself, as you may desire. Elizabeth would copy it, I know, for me, if you were willing I should have it, and do not like to do it yourself.

I believe you never saw Richard's lines, that they were shown to Lidian, but not to you. At the risk of your having seen, I will copy them, for though rude and simple[n] I think they describe so truly[n] some of the feelings that were inspired.

> Thou fairy child, a gift so sweet
> So swiftly taken; as if meet
> Ere we may come, for heaven's abode
> Wast lightly freed from mortal load.
> How fair wast thou! on thy high brow
> In heavenly lineament—
> Was writ with such significance
> That they exchanged an asking glance
> Who knew to read the fingering
> Of heaven
> But now, as in Belshazzar's hall
> The Chaldees failed the heavenly call
> To tell, so it o'er tasked their powers
> To fathom what in thee was ours.
>
> Thoughtful and sad, thy earnest eye
> Sparkled the question ever— *Why?*
> The many bask in nature's rays,
> But in the centre passed thy days,
> Unspeaking, oft thou seemd'st the thought
> A sage had into marble wrought;
> Now had concentered here the sage
> The fruit of all his thoughtful age.
> Perchance when God thy spirit breathed
> And myriad charms about thee wreathed.
> He meant thee for a future race,
> Whereto we grow with lazy pace;
> But too soon he gave thee birth
> Into the yet unready earth.
> So he has ta'en thee from the scene
> Back to the courts of heaven serene &c—

I leave out the words that are less expressive. But several traits are full of expression to me. Especially as the form "fruit of the sage's concentred thought" thus he always seemed to me the child of my friend's mind, born to fulfil his life, for he too always asks the Why though with the same calmness.

I suppose Lidian told you of Miss Parson's reading a letter of yours under Mesmeric influence (of which you make light, so wittily) but as she may not remember all she heard I shall try to write down exactly what James and Sarah told me about it.[3] It was at James's house and only themselves and the Buchanans present.[4] She was tried with five or six autograph letters.[n] On one (of[n] General Wayne's) she passed what they supposed to be a false judgment.[5] On one of Miss Martineau's,—she said "here are so many impressions and so entangled, one coming so quick after the other I cannot feel any thing clearly."[6] They asked her if it was not a good person, she said "the person means well, but would be likely to deceive himself"—

A letter of J. S. Buckminster written when he was a boy being put into her hand, she was averse to hold it and said "it is good for nothing throw it away"[7] On their urging her more and wishing to know of[n] the moral qualities of the person she said "he seemed to her false" and would have no more to do with it. This at first amazed the spectators, but afterwards, considering that the letter was one of those written *to order* about being "schooled by his honored papa" and the like they thought there might be ground for the impressions of the magnetized in this instance, though so contrary to their expectations.

One of Mr Alston's letters affected her at once making her very pale and sick. Buchanan took it from her, saying "it might injure her as the person was recently dead"!![8] But James[n] observed that, on a previous occasion, she had been very agreeably affected by one of Dr Channing's.

Then was given her one from you to James containing a copy of "The Humble Bee."[9] She expressed pleasure and serenity at once from this contact. "The writer" said she "is holy, true, and brave"

Buchanan,— Brave! how do you mean? Would he fight for the Greeks?—

—He does not fight with such weapons; he has arms of his own.

Buchanan— Arms of reasoning, I suppose.

—Is there not something above reasoning?—

Sarah said that in all she said about you, but especially in her way of putting this question she assumed a tone and emphasis that reminded her of you.

She expressed pleasure in other ways I have forgotten, but then said, He is not perfect, though; there is something wanting.

James urged her to name the "fault"

—It is not fault, it is defect—it is underdevelopment; it puts me in mind of a circle with a dent in it.

They could not get her beyond this for sometime, and at last Buchanan proposed, on her saying she could not *criticize* the person, to magnetize the organ of self esteem that she might overlook him.

—You cannot get me up so high that I can overlook him. I might many, but not him. At last, after much questioning, she said with apparent difficulty "If he could sympathize with himself, he could with every one"—which is, in my opinion, a most refined expression of the truth, whether obtained by clairvoyance or any other means.

Her hand was then placed on the poem. This J. and S. said was to them the most interesting part of the scene, for if they could suppose her to have got from sympathy with what was in the minds of those present what she had said previously, they could not here, for they had nothing in their thoughts but expectations whether she would know it to be a poem and pronounce on its poetical merits.

As she said nothing for some time, J. asked her whether that was something good she had under her hand.

She expressed displeasure. Why did you speak to me, she said. I was not thinking of such things. I was in the country[n] in a sweet place, like the woods at Hingham.— She said it was a place where you would want to lie down on the grass.—not sit down.

They changed the letter for one of Aaron Burr's

She expressed aversion, and for a time would not hold it.— When she did, she made some good remarks, that he was a man all for ambition, yet fond of his family—very fond.

—Would he be successful with ladies, said J.

Too much so, she said.

Then she laughed and said "How he would look down on the last one I was thinking of!

J.— And how would that one regard him

—He is so high above him, that he could not even see him!

On their questioning more, she said, I am only guessing now, the other one I saw, a form seemed before me.

Buchanan Can you not guess whose form?

—It seemed something like Mr Alcott, but not exactly. It might have been Mr Emerson, but I do not know about him well enough to tell.

So much for the clairvoyante, who seems to me a very good and innocent girl.—I am going to see her tried myself, next week, probably. This time I believe I have set down exactly what (not all) that was told me.

This is the first time I have been able to write a word without pain, or read either for four days, during which my head has ached day and night. So today is as good as heaven to me. Yet, you may imagine I accomplish nothing, at least outwardly. These last weeks I have been much happier than in the month of dark December, for I have enjoyed a consciousness of inward ripening and accessions of light. It cannot always be so bitter cold; when it is not, I hope to be able to use my eyes and hands also. Meanwhile expect from me no good works, but write me yourself one letter and think affectionately of your friend

MARGARET.

Is your lecture in town the 7th Feby.[10] What is Mr Lane's address. I shall not write to him now, but should like to be able, when I feel like it. His letter has the true deep tone of his real self, and it is pleasant to see that when he is in his true place, he cannot help seeing *you*

ALS (MH: bMS Am 1280 [2373]). Published in Rusk, *Letters of RWE*, 3:235–38. *Addressed:* R. W. Emerson / Concord / Mass. *Endorsed:* Margaret Fuller / Jan 1844.

being ought,] being ⟨should⟩ ↑ ought ↓ ,
and not] and ⟨o⟩not
feel at this distance of time] feel ↑ at this distance of time ↓
rude and simple] rude⟨ly⟩ and simpl⟨y⟩e
so truly] so t⟨h⟩ruly
six autograph letters] six ↑ autograph letters ↓
one (of] one (↑ of ↓
know of] know ⟨?⟩of
But James] ↑ But ↓ James
was in the country] was ↑ in the country ↓

1. January 27 was the second anniversary of Waldo Emerson's death. After thanking her for her sympathy, Emerson said: "I have had no experiences no progress to put me into better intelligence with my calamity than when it was new" (Rusk, *Letters of RWE*, 3:238).

2. Immediately after his son's death, Emerson began to record memories and impressions that later developed into his elegy, "Threnody." Early drafts of lines for the poem may be found in *JMN*, 8:163–66, 451–57, 473–74, and 530. Emerson replied to Fuller's request: "I will try, since you ask it, to copy my rude dirges to my Darling & send them to you" (Rusk, *Letters of RWE*, 3:239).

3. Anna Quincy Thaxter Parsons (1812?–1906), daughter of Nehemiah and Anna Thaxter Parsons of Haverhill, was active in religious and reform groups. She wrote for the *Harbinger* and the *New-York Daily Tribune*. One of the founders of the Boston Religious Union of Associationists, Parsons also founded the Boston Women's Association-

ists Union (Haverhill VR; Suffolk Probate, no. 135649; *Boston Daily Advertiser*, 20 September 1906; Marianne Dwight, *Letters from Brook Farm, 1844–1847*, ed. Helen D. Orvis [Poughkeepsie, N.Y., 1928], p. xiv).

4. Probably Joseph Rodes Buchanan (1814–99), the eccentric author of books on healing and creator of "Psychometry." He was a Kentucky native whom Clarke probably knew during his days at Louisville (*DAB*).

5. Presumably General "Mad Anthony" Wayne of the American Revolution.

6. Fuller met Harriet Martineau, the English reformer and writer, in 1835 and afterward corresponded with her.

7. Joseph Stevens Buckminster (1784–1812), Fuller's distant relative, had been a powerful and popular minister at Boston's Brattle Street Church (*Heralds*, 2:134–53).

8. Washington Allston, the New England painter, had died on 9 July 1843.

9. Emerson's poem. Emerson's letter of 7 December 1838 has been published in *James Freeman Clarke: Autobiography, Diary, and Correspondence*, ed. Edward Everett Hale (Boston, 1891), p. 123.

10. Emerson delivered his lecture "The Young American" on 7 February to the Mercantile Library Association in Boston (Charvat, "Emerson's Lecture Engagements," p. 505).

444. To Ralph Waldo Emerson

Boston, 2d Feby 1844.
3 Louisburg Square

My dear Waldo

I gratefully received your packet, other than this, there is no time to say. At James Clarke's there are to be, next Monday evening *Mesmeric* experiments of reading letters &c tried on the same Lady of whom I wrote you in my last. Sarah desires me to invite your presence, in case you shall or can be in town so early as Monday. No one is to be there but myself and S. and A. with whom I am staying.[1]

At any rate we shall be at your lecture Wednesday eveg and go after to Miss Peabody's who has invited E. Hooper, A Shaw and other bright forms.

Perhaps, if you come to town in the morning we shall see you here in aftn of that day.

With love to Lidian yr affece

MARGARET.

ALS (MH: bMS Am 1280 [2374]). Published in Rusk, *Letters of RWE*, 3:240. Addressed: R. W. Emerson / Concord / Mass. Endorsed: Margaret Fuller / Feb 1844.

1. The Wards.

445. To Richard F. Fuller

Boston 2d Feby 1844.

My dear Richard,

I assure you we had a real fright about you from Ellery's letter. There was nothing to give us any notion he was in jest, however, we are very glad to find it was so. I think I may have to defer showing you Arthurs letters &c till you come, for reasons that would be tedious to detail.

I want you to look at and if you can to go over the old house opposite Mr E's for sixty dollars a year. We think of taking that, but say nothing yet, lest the refusal be snatched from us, and perhaps there be no chance to go to Concord to which we much incline.

Your piece I have read with many thoughts but am not likely to get time to write them, before you come home. They will keep till then.

Am sorry not to have time to write you good letters during yr pleasant seclusion. But so it must be. This world brings so many claims, yet yours I think will be satisfied in fine. Yr sister and friend

M.

ALS (MH: fMS Am 1086 [9:102]); MsC (MH: fMS Am 1086 [Works, 2:729–31]). *Addressed:* R. F. Fuller, / At the Red Lodge.

446. To Ralph Waldo Emerson

[14? February?] 1844

Sarah Clarke had fully intended to invite our new Ecstatica for Monday Evening, and submit to your eye the same revelations as to ours, when she was informed by Caroline that you had spoken of such experiments as "peeping through the keyhole," and such like. Sarah then says, "Have I a right to expose this delicate girl, whom I highly respect, to the scrutiny of one before whom she is to appear as a suspected person?"

M. It is to be remembered that many of his friends have been obliged to approach Mr E. in that character. I myself occupied it opposite him for some years.

Sarah. Yes, but his friends consent of their own free will to meet

181

him thus, because of their value for him. *We* shall put Miss Parsons into this position, while she will suppose herself opening her heart to friendly ears, and minds inclined to trust.

M. I do not like to have Mr E. deprived of the opportunity. Shall I write to him, and ask him if he can go to look, believing the actor, as all law divine or human demands, innocent until proved guilty?

Sarah. And make him aware that she neither makes a show of herself, nor seeks excitement, but comes to our house as to that of a friend, where she may expand, and give pleasure by the use of what seem to us real and uncommon powers.

MsCfr in Emerson's hand (MH: Os 735Laa 1844.10.14). Published in Rusk, *Letters of RWE*, 3:240–41.

Although this copy is dated "Oct 14 1844," it clearly belongs to February. On 16 February, Emerson wrote to Fuller in response to this letter, saying he could not come to town and promising to "write now to Sam W. that I am not to come & I will also write a note either to Mrs Hooper or to Anna Shaw" (Rusk, Letters of RWE, *3:241). It is not clear whether Fuller ever persuaded Emerson to participate in one of the mesmeric evenings.*

447. To William H. Channing

[March? 1844]

[   ] Mr Emerson preaches in town next Sunday. See how straight[n] and fast onward is the march of thought. Tis not more than three years since they left off asking him to enter pulpits because he appeared there once and made no formal prayer, and now a large assembly waits to hear him utter what he pleases, as he pleases. Verily it is a speaking comment on the text Sit still and let things come to thee (if only the inner temple be hallowed more and more by the Presence to receive the gift.) [   ] was good and pretty in their [   ] [E]llery left off chopping wood wh [   ] the strength of his hand, and [   ]

ALfr (MH: bMS Am 1280.226 [3908]). *Addressed:* To / William H. Channing / New York City.

Dated from Fuller's statement that Emerson was to "preach." He spoke at Boston's Amory Hall on 3 March and at the Second Church (his old pulpit) on 10 March (Charvat, "Emerson's Lecture Engagements," p. 505). Fuller's language suggests the latter date.

how straight] how str⟨ait⟩aight

448. To Lydia Francis Child

Boston 13th March 1844.

My dear Mrs Child,

Now that I am sending directly to you, I must take the oppory to thank you for giving me your book. I have done so, in a scanty fashion, through a little notice in The Dial, but it may not have met your eye in that generally eschewed periodical and I wish to say beside, how much I was pleased, not only to possess the book, but at your holding me in remembrance.[1]

So busy and various has been your life, since I knew you, and I was so young at that time, that I have doubted when we met, whether you remembered much about me. Now, however, that I know you do hold me in friendly regard, I shall come forward to offer the hand, when we meet again, and perhaps circumstances may favor a renewal of acquaintance. In former days, you used to tell me much which I have stored in memory as I have in my heart the picture of your affectionate, generous, and resolute life. *Now*, if we were to meet, we might have more topics in common; At least I ought to have something to impart, now so many pages of the great volume have been opened to my eye. In the hope that it may be so I remain yours

S. MARGARET FULLER.

ALS (MHarF). *Addressed:* Mrs Child, / New York City.

Lydia Maria Francis had been Fuller's friend in Cambridge. They read philosophy together in the 1820s but saw each other seldom after Francis's marriage to David Child. She was an ardent abolitionist and successful writer.

1. Fuller reviewed Child's *Letters from New-York* (New York, 1843), calling it "a contribution to *American* literature, recording in a generous spirit, and with lively truth, the pulsations in one great center of the national existence" (*Dial* 4 [1844]:407).

449. To Abigail Clarke Stimson

Cambridge 16th March, 1844.

Dear Mrs Stimson,

I have delayed writing to you about coming to Providence, because a thousand uncertainties have impeded my decision At one time I thought that, if a class were formed, it might be possible for me to go to P. once a week while retaining my classes here and in Boston. But my strength decreasing as usual[n] as spring draws near, I am warned not to attempt too much lest I fail in all.

Thus, perhaps, I may be obliged to postpone coming so long that you will not wish to have me at all. But, as the evenings in May are still more than two hours long, and this is as much time as I can give to these sessions, you may think this month will answer.

I could come to Providence the 6th May, for a fortnight. I should like to have six meetings, three in each week, on the alternate evenings.[n] I would come for a hundred dollars, and meet, for that, a circle of thirty, if so large a one[n] can be collected. I thought originally that I ought to ask a hundred dollars beside my expenses, as I must be from my home, and the excitement and fatigue probably considerable, but supposed from Mrs Newcomb's remarks that there might not be a class of more than twenty collected, in which case a hundred dollars for the six meetings would be about in proportion to my usual terms. I am as willing to meet a large as a small circle, and of gentlemen as[n] well as ladies, if the members will be friendly, will consider me, and aid with good will and a sincere interest to make these meetings a source of pleasure and profit to us all. In meeting such persons, my sense of responsibility does not oppress me long. But the presence of minds not animated by sincere good will is very disadvantageous to me and to all.

Any other particulars I gladly leave to your kindness and discretion I think you will find that some of my old friends will second you. I should like to know whether[n] you shall at this time, and on these terms desire my presence as soon as your convenience permits.

I direct this letter to care of Mr Hall,[1] because though I believe Mr. Stimson's name is *John H*, I am not quite sure, and if I mistake, the letter may not reach you. With best regards to him and to you

S. MARGARET FULLER.

ALS (RPA). *Addressed:* Mrs Stimson / Care of Revd Mr Hall / Providence / R. I.

Abigail Clarke (1798–1882) of Norton, Massachusetts, married John H. Stimson (1798–1860) in 1828 (Norton VR; Rhode Island VR, vol. 16; *New England Historical and Genealogical Register* 14 [1860]:293).

strength decreasing as usual] strength ⟨always liable to fail me⟩ ↑ decreasing as usual ↓
alternate evenings.] alternate ⟨meetings⟩ ↑ evenings ↓ .
large a one] large a⟨n⟩ one
gentlemen as] gentlemen ⟨of⟩ as
know whether] know ⟨now⟩ whether

1. Edward Brooks Hall (1800–1866) of Medford graduated from Harvard and from the Divinity School. He was ordained in Northampton and later became minister

at the First Church in Providence, where he served for thirty-four years. After the
death of his first wife, Hall married Louisa Jane Park, daughter of Dr. John Park of
Boston, Fuller's former teacher (*Heralds*, 3:150–51).

450.   To James F. Clarke

Thursday 21st March. [1844]

Dear James,

   I dont know but you thought from what Mr E. said that I had been
pluming myself in borrowed feathers as the author of your Triformis.
I showed it to Mr E. and would not tell him who wrote it, so it seems
he inferred (knowing my great modesty) that it was mine. But I had
and have still a little reason for letting him find out as he can. I have
put it in now without motto, also have stolen some remarks of yours
for a little dialogue but suppose, if your *sermons* are not pilfered from,
you dont care where else[n] I go in the more uncultivated regions of
your mind, picking up the wayside flowers.[1]

   Yr affectionately

MARGARET.

ALS (ViU).

where else] where ⟨I⟩ else

   1. Clarke had written Fuller and sent a Latin motto for his poem "Triformis":
"Terret, lustrat, agit, Proserpina, Luna, Diana, / Ima, superna, feras, sceptre, fulgore,
sagitta" (*Letters of JFC*, p. 144). John Buck translates the passage: "She quells, cleanses,
and drives the untamed / With sceptre, radiance, and dart— / Proserpina, Luna, Diana:
deepest and highest at once." Buck goes on to note that "in a sense, the poem is a conventional celebration of the civilizing, domesticating power of the feminine. If it verges
on sexism, however, it also qualifies the sexism almost out of existence with the energy
of the verbs and the power of the goddesses' instruments. The poem does not repudi-
ate the feminine responsibility to domesticate and civilize, but it deifies, gives energy
and makes heroic that feminine power."

451.   To Elizabeth Hoar

[April? 1844?]

I send you 3 papers written for my class, two by S Clarke, one by
Marianne Jackson. Our last meeting yesterday was beautiful; how no-

James Freeman Clarke. Courtesy of the Unitarian Universalist Association archives.

ble has been my experience of such relations for six years now, and with so many, and so various minds! Life *is* worth living—is it not?

MsCfr (MH: bMS Am 1280 [111, p. 109]). Published in part in *Memoirs*, 1:351; published entire in *JMN*, 11:478.

452. To Frances Hastings Fuller

Cambridge, 2d April, 1844.

My dear Frances,

I have been looking every where for a few lines Ellen wrote you to begin a letter. But I cannot find them. Their substance was merely to inform you how delighted she was with your presents, to express her love towards you and her brother, and say, what is true, that the state of her health does not permit of her writing but a few lines at a time.[1] She is doing very well, but we are anxious to have her careful, as if she gets well through, she *may* have health for the rest of her life

She looked very pretty when here, so meek and soft. I hope she may have a child that will be great pleasure to her now and solace by and by. Perhaps it will be happy if the eldest is a little girl, the eldest daughter becomes the Mother's friend, as I hope Cornelia will to you.

It gives *me* a great deal of pleasure to see *you* take so much in your children.[2] I am sure they are uncommonly sweet ones. It is sad for us that we cannot see them at this charming age, especially Mother would be gladdened by it. I wish dear Mother may sometime visit you, as you propose. She seems very delicate, passes her time as usual in devotion to others, but the life we lead here is too monotonous, and under too many depressing influences for her. I dread for her, too, the anxiety she is to undergo about Ellen. The affection of her heart makes all agitation bad for her.

I rejoice to hear that William has such a friend in Mr Robert. An earnest friend is a jewel not easily unearthed. Uncle Abraham promises to write to Wm about his affairs which have, now, come to a close. He says W. has nothing to receive except the 240 at this final distribution, and he still, I believe holds his share in the C. P. estate.[3] (The house there is now in a very bad state, and unless a good deal is done to it, we shall have no tenants, and these repairs, if made will eat up all profit for some time to come.) I understand W. had his share from the Groton estate. I suppose that was not included in the acct Eugene

187

sent me. We each receive in the whole about two thousand dollars. But let W. hold a final communication with Uncle A. and wind up. He can receive his share of the final distribution now whenever he draws for it.

We see no way into the future, have no plans or I would tell them you.

Of Boston news there is little. Hannah Jackson is engaged to Dr Cabot, son to Mr Sam Cabot.[4] Ann Whiting is engaged to a Mr Whipple. Mr Hibes[?] continues his (unpermitted) engagement with Elizh Shaw.—[5] S. Ward leaves business and goes into the country next month. He thinks he shall go to Berkshire this summer to board, and if the air there suits Anna's health and they like it, take a farm there, if not take one perhaps near Boston.[6] Anna makes considerable sacrifices to this plan, and encounters more care than is good for her, as she is not at all well, but she shows a cheerful resolution.

I am greatly obliged, dear Fanny, by the pretty collaret. It looks like you. I still wear a ruff you made me while here.— I am quite unwell this spring and feeling the raw east winds, must congratulate those who are out of their reach. With love to William and kisses to the children [   ]

Jane Tuckerman has a very pretty baby and is perfectly happy in it.[7]

Mrs Mann and Mrs Hawthorne have given to the tree of Peabody lineage two new branches, a little Horace Mann, and Una Hawthorne.[8]

[   ] Miss Howe of Cambridge. I wish you [   ] call and see her; she can tell you all the news from "*this way*"

ALfr (MH: fMS Am 1086 [9:118]); MsCfr (MH: fMS Am 1086 [Works, 1:193–97]). *Addressed:* To / William H. Fuller / for Mrs Fuller / Cincinnati / Ohio.

1. Ellen was at this time eight months pregnant.
2. A second daughter, Margaret Ellen (1843–73), had been born to Fanny and William Henry the preceding July (William Hyslop Fuller, *Genealogy of Some Descendants of Thomas Fuller of Woburn* [Palmer, Mass., 1919], p. 145).
3. The second distribution of Timothy Fuller's estate took place on 19 March 1844. Each of the children received $252.88 (Middlesex Probate, 1st ser., no. 8792).
4. Hannah Lowell Jackson (1820–79), Marianne Jackson's cousin, married Samuel Cabot (1815–85). Cabot, a grandson of Thomas Handasyd Perkins, was a doctor and prominent antislavery reformer. His father, Samuel Cabot, Sr. (1784–1863), made a fortune in the China trade (Briggs, *Cabot Family*, pp. 281, 325–26, 685; James Jackson Putnam, *A Memoir of Dr. James Jackson* [Boston, 1905], p. 96).
5. Both engagements were broken: Ann Whiting (1814–67), daughter of William and Hannah Whiting of Concord, never married; Elizabeth Shaw (1823–50), Frank Shaw's sister, married Daniel Oliver (1817–50) in 1846 (William Whiting, *Memoir of Rev. Samuel Whiting, D.D.* [Boston, 1872], p. 255; *Memorial Biographies of the New England Historic Genealogical Society* [Boston, 1880], 2:61; Arthur Winfred Hodgman, "Elias Parkman of Dorchester and His Descendants, 1633–1929," NEHGS, p. 98).

6. The Wards had a home in the Berkshires near Lenox, Massachusetts.

7. Alice King, the first of Jane's two daughters, died on 10 May 1846 (*Pedigree of King* [Lynn, 1891], n.p.).

8. Horace Mann, Jr. (1844–69), was born on 25 February and Una Hawthorne (1844–71) on 3 March (Tharp, *Peabody Sisters*, p. 163; *New York Times*, 12 September 1877; George S. Mann, *Genealogy of the Descendants of Richard Mann* [Boston, 1884], p. 28).

453. To Anna Barker Ward

Sunday, 14th April. [1844]

My dear Anna,

I should go and see if I could get the girl, Anne Stephens, for you, as E. Hoar says you wished, but that I feel sure it would be useless. She is engaged to a young mechanic in this place, and all her pleasure is to see him often.

I think your father must have come this beautiful day.[1] I shall be in town Tuesday[n] morng, if fine, and then call to see you, if you have a few minutes disengaged. Soon we shall be far apart, dear Anna, dear Sam. I cannot choose but shed some tears at times that it should have been mine to infuse some foreign element into the last days of habitual intercourse. But we are what we are and can only pray Heaven to make us by all this long evil of life somewhat wiser and better.— I hear you are tolerably well now, Anna, of that I am glad. I should have come to see you on my way back, but had so many little things to do, I could not have staid more than a moment, and preferred waiting till I felt less tired and in better spirits

Your friend

MARGARET.

ALS (MH: bMS Am 1465 [924]).

town Tuesday] town ⟨Thursday⟩ ↑ Tuesday ↓

1. Jacob Barker was a New England Quaker who made and lost a fortune in New York City before moving to New Orleans, where he became very successful.

454. To Arthur B. Fuller

Cambridge 22d April
44

My dear Arthur

Your letter to Lloyd gives a brighter picture of your affairs and health, yet, I suppose the main facts are still as when you wrote to me.

Immediately on my return from N. J. I went to see James. He read me a letter from Mr Conant, speaking in the highest terms both of yourself and your success.[1] We talked over the whole matter, but all the result is that Mr Briggs means to propose to the A. Unitarian association to vote $100 to Belvidere.[2] He (J.C)[n] says "for books, apparatus &c We think they will grant it. Nothing will be known of this matter,—at least not for a year, and then only to those who happen to mouse about among the accounts of the A. U. A.—I see no objection to taking it on that ground. Arthur will not be expected to do anything but to apply it for these and report accordingly. I see no prospect of getting more than this done." Now, you say in yrs that you do not want to be fettered that it is not an object under present circumstances to have money for these purposes. If you continue to think so, you can decline, shd the offer be made.

I do not think you will get anything freely done here for you. But shd you leave the school, and want money for purely Unitarian purposes, I daresay they will let you have it by and by. I would not make useless applications to them, if I could help it.

You are much likelier to get a little help near, from some ladies' fair at one of the Western towns[n] perhaps. And what was given so, if little, would be freely given.

But after all, if you can realize nothing from yr school, well patronized as it is, before the end of 18 mos, it seems not worth the sacrifice of so large a portion of yr young energies.

But you must act[n] very wisely and cautiously, for any appearance of lightness, after all that has been said and done, will injure yr reputation. William Clarke thinks you had much better offer back the place to the trustees, and thus if you hold it, hold it free. But on the other hand will not your readiness to do so lower the reputation of the property and make it difficult for *you* to sell it?

If you could carry through yr plan, establish the reputation of the school and then sell it a good bargain, it would be a brilliant starting point for you.

But if it will injure yr health, leave you poor, and too late with your profession, the game, to use the French proverb, is not worth the candle light[3]

I do not feel able, at this distance, to advise you, except to[n] hold counsel perhaps with Mr Wilson, and other friends[n] and not to act, if possible, till you have been at Chicago.[4] I have confidence that you will act wisely and that it will not end a bad business.

Should you leave, would it not be well to go to St Louis, and study a few months with Mr Eliot as you earlier proposed?—[5] If you do *not* permanently leave,[n] I hope you may be able to go there in the course of the season, as you propose.

I need not say, do not act at this important crisis from any temporary feelings of depression. I will say rather, do not overstrain yr constitution or injure yr health at any rate, for when these are gone, A's gone.

I think it is clear that if yr school cannot sustain itself, it will not be sustained by aid from here, nor probably is it desirable that it should; if the country wanted it, it would be sustained, if it does not, th utmost efforts, and all yr personal [energies] will not win for it a real success.

There seems no chance of Eugene, R. or Ellen going to you. Mother is now with E. who expects her confinement soon. She is pretty well.

We sent to day yr box, containing, I think, all you asked for except "dramatic dialogues" wh we could not find and the other book you mentioned in letter to L. we never owned. Mrs Farrar sent three or four books, among others her *Crusoe* may be good to read in yr school. I send "yng Lady's friend" and "Lives of the Painters" thinking they might be of use, but return them to me sometime, as they are presentation copies.[6] Kuhns sent Tracts for wh thank them in yr next[n] (Mr K. is almost well now) I did not send yr celestial globe this time, as, if we had, must have got a very large box, and it is uncertain whether you will want it there.— only 4 or five letters from McLaughlin, Richard, Ellen and Lloyd.[7] Forgot G. Livermore till too late will let him know W. C. is to go the 1st May.[8]

Richard, I suppose, has let you know about his settlement with Uncle A. He will have enough, with great economy to get through the study of law. Lloyd too, is tolerably well off.— He improves much, was delighted with yr letter. I would give much he could be in active employment near you for a time, as teacher of a primary school or otherwise, but suppose it cannot be. His faculties are a good deal called out where he is, but not enough.

Richd is very busy now, preparing his part, the Greek Oration.[9] Nothing has happened, I had a pleasant time in N.Y. was very unwell when I went, but returned better. Mr Greeley asked after you, I think, so most particy did Mrs Howe, who was here today.[10] Dr Francis says he would like to send you some books, if he knew what kind you want, wishes to know if you want some *theological* or what?[11]

Farewell, my dear Arthur, I shall be very anxious to hear from you again. I own I am much disappointed that our bright hopes and efforts are crowned with no more success. If they had been I should have felt repaid for many bitter and sorrowful moments at the West. But I know it will be noway yr fault that there is not a brighter result. You have done all you can and done a great deal, what very few of yr age and experience could. If not there you will do well elsewhere May Heaven take care of you, granting wise counsels and mature thoughts prays your sister

MARGARET.

ALS (MH: fMS Am 1086 [9:64]); MsC (MH: fMS Am 1086 [Works, 1:645–55]). *Addressed:* To Arthur B. Fuller / Principal of the Academy / at Belvidere, Illinois. *Postmark:* Cambridge MS Apr 23.

He (J. C)] He ↑ (J. C) ↓
Western towns] *Here Fuller later added:* When you go to Chicago you *may* interest some such ladies.
must act] must a⟨t⟩ct
you, except to] you, ⟨I advise⟩ ↑ except to ↓
Wilson, and other friends] Wilson, ↑ and other friends ↓
not permanently leave,] *not* ↑ permanently ↓ leave,
Tracts for wh thank them in yr next] Tracts ↑ for wh thank them in yr next ↓

1. Augustus Hammond Conant (1811–63) of Brandon, Vermont, emigrated to the Des Plaines River, west of Chicago, in 1835. In 1840 he attended the Divinity School at Cambridge for one year, then returned to Illinois to settle at Geneva, where Fuller visited him on her trip in 1843. Not only did Conant build a church there in 1844, but he served for several years as a Unitarian missionary in the West (*Heralds*, 3:128–30). Arthur Fuller had bought a school at Belvidere, Illinois, a community of 800 inhabitants. He paid $455 for a two-story building and two acres of land. By May 1844 he had one hundred students, but he later sold his academy to begin study for the ministry (*Heralds*, 3:128–30; Arthur Fuller to Eugene Fuller, 9 December 1843 and 28 May 1844, MH).

2. Charles Briggs (1791–1873) was secretary of the American Unitarian Association from 1835 to 1848 (*Heralds*, 3:215). In his letter of 1 March to Clarke, Conant had asked for a $500 contribution for the school, saying that it should come from private contributors because open support from the the Unitarian church would ruin Fuller's reputation among the Trinitarians. Conant did go on to say that if private contributions were insufficient, the AUA could quietly increase the fund (AUA record books, MH-AH).

3. "Le jeu ne vaut pas la chandelle." According to Hugh Percy Jones, "it was an old custom for poor folk to meet in a neighbour's house to play cards. At the end, they each subscribed something towards the expenses of the entertainment. If they were stingy, their host found that the gifts were less than the cost of the candle which he had provided" (*Dictionary of Foreign Phrases and Classical Quotations* [Edinburgh, 1908], p. 278).

4. Probably, though not certainly, Edmund B. Willson (1820–95), who taught at the academy at Leicester and who had recently been ordained at Grafton, Massachusetts. The month following this letter Willson married Martha A. Butterick (*Heralds*, 3:384–87).

5. William Greenleaf Eliot (1811–87) was minister of the Unitarian church in St. Louis. Prominent in community affairs, Eliot founded Washington University. He was Christopher Cranch's brother-in-law and a founder of the *Western Messenger* (*Heralds*, 3:90–98; *DAB*).

6. Eliza Farrar, Fuller's good friend, wrote *The Young Lady's Friend* (Boston, 1836).

Hannah Farnham Lee, whom Fuller knew in the 1830s, wrote *Historical Sketches of the Old Painters* (Boston, 1838).

7. Probably Arthur's classmate Henry Bartlett Maglathlin (1819–1910), son of Bartlett and Maria Chandler Maglathlin. Young Maglathlin graduated from Harvard in 1843 and from the Divinity School in 1846. He later became a doctor (Harvard archives).

8. George Livermore (1809–65) was a Cambridge merchant known for his avid book collecting (Walter Eliot Thwing, *The Livermore Family of America* [Boston, 1902], pp. 129–34).

9. Fuller mistakes her brother's part in the Harvard commencement of 1844. Richard's assignment was the "English" oration, one that was not read at the ceremony, a slight that he deeply resented (Richard F. Fuller, *Recollections of Richard F. Fuller* [Boston, 1936], p. 71).

10. Horace Greeley (1811–72), son of Zaccheus and Mary Woodburn Greeley, of Amherst, New Hampshire, first became a printer, then a journalist with strong Whig principles. In April 1841 he founded the *New-York Daily Tribune*, which by 1846 was considered the best all-purpose paper in New York. Embracing abolition and Fourierism, Greeley was a tireless worker for many reform movements *(DAB)*. Mrs. Howe is Julia Ward Howe, with whom Fuller was quite friendly at this time.

11. Convers Francis, the Parkman Professor of Pulpit Eloquence and Pastoral Care at the Divinity School *(General Catalogue of the Divinity School of Harvard University, 1901* [Cambridge, Mass., 1901], p. 5).

455. To William H. Channing

Cambridge, 28 Apr 1844.

It was the last meeting of my class. We had a most animated meeting. On bidding me goodbye, they all and always show so much goodwill and love, that I feel I must really have become a friend to them. I was then loaded with beautiful gifts, accompanied with those little delicate poetic traits of which I shd delight to tell you, if we were near. Last, came a beautiful bunch of flowers, passion flower, heliotrope, and soberer flowers. Then I went to take my repose on C's sofa, and we had a most sweet afternoon together.—

MsCfr (MH: bMS Am 1280 [111, pp. 106–7]). Published in *Memoirs*, 1:351, and *JMN*, 11:478.

456. To Caroline Sturgis

Friday evening, May 3d [1844]

I hasten to inform thee, Caroline, how well thou art guarded with talismans. The Greek meaning of Amethyst is Antidote against intoxication. It was used by the ancients as a talisman for this, also to give good thoughts and understanding.

The Agate preserves against the sting of the Scorpion, and, worn on the left arm, or hand, makes the owner wise and attractive. If laid under the head of the sleeper, it brings him manifold dream-pictures.

How sweet it is after the thunder-shower! but you are not among the blossoming trees.

Just now, looking in Pericles and Aspasia for something else (which I could not find) I came upon the poem, "You build your nest Aspasia" &c[1] I had forgotten how beautiful it is; look and see if it be not the right kind of nest.

You gave me this book, and Festus,[2] if ever you find a book as good, or (possible?) better, be sure and give me that too.

MARGARET.

The *diamond* is an antidote against poison, wild beasts, and evil spirits. The Dantes in their thick forests need the diamond.[3]

The Carbuncle is called so from carbo, because like a live coal.

> Slow wandering on a tangled way
> To their lost child pure spirits say
>   The diamond marshal thee by day;
> By night the carbuncle defend
>   Hearts-blood of a bosom friend;
> On thy brow the Amethyst,
>   Violet of secret earth,
> When by fullest sunlight kist
>   Best reveals its regal worth,
> And when that haloed moment flies
> Shall keep thee steadfast, chaste and wise.[4]

ALS (MH: bMS Am 1569 [1350]). *Addressed:* Miss Caroline Sturgis / Summer St.

1. Walter Savage Landor's imaginary conversation, *Pericles and Aspasia* (London, 1836), was a favorite of Fuller's. Of it she said: "Love and Friendship have never been painted in more lonely and dignified relations" (*New-York Daily Tribune*, 28 March 1845). The line she quotes begins sec. CCXXVI (*The Complete Works of Walter Savage Landor*, ed. T. Earle Welby [London, 1929], 10:234):

> You build your nest, Aspasia, like the swallow,
> Bringing a little on the bill at once,
> And fixing it attentively and fondly,
> And trying it, and then from your soft breast
> Warming it with the inmost of the plumage . . .

2. Philip Bailey wrote *Festus*, a book-length poem, in 1839. Fuller, who greatly admired the work, reviewed it in *Dial* 2 (1841):231–61 and in the *New-York Daily Tribune*, 8 September 1845.

3. The Dark Wood of Error at which Dante finds himself at the opening of the *Commedia*.

4. Fuller later copied these verses into her journal, saying that they had "a mystical, a prophetic meaning" (Margaret Fuller 1844 journal, MHarF).

457.   To Anna Loring

Tuesday evening, May 7th. [1844]

I am truly disappointed, my dear Anna, not to have you with me today, and sorry you are hurt and shut up, when the weather is so beautiful. The Exhibition is now lost,[1] and some amusements we had this afternoon, but as to your visit to me, I think you cannot fail to be well enough a week from next Saturday, and you must come then and spend Sunday with me.

Your kindest Mother, in having my bracelet so beautifully reset, for which you must thank her for me, has also gratified a wish of mine in having this lava which was once its clasp set for you. I thought you would like to wear an ornament which matches with one of mine, and it is thus the gift both of your mother and me. It is stamped in pure white with the head of Raphael, one of those rare beings in whom a mind of transcendant genius was[n] associated with an outward form of beauty and a temper which won to him the tender love of all men. However long you may live, or much you may learn, every advance will only enable you to know and revere the better this painter who, beyond all others, was worthy to depict the holy Virgin, the Mother of a holy child. You will always, I am sure, like to keep this simple pin. I meant to have given it you and worn the bracelet with you today, but we shall have occasions enough for this.

Send word by Lloyd whether you are better. If I can, I will see you on Thursday. I shall be in town on my way to West Roxbury. Affectionately your friend

S. Margaret Fuller.

ALS (MCR-S).

Anna (1830–96), daughter of Ellis and Louisa Loring, married Otto Dresel (1826–90), a pianist and composer, in 1863. During the Civil War she was a vice-president of the Sanitary Commission in Boston (Pope, *Loring Genealogy*, p. 256).

genius was] genius ⟨is⟩ was

1. A group of "chemical paintings" exhibited in illumination "in the style of the celebrated Daguerre of Paris" went on display in Boston on 8 April. The exhibition closed on 6 May (*Boston Daily Advertiser*, 6 May 1844).

458.   To Ralph Waldo Emerson

Cambridge May 9th [1844]

Dear friend,

The printing is begun, and all looks auspicious, except that I feel a little cold at the idea of walking forth alone to meet that staring sneering Pit critic, the Public at large, when I have always been accustomed to confront it from amid a group of "liberally educated and respectable gentlemen"[1]

Have also your note of this morng and will settle with Sarah about the Etchings.[2]

If you *do* come to Boston cant you arrange to dine, or *better*, spend the night here" and let the stage take you from here that I may have a chance to see you.

In greatest haste,

MARGARET.

Do you remember some lines I wrote you from Canton about a Cherry tree in blossom before my window Will you let me have them to copy into my journal of this month I have an apple tree in full blossom before it *now*.

ALS (NNC). *Addressed:* To / R. W. Emerson / Concord / Mass. *Postmark:* Cambridge MS May 9. *Endorsed:* M Fuller / May 1844.

night here] night ↑ here ↓

1. Fuller was completing *Summer on the Lakes*.

2. Sarah Clarke made a set of drawings for the book, but they were not included until a second issue (Joel Myerson, *Margaret Fuller: A Descriptive Bibliography* [Pittsburgh, 1978], p. 11).

459.   To Caroline Sturgis

Cambridge,
May 25th [1844]

dear Caroline,

I dont know whether Ellery will adapt Waldo's plan of notifying his friends severally of such events, but, if not, you will like to know that his child is come and Ellen safe.[1] It is a girl and[n] was born day before yesterday, my birthday. Our youngest brother Edward, who died while I held him, was born on my eighteenth birthday, and given to me.[2] I did not know then I should have such a large family of sons, and mourned for him much, for he was a beautiful child. Ellen has often expressed a wish that hers might be born on that day, and since the event was deferred she began to hope it would. She spoke of it in a letter to me last week.

On Thursday I finished my book just at dinner time and passed the afternoon at Mt Auburn.

I thought much of the time when I, too, should drop this mask of flesh, and who would finish my work. I had a fancy the child was born that day, and hoped it would have been[n] a boy. However my star may be good for a girl, educated with more intelligence than I was. Girls are to have a better chance now I think. She will have my saint's day, and you for a godmother. She will have friends such as I wanted, when a child.

To day is the same day we set out on our journey last year.

Adio

MARGARET

If this child dies, too, her uncle will be grown to about the angelic size in the other world and can take care of her. He had beautiful blue eyes and golden hair as angels, little and great, are described, and perhaps, growing up *there,* his beauty is not tarnished, but only unfolded.

ALS (MH: bMS Am 1221 [246]). *Addressed:* Miss C. Sturgis / Summer St.

It is a girl and] It ↑ is a girl and ↓

would have been] would ⟨be⟩ ↑ have been ↓

1. Margaret Fuller Channing (1844–1932) married Thacher Loring (1844–1928) in 1870 (MVR Boston 1932 6:229, 1928 1:310; Pope, *Loring Genealogy,* p. 298).

2. Edward Breck Fuller, youngest of the Fuller children, was born on Margaret's birthday, 23 May 1828, and died on 15 September 1829 *(CVR).*

460. To Charles C. Little

May 30th, 1844.

To Mr Little

Dear Sir, I understand my book cannot be out for three or four days. In that case, please let Mr Clarke have the sheets. I will answer for his care. With respect

S. M. FULLER.

ALS (NBLiHi). *Addressed:* To / Mr Little. *Endorsed:* S. M. Fuller / May 30th 1844 / order.

Charles Coffin Little (1799–1869) was a partner in the firm of Charles C. Little and James Brown, which published Fuller's *Summer on the Lakes (DAB).*

461. To William H. Channing

[June? 1844]

[   ] think I have written too sweetly or in too fair words, hush the moral voice with mindfulness that such is always the Poetry of Truth.

I want to send you an eagle's feather from the Eagle's nest at Oregon.[1] Sarah gave me three the other day; one I have given to Cary, one I keep, one is for you. I never expect to use mine, but perhaps you will write me *the* letter sometime with yours. I may not have opportunity to send it soon; eagles' feathers wont go into parcels of a common shape.

As to my book, there are complimentary notices, in the papers[n] and I receive good letters about it.[2] It is much read already, and esteemed "very entertaining"! Little and Brown take the risk and allow a per centage. My bargain with them is only for one edition; if this succéeds, I shall make a better. They take their own measures about circulating the work, but any effort from my friends helps, of course. Short notices by you, distributed at Phila New York and even Cincinnati would attract attention and buyers!![3] Outward success in this way is very desirable to me, not so much on account of present profit to be derived, as because it would give me advantage in making future bargains, and open the way to ransom more time for writing.

The account of the Seeress pleases many, and it is amusing to see how elderly routine gentlemen, such as Dr Francis and Mr Farrar, are charmed with the little story of Mariana. They admire, at poetic distance, that powerful nature that would alarm them so in real life. How canst thou be willing that any should see me as Mariana?— I shall always do so.— I feel that the inmost passages are only for God, music, and love. Imagine prose eyes, with glassy curiosity, looking out for Mariana. Nobody dreams of its being like me; they all thought Miranda was, in the Great Lawsuit.[4] People seem to think that not more than one phase of character can be shown in one life.

Sylvain is only a suggested picture, you would not know the figure by which it is drawn, if you could see it. Have no desire, I pray thee, ever to realize these ideals. The name I took from Fanny Elsler's partner.[5]

In the bridal dance, after movements of a birdlike joy, and overflowing sweetness, when he comes forward, she retires with a proud, timid grace, so beautiful; it said "see what a man I am happy enough to love". And then came forward this *well-taught dancer*, springing and pirouetting without one tint of genius, one ray of soul; it was very painful and symbolized much, far more than I have expressed with Sylvain and Mariana.

Write me any thing more that strikes you, then will the book become very interesting to me.

Have you begun the memoir?[6] I hope next Sunday to write out what I have to say about your uncle, and then will send it. They have built a mean house close to his willows. I wish they had waited for me to be gone.

Cary has been staying with me for near a fortnight, pleasant is our independent life in the still house. There are many things I might tell you, but must wait for time is not abundant with me just now. With blessing Farewell.

If you dislike my version of your visions, will not you burn it and write them out for me yourself.

ALfr (MB: Ms. Am. 1450 [52]). Published in part in Higginson, *MFO*, pp. 198–99. *Addressed:* William.

notices, in the papers] notices, ↑ in the papers ↓

1. Oregon, Illinois, where she had been on her trip.

2. Reviews of *Summer on the Lakes* appeared in the *Boston Courier, Boston Post,* and *New-York Weekly Tribune* in June (Joel Myerson, *Margaret Fuller: An Annotated Secondary Bibliography* [New York, 1977], p. 7).

3. Apparently Channing did not review the book.

4. So did she: "Last year at this time I wrote of woman, and proudly painted myself as Miranda" (Margaret Fuller 1844 journal, MHarF). Fuller refers to her *Dial* essay "The Great Lawsuit," which became *Woman in the Nineteenth Century.*

5. Fanny Elssler, the celebrated Austrian dancer, had performed in Boston in 1840 and 1841. Her partner was James Sylvain (born Sullivan) (Ivor Guest, *Fanny Elssler* [Middletown, Conn., 1970], pp. 130–47, 177).

6. Whether Channing had begun his memoir of Dr. William Ellery Channing is unclear. He published it in three volumes in 1848.

462. To Caroline Sturgis

3d June. [1844]

Dear Caroline

I look forward with desire to having you in the house and hope your mind will not change about coming, and may be contented for a few days. Am glad, however, you did not come while L. staid, as I have had to devote myself to him in ways that might have disturbed you. He goes tomorrow at 3. I shall come to the Concert tonight and will stay at your house[1] Shall I not then take out your things with me next morning in Omnibus and you walk out in aftn.

I go to Concert with Richard, if you have made no arrangement you like better and wish, you might go with us. I shall be at your house a few minutes before going.

I have fixed the little room next mine for your sitting room. The window has the same view as mine, only prettier, as the river can be seen more completely. I hope you will like the window, if you feel like writing or drawing

MARGARET.

ALS (MH: bMS Am 1221 [200]). *Addressed:* Miss C. Sturgis / Summer St.

1. On that night at the Concert Hall in Boston, Palmo's Concert Company gave a program of "Songs, Duets, Choruses" from several operas (*Boston Daily Evening Transcript,* 3 June 1844).

463. To Little and Brown

Monday 3d June. [1844]

Messrs L. and B.

If "Summer on the Lakes" is out, will you send me by the bearer seven copies, otherwise let me know whether I can have them tomorrow morning, if I send.

Will you let Mr Greeley of the N. Y. Tribune and N. P. Willis have copies as early as possible[1] They have promised their best support to circulate the book in N. Y.

With respect

S. M. FULLER—

A copy I suppose will be sent Mr Emerson at once. I do not know what message he has left about[n] it, but if none please send him one, so soon as any are ready.

ALS (ViU). *Addressed:* Little & Brown / Washington St. *Endorsed:* Miss Fuller.

left about] left ⟨acknowl⟩ about

1. Nathaniel Parker Willis (1806–67), a popular poet and dramatist, was an editor and writer for the *New-York Evening Mirror* (which did not review *Summer on the Lakes*) (*DAB*).

464. To Charles K. Newcomb

9th June. [1844]

Dearest Charles,

I think the reading of you in many respects excellent, of the "eastern magician," the gleams of sunlight across the dark pine woods, and trailing the little switch.[1] She has seized with force several leading traits, and went much deeper than she did with mine.

I wish you would have it copied for me, and, when you come here, bring the leaves of your journal and read aloud. Was it the 23d of this *last* May that is my birthday and was marked this year with deep strokes in the life of my mind. I should like to know what was passing in yours.

Will not you come and pass a day or two with me? I am much alone now, and it is very still here. I may not come to the Farm. Bring some things to read to me if you *do* come. There is a place on the river bank pretty enough, though not like the pine woods. I wish you would read me Edith again. And you know you promised me something for my self that was to tell much.

With salutation from the Madonna heart your

Did you hear Ole Bull play the Adagio Religioso?[2]

AL (MH: fMS Am 1086 [10:143]). *Addressed:* Charles.

1. It appears that Anna Parsons "read" Newcomb's character in one of her mesmeric sessions.

2. Ole Bornemann Bull, a Norwegian violinist, completed a five-concert stay in Boston on June 4. The very popular performer often played his "Adagio" as well as his compositions that grew from his American experiences: "Niagara" and "To the Memory of Washington" (*Boston Daily Evening Transcript,* 3 and 5 June 1844).

465. To Barbara Channing

Cambridge
14th June, 184[4]

Dear Barbara,

I was truly obliged by the hearts ease which looks luxuriant and fair as a plant by that name should.

Did you go to see Ellen, and if you did how did you find her and how did the baby look? Affecy yours

S. M. FULLER.

ALS (MBAt). *Addressed:* Miss Barbara Channing / Tremont St.

466. To [?]

[Summer] 1844

Every day, I rose and attended to the many little calls which are always on me, and which have been more of late. Then, about eleven, I would sit down to write, at my window, close to which is the apple-tree lately full of blossoms, and now of yellow birds. Opposite me was Del Sarto's Madonna; behind me Silenus, holding in his arms the infant Pan.[1] I felt very content with my pen, my daily bouquet, and my yellow birds. About five I would go out and walk till dark; then would arrive my proofs, like crabbed old guardians, coming to tea every night. So passed each day. The 23d of May, my birth-day, about one o'clock, I wrote the last line of my little book; then I went to Mount Auburn, and walked gently among the graves.

ELfr, from *Memoirs*, 2:120.

1. Andrea del Sarto (1486–1531) was a Florentine colorist. He did many Madonnas, but his best known is the *Madonna of the Harpies* (1571). Silenus, father of the satyrs, served Dionysus. He is sometimes called the son of Pan, sometimes the brother.

467. To Arthur B. Fuller

Cambridge 3d July, 1844.

My dear Arthur,

It seems a good while since I wrote[n] and yet there have not been many and important events of which I should write.

Mount Auburn Cemetery, Cambridge. From *American Scenery*, ed. N. P. Willis (London, 1840); courtesy of the Pennsylvania State University Libraries.

Richard will write you word as how he has sold the C. P. house. I think we shall always be glad of it, *am sure I* always shall. At Concord they are stumbling along Baby fretting much, parents astonished to find there really comes a great deal of care with a child.[1] Mother unwell, but I hope she will cease to be so when she gets home here and has had some rest. She is coming in a day or two, and I shall leave a blank space in this letter for her to fill up.

We were very glad to get yr parcel containing the books about yrself and the flowers for Praeses[?] at which I judge he will stare, and yet, probably, be pleased, too. Mr Conant's letter just published in the Christian Register does you good here.[2] All from yr part of the world give as high an opinion of yr efforts and merits as you yourself could; can I say more?

Without joke, I am satisfied that yr success and the tact and energy by which you have attained it are extraordinary. I think of you with great pleasure and am only anxious about your health. Write in yr next, under what circumstances and with what means you are to travel in the summer vacation. Mr Patton thought you would be paid as a missionary, then.

The Pattons will do all they can to enlist interest here in yr behalf.— I have been to see them and urged them to make me a visit, and they have called, but have so many engagements; it is not certain they will do more.

The Harringtons I have not seen.[3] I shall, if I can, but if not, you need not be uneasy. Ministers are expected to do for those placed as you are what Mr H. did for you and it does not oblige yr family to any thing. Still I will see them if I can.

R. will send you a copy of my book. He wishes to give it you. It seems to be selling very well is much read, and a number of favorable notices in the Boston and N. Y. papers. I shall be surprized if it is not assailed in some of the reviews.

I do not wish to send yr globe by the Clarkes. If you are not to stay more than a year longer, I would not have it at all, if I were you. You will not wish the trouble of bringing it hence again, you will not want to leave it there, as Mr Farrar's gift. If you *do* want[n] it, Hines,[4] if he goes, had better take it and if you will mention in time what sort of books you want, you know Dr Francis offered to send some[n] to you. If you are to stay more than a year, I do wish Lloyd might go out to you with Hines. With judicious care it might be the making of him and he is much improved and most anxious to improve. But, if you do not stay, I suppose it would hardly be worth while to risk the expense of such an experiment.

I will now leave room for Richard to tell you about his new bargain and remain dear Arthur yr well pleased and affece sister

MARGARET

I may close this letter without waiting Mother's return, if so she will write by the Clarkes. They set out 22d July.

July 4th

Richard says he shall have to take a whole sheet for himself, so as to send the instrument for you to sign about the sale, so I will close this myself. You will receive this in a few days and Mother will then reply about yr books. Yr letter was forwarded to her at Concord and she sent word you had sent for some books, but not the list or money for us to buy them. She will be at home tomorrow.

R. says Praeses was truly delighted with the flowers and took yr address for the purpose of writing to you, though I should judge this design might fall through as the good gent. falls asleep, even when sitting for his portrait

Uncle A. sent me a letter recd by him eight or nine months ago from Mr Whittier to the following purport "I intended to have named to you a young man of this town (Hallowell)[n] by the name of George Mulliken 19 years of age just out of College.[5] He is, I think, just the one for our friend Arthur F. at his establishment. He is a sober, if any thing too sober, exemplary young gentleman, just the one to give such an establishment as A's a character for every thing that is amiable, moral, "lovely and of good report. Said to be a fine scholar, and not anxious for money; his whole wish seems to be to do good.— Will you communicate with A. and then write me. I feel quite an interest both in A and this young man, whose heart I dont think an evil thought ever entered."

This M. is probably engaged now. I suppose Uncle A did nothing about it at the time. But in case you dont suit yr self entirely otherwise, it might be worth yr while to inquire at Hallowell

Miss Bartlett was speaking of yr being at Nahant and how fond Mrs Codman was of you.[6] You possess the talent of making friends, may they prove dear and valuable friends.

Once more farewell, and all good keep with you!

Mrs Clarke has a famous plan, she thinks, to propose to you. I hope you will be able to go to Chicago and see her, they will be well settled by the end of August.

ALS (MH: fMS Am 1086 [9:122]); MsC (MH: fMS Am 1086 [Works, 1:655–63]). *Addressed:* Mr Arthur B. Fuller / Principal of the Academy / at Belvidere / Illinois. *Postmark:* Cambridge MS Jul 5.

I wrote] I ⟨?⟩ wrote
you *do* want] you ↑ *do* ↓ want
send some] send ⟨them⟩ ↑ some ↓
town (Hallowell)] town ↑ (Hallowell) ↓

1. The Channings.

2. The *Christian Register* for 29 June reported that Augustus Conant had preached at Belvidere, where he found Arthur Fuller well liked, even by the local Trinitarians. Conant emphasized the respect Fuller had won in the area and called for a missionary to settle there. Arthur then wrote a letter that appeared on 6 July, making another plea for a resident missionary for Belvidere *(Christian Register,* 29 June and 6 July 1844).

3. Joseph Harrington, Jr. (1813–52), graduated from Harvard in 1833, studied theology with George Putnam in Roxbury, was ordained an evangelist in 1839, and went to Chicago, where he was a missionary until the summer of 1844. He later served in pulpits in Boston, Hartford, and San Francisco. In 1841 Harrington married Helen Griswold of Baltimore (Waldo Higginson, *Memorials of the Class of 1833 of Harvard College* [Cambridge, Mass., 1883], pp. 30–32).

4. Ebenezer Pierce Hinds (1821–62), Arthur's classmate, had been a schoolteacher before he joined the Harvard class of 1844 in 1843. His classmates remembered him as "eccentric and reticent to excess" (Edward Wheelwright, *The Class of 1844, Harvard College, Fifty Years after Graduation* [Cambridge, Mass., 1896], pp. 120–23).

5. Mr. Whittier is probably Simeon Chase Whittier, who married Fuller's aunt Martha Williams Fuller in 1809. George Samuel Mulliken (1824–60) of Manchester, Maine, a Bowdoin graduate in 1843, became a lawyer and then a judge in Augusta *(General Catalogue of Bowdoin College* [Brunswick, Maine, 1950]).

6. Which Miss Bartlett Fuller means is unclear, but Mrs Codman is probably Mary Cushing Codman (1774?–1846), wife of Stephen Codman (1757?–1841), a Boston merchant who was "one of the earliest of the Nahant cottagers" to open his summer home. Fuller may, however, mean their daughter-in-law, Catharine Amory Codman (1796–1850), wife of Henry Codman (1789–1853), the Fullers' neighbor in the Willow Brook section of Roxbury ("Codman Family," NEHGS; Cora Codman Wolcott, *The Codmans of Charlestown and Boston, 1637–1929* [Brookline, Mass., 1930], p. 68).

468. To Charles K. Newcomb

Cambridge
8th July. [1844]

I grieve, dear Charles, that you should have been disappointed at not receiving a copy of my book *from myself.* But we authors buy our own books just the same as other people do, and though the inner circle of relations is not very large with me, yet that of persons from whom I have received all those marks of regard that would justify them in expecting this from me, if I did it at all, is very large; it would amount if not to the "dear five hundred," certainly to sixty or seventy persons.[n] Mr Emerson, in making the bargain for my book, felt this, and requested that I would not give it to him or Ellery that he might be able to say to other friends that I had not, thinking they would perceive the reason.

You must not then be surprized if you receive from me now or at any time some other" mark of remembrance rather than my own book. For when I shall not receive a hundred dollars from the entire edition, I cannot afford to have fifty deducted for copies. If I ever become so popular that my books are sure to pass through several editions, then I shall indulge myself in giving them to all whom I am anxious to have read them.

You did not have your character copied for me. You must not so neglect the request of your friend

MARGARET.

I go to Concord this p.m. for a week or more.

ALS (MH: fMS Am 1086 [10:144]).
seventy persons.] seventy ↑ persons ↓ .
some other] some ↑ other ↓

469.   To Ralph Waldo Emerson

Friday—
[ca. 10 July 1844]

I pray thee, O friend, if thou dost walk forth today, to visit the spot in Sleepy Hollow where we sat down awhile and look on the ground to see if perchance my eyeglass may be glittering there, for the want of it plagues me. But dont look any where else; it is there or no where. I think I may have loosened it, when I put the letter into the bosom of my dress.

The little messenger will also bring a pair of shoes that I left under the entry table. I send a letter from Georgiana Bruce, I thought you would like.[1] I will take it again tomorrow, if I come at noon to hear you read.

The little Edith mingles in my dreams She seems one of the good messengers.

MARGARET.

Dont show the letter at all. Is not what she says of the mulatto women much better than Sue's attempt to paint that specimen? what *was* her name?

207

ALS (MH: bMS Am 1280 [2381]). *Addressed:* R. W. Emerson, / at the White House! *Endorsed:* Margaret Fuller.

Probably written in the summer of 1844, when Fuller was visiting Concord and staying with the Hawthornes in the Old Manse.

1. Georgiana Bruce was a young Englishwoman who was employed by the women's prison at Sing Sing. She had been a Brook Farm resident and was Fuller's good friend.

470. To Richard F. Fuller

Thursday 11th July [1844]

Dear Richard,

I write to you rather than Mother to tell you about Ellen. She still holds out and she says the baby does better than it has. Still her situation is quite unbearably fatiguing and laborious; she could not hold out so long.

Will you go to Mrs Farrar and tell her with my love that, if Deborah *can* find a girl for her, as she thought she might now at the beginning of the vacation, it will be doing E. and myself the greatest possible kindness

E. feels, as I thought she would, that she would rather have nobody, than have one sent on whom she cannot, with good reason, depend. She lays little stress on the person's experience with children compared with her being a good and kind person fit to do her other work. She thinks if she had not the care of that, she could get along with[n] the baby and should want to take the chief[n] care of it, at any rate.

At home, will you give my love to Mother, tell her I am having a pleasant time and flatter myself she is taking good care of her health. Ask Abby to send me by Ann the *white muslin sleeves* that are in my *purple muslin dress*[n] and more stockings if she has any for me.

Tell Ann her sister Abby depends on seeing her next Saturday and wants to know if it is not possible for her (Ann) to bring a cook for Mrs Emerson.

Mr E. has now another son, born yesterday morning. I am going to spend the day there.[1]

Expecting to hear from you on Saturday at latest, I am affectionately yours

MARGARET.

I have not see H. Thoreau.

ALS (MH: fMS Am 1086 [9:95]); MsC (MH: fMS Am 1086 [Works, 2:703–5]). *Addressed:* Richard F. Fuller / Cambridge / Mass. *Postmark:* Concord Mass Jul 11.

along with] along ⟨in other respects⟩ with
the chief] the ↑ chief ↓
mulsin dress] *mulsin* ↑ *dress* ↓
1. Edward Waldo Emerson (1844–1930) was born in 10 July (*DAB*).

471. To Ralph Waldo Emerson

The Parsonage, 13th July. [1844]

It seems rather odd, dear Waldo, to send you a rude thing like this, just as you have been showing me your great results, sculptured out into such clear beauty.[1]

But your excellence never shames me, nor chills my next effort, because it is of a kind wholly unattainable to me, in a walk where I shall never take a step. You are intellect, I am life. My flowers and stones however shabby interest *me*, because they stand for a great deal *to me*, and would, I feel, have a hieroglyphical interest for those of like nature with me. Were I a Greek and an artist I would polish my marbles as you do, as it is, I shall be content whenever I am in a state of unimpeded energy and can sing at the top of my voice, I dont care what. Whatever is truly felt has some precious meaning. I derive a benefit from hearing your pieces as I should from walking in the portico of a temple, amid whose fair columns the air plays freely. From it I look out upon an azure sea. I accept the benignant influence. It will be eight years next week since I first came to stay in your house. How much of that influence have I there received! Disappointments have come but[n] from a youthful ignorance in me which asked of you what was not in your nature to give. There will be little of this, if any, in future. Surely! these essays should be a sufficient protest against such *illusions*.

The piece I send you pleases me as the "Herberts" and that "Dialogue" did as being each the thought of a day.[2] Here are three days of life in[n] the past year during which my mind pursued its natural course uninterrupted from sun to sun. They please me by recalling these three bright days. Anyone who, in reading them, considered it as spending the day with me might find an interest in them, if in my mind at all.

The horse, konic belongs to Frank Shaw. S. Ward it was who likened Sarah to the sweet fern. The Sistrum I have shown you, and I believe[n] the Serpent, triangles, and rays which I had drawn for me. The other two emblems were ascribed to me by others, and the Winged Sphinx I shall have engraved and use, if ever I get to look as steadily as she does.[3] Farewell, O Grecian Sage, though not my Oedipus.

I wish I could have Edith up here a little while, some day. I want to see her with Una,—but I suppose she could not walk so far, could she?

The Egyptians embodied the Sphinx as in body a lion, in countenance of calm human virgin beauty. It was reserved for the Greek to endow her with wings.

I have just had a very pleasant visit from Henry. No Atlantides though!

AL (MH: fMS Am 1086 [9:109]). *Addressed:* To Waldo.

come but] come ↑ but ↓
life in] life ⟨during⟩ ↑ in ↓
you, and I believe] you, ↑ and I believe ↓

1. Fuller's comment at the end of the next paragraph suggests that she had been reading the manuscript of at least part of Emerson's forthcoming *Essays: Second Series.* She was staying with the Hawthornes in the Old Manse.

2. Fuller may well have sent Emerson a copy of her "Life on the Prairies," a piece she republished from *Summer on the Lakes* in the *New-York Weekly Tribune* of 15 June. Her works that she mentions are "The Two Herberts," *Present* 1 (1844):301–12, and "Dialogue," *Dial* 4 (1844):458–69.

3. Fuller refers to several occult symbols that she sketched on the letter.

472. To Georgiana Bruce

[16 July 1844]

I tell you this now, that when future silences occur you may have patience with my disabilities, as others have, and not mistake my interest in yourself, which is strong. [   ] I must be glad to see you thrown so completely on yourself, both as to outward and inward life: thus shall you learn; thus shall you teach. But it seems to me you are too restless. I know not how far this is inevitable, but I wish you may have patience to extract the honey from every field you traverse in your adventurous course. The materials for future thought afforded by your life at Sing Sing are of rare value. I can see by your letter what they must become to yourself. I would not have you lose or abridge so fine an occasion and one which will not return. [   ]

I am staying here with the Hawthornes. I do not see B. or G., nor do my friends seem to be in the habit of meeting them.[1] [   ] It is at present the world of infants. The Hawthornes have one of great beauty; my sister Ellen, one born on my birthday and named for me; Mr. Emerson, a son born one day after I came. Having enjoyed several days of laziness playing with the children and hearing the wind blow through the old trees around this parsonage, I break upon it the first time this morning to write to you.

Let me hear from you again. Believe that I prize your letters, and am, with some understanding,

Your friend,

MARGARET F.

ELfr, from Kirby, *Years of Experience*, p. 210.

Dated from a notation in Fuller's 1844 journal (MHi).

1. Burrill and George William Curtis, sons of George and Mary Burrill Curtis, had lived at Brook Farm but were staying in Concord in the summer of 1844. Burrill (1822–95) graduated from Cambridge University in 1858 and became an Anglican clergyman. George William Curtis (1824–92) married Anna Shaw, daughter of Fuller's close friends Frank and Sarah Shaw, and became a popular author and the editor of *Harper's Weekly* (Joel Myerson, "James Burrill Curtis and Brook Farm," *New England Quarterly* 51 [1978]:396–423; Ellen Mudge Burrill, "The Burrill Family of Lynn," *Register of the Lynn Historical Society* [1907], pp. 114–15; *DAB*).

473. To Charles Lane

[17 July 1844]

To Charles Lane,

Although I have not seen or *heard* directly from you now for sometime yet I have not forgotten your appeals which seemed to me conceived in a spirit so gentle and sincere. I have supposed that I could be of no use to you in the path your mind has taken, and that you therefore did not care to address me, but that, if you thought of me, it was as I have of you as a *friend*. For, with me, that title is not given lightly, and therefore cannot be lightly withdrawn. I suppose it is the same with you.

The act by which you have externized your later views of what is best for the soul in these places and ages, though it does not command my sympathy, does my respect. It seems to me that C.L. might have aided himself and the world more wisely than by becoming a

Shaker, but I doubt not that he has obeyed his conscience in so doing, therefore this part of his history does not seem inharmonious with the good I have known or thought of him.

But other things there are which reach me by hearsay and which disturb the image of you I would wish to retain, and I am anxious to hear from yourself the true version of certain facts.

If you do not answer, or fail to satisfy me, I shall be disappointed but at least, shall have appealed to yourself, instead of lending an easy ear to others.

I said to you once that I thought you would do as you felt you ought. Such has been my confidence I shall leave aside some points in which I myself can find an excuse for seeming fault in you and ask only.

How, with your views about property and having published to the world that the Harvard farm had passed out of human ownership, can Mr Emerson hold it, at your desire, in trust as property of yours?

How can you make it, if you call it yours, a pasture for the cattle of your new colleagues, as it is said you do, with your views as to the use of cattle?

How is it that you are selling the library, which we understood to be left in your care by Mr Greaves for the profit of scholars in the noblest provences to whomsoever has a mind to buy? For I am told you not only part with these books for money to those who, like Mr Emerson, you know will make a good use of them but are anxious to do so in Boston through the agency of Mr Loring to any purchaser that can be found.[1] You are also accused of a course with regard to the Alcotts not to your honor, but I will not ask you about this, as I can find in my own mind an explanation of your acts, though I should be glad to know the exact truth.[2] By answering on these points, you will both give me satisfaction in my own mind, and as enabling me to answer the sorrowful doubts of those who begin to think that those who talk most nobly will infallibly act the least so.

If you will write direct &ce

in trust and hope your friend &ce

ALC (MHi).

The text is a copy made by Fuller in her 1844 journal (MHi), pp. 57–60.

1. When he came to the United States in 1842, Lane brought with him the large library that J. P. Greaves had assembled. When he left Alcott, Lane took the books and later offered them to Emerson. As late as 1854 Lane was still bargaining with Emerson, who had apparently gotten all the books by 1847 (Rusk, *Letters of RWE,* 3:331, 381, 389, 391 and 4:234, 478–79; Edgell, "Bronson Alcott's 'Autobiographical Index,'" p. 714). Ellis Gray Loring was a Boston lawyer who was prominent in the antislavery movement.

2. Lane, in a misguided effort to "save" Alcott, quite clearly tried to separate the Alcotts in order to eliminate their sexual activity (Roger William Cummins, "The Second Eden: Charles Lane and American Transcendentalism," Ph.D. dissertation, University of Minnesota, 1967; Shepard, *Pedlar's Progress*, pp. 376–80; F. B. Sanborn, *Bronson Alcott at Alcott House* [Cedar Rapids, Iowa, 1908], p. 66).

474. To Ralph Waldo Emerson

[20? July 1844]

My dear Waldo,

Did you notice that, when you refused to go to walk and declared the dark aspect of your mental fortunes, the clouds that had been hanging lightly full of silver lustre, grew dark too, bent heavily, and soon began to weep It was as miraculous a coincidence as many that have showed the servitude of Nature to Saint or Prophet! In this instance, I fear me, it bodes no good to the hapless Africans (not Afrites!)[1] let me see how many millions, who will be none the better for your silver tongue!

I always thought the saddest position in the world must be that of some regal dame to whom husband, court, kingdom, world, look in vain for an heir! She is only supposed to eat breathe, move, think, nay![n] love, for the sake of this future blessing. The book[n] of her life is only permitted[?][n] for the sake of its appendix. Meanwhile she, perhaps, persists in living on as if her life by itself were of any[n] consequence, is the mother of no Prince or has even[n] the impertinence to[n] encumber the kingdom with a parcel of Princesses, girls who must be "weel-tochered" to make them of any value.

But what is this pathos compared to that perceptible in the situation of a Jove, under the masculine obligations of all-sufficinyness, who rubs his forehead in vain to induce the Minerva-bearing headach! Alas! his brain remains tranquil, his fancy daughterless! Nature keeps on feeding him and putting him to sleep as if she thought the oak was of consequence, whether it bear the miseltoe or not!

Heaven help thee, my Druid! if this blessed, brooding rainy day do not. It is a fine day for composition were it not in[n] Concord. But I trow the fates which gave this place Concord took away the animating influences of Discord. Life here slumbers and steals on like the river. A very good place for a sage, but not for the lyrist or the orator

Gentle River
stealing on so slowly ever

from reeds that grow thy bank along
easy would flow the pastoral song

    But the shell
Which may be strong for lyric swell
    Or trumpet spire for oratory
    Seek these mid the Tritons hoary,
Where an incalculable wave
Wrecks the warship[n] tall and brave,
Rushes up a mile-long strand
Hails the stars, and spurns the land
Pushes back the noblest River
Seeking in vain its love forever,
    There mightst thou find a shell
Fit to be strung for strains of Delphian swell

But, Waldo, how can you expect the Muse *to come to you*. She hovers near. I have seen her several times, especially near night. Sometimes she looks in at your study windows when she can get a chance, for they are almost always shut, then

    Seeing seated, pen in hand,
By a gentle dubious[n] light,
    One whose eyebeam, purely bright,
Marks him of her chosen band,[n]
    She thinks, "at last I may draw near
And harbor with a mortal find
In the wide temple of his mind
No jangling notes can rend my ear."
    So she furls her various wings,
Breathes a soft kiss on his brow,
    And her lark-like song she sings
As clear as Earth's dull laws airs[n] allow;
    But why sudden stops the strain
Why backward starts that music-form
    Flutters up the heavens again
With backward wings that rouse the storm
    Rouse thunder-peal and lightening glare
In the repelled, earth-wooing air?

    In that temple so divine
She sought at once the inmost shrine
    And saw this thought there graven,—

"Earth and fire, hell and heaven,
Hate and love, black and white,
Life and death, dark and bright,
    All are One
    One alone
  All else is seeming
  I who think am nought
  But the One a-dreaming
  To and fro its thought:
  All is well,
  For all is one;
  The fluid spell
  is the cold stone;
  However voluble
  All life is soluble
  Into my thought;
  And that is nought,
  But self-discovering
  self recovering
  Of the One
  One Alone."

"Ciel!" cried the muse "what then is my music?"
"That" says the oracle "is soul fallen sick,
  To motion excessive
  And by curves successive
  Circling back again
  On the sea a drop of rain."

  "What" says she, "has my song,
My most creative, poised and long
  Genius-unfolding song
No existence of its own?—
Have I no eternal throne
  Deeper based[n] than Fate?
  I thought mine a state
  Permanent as Truth,
  Self-renewing Youth!"
  "It *seemed* so," quoth he
"But there's no Eternity
  Except Identity."
"I dont know what you mean" she cries
"But this I feel

At your cool replies
On my just now so clear eyes
　　Sad films steal;
　　And in my dry throat
　　Rises no clear note;
　　And each wing
To my cold side^n begins to cling;
　　I must away
　　Where the day
　　With many-colored ray
But now an aspect gave
To the worlds, more fair
　　Than they show in this cave,
　　Shut from the living air;
　　Dont lure me here again with your sweet smile
As the sweet herbs that on the mountain grow
Allure the chamois to the path of toil
　　And to the clefts beguile
Through which he falls into the caves below
Where in age-treasured snow buried!—
　　He yields his breath,
Quite unconvinced that life no better is than Death"

AL (MH: bMS Am 1280 [2375]). Published in part in Higginson, *MFO*, pp. 70–71; published entire in Rusk, *Letters of RWE*, 3:252–54, and Miller, pp. 133–34. *Endorsed:* Margaret Fuller / July 1844.

think, nay!] think, ⟨?⟩nay!
The book] ⟨her⟩The book
only permitted] only per⟨?⟩tted
of any] of ⟨no⟩any
Prince or has even the impertinence to encumber] Prince ⟨and⟩ or has ⟨perhaps⟩ ↑even↓ the impertinence ⟨even⟩ to encumber
were it not in] were it not ⟨for⟩ in
Wrecks the warship] Wrecks the w⟨?⟩arship
gentle dubious] gentle du⟨p⟩bious
chosen band,] chosen ba⟨?⟩nd,
as Earth's dull laws airs] as ⟨d⟩ Earth's dull laws ↑airs↓
Deeper based] Deeper ↑based↓
cold side] cold side⟨s⟩

1. Fuller undoubtedly refers to Emerson's "Address Delivered in Concord on the Anniversary of the Emancipation of the Negroes in the British West Indies," which he read on 1 August (*The Complete Works of Ralph Waldo Emerson*, ed. Edward Waldo Emerson [Boston, 1903–4], 11:99–147). Afrites are the second most powerful class of devils in Muslim mythology.

475. To Jane F. Tuckerman

Concord, July 22, 1844

Today I was to end my visit to the Hawthornes and go home, but Ellery being absent in Berkshire, Ellen was seized with a desire to make mother a visit and consult Dr Wesselhoeft, about herself and little one; so I abide and keep her house.

This is very pleasant for me too; I have an excellent sable "help" who shews her teeth with good-humored acquiesence in my every wish; Ellen's house is very still and prettily arranged. I have got my books and writing materials, and such flowers as may be had now, just the same as at home; that fine head of Julius Caesar and Domenichino looking at me from the wall. I have only to go up the hill behind the house to be in Sleepy Hollow. It is very pleasant to be Mr Emerson's neighbor, and to have E. Hoar and the Hawthornes within visiting distance.

At the Parsonage I had a most delightful time; it was so pleasant to be in the old old house with its avenue of whispering trees. The orchard sloping down to the river's bank is delightful, and two hills are near which command the best prospects. Hawthorne has a boat in which he sometimes took me out in the late afternoons. I enjoy being with him much. Mrs H. is very happy, and truly wise in her conduct of life; and the baby, oh Jane! as I have not seen thine since it was very little, I shall dare to say Una is the most beautiful I ever saw. Such harmony of lines and features, such softly-beaming, gracious smiles, such living peace, such sweet little thrills of joy, and such noble bearing; in this last she is like little Waldo, and both different from any infants I have ever seen; Una has more positive *beauty* than Waldo had, though no child could ever be so fair to me!

Ellen's little one, Greta is her pet-name, has suffered much; it has an interesting, almost pathetic look of premature intelligence; I hope it will have more tranquillity now. This is the world of babies! E. H.'s little niece is just dying of water on the brain;[1] this casts a shade. Mr Emerson has another son; I hope they will not call it Waldo,—this would be painful to me.

MsCfr (MH: fMS Am 1086 [Works, 1:103–7]).

1. Probably Elizabeth Howe Storer, who was born on 17 October 1842. She was the daughter of Robert Boyd Storer (1796–1870) and Sarah Sherman Hoar (1817–1907), Elizabeth's younger sister (Malcolm Storer, *Annals of the Storer Family* [Boston, 1927], pp. 52–53, 60–61).

476. To Charles Lane

[26 July 1844]

To Charles Lane;

Thanks for the letter. I cannot doubt that your tendency is upward and onward. May truth be ever more deeply and thoroughly revealed to you!

You are a little sarcastic toward me, I think. This is not quite right. You could not seriously think that, in saying any act of yours did not entirely commend itself to me, I meant to intimate that I myself am in possession of a higher wisdom. I am in no way entitled to counsel or reprove "and to your own" higher sphere the genius of your own life alone could call you.

But, maugre the slight scintillation I think you in the main, received me as I meant. As I should have recd any similar appeal from you.

And so, with thanks once more, I remain your friend. etc.—

ALC (MHi).
The text is a copy made by Fuller in her 1844 journal (MHi), pp. [88]–89.

477. To Caroline Sturgis

Sunday 4th August [1844]

My Caroline, are you prisoned in the little room today, which has fostered Henry Thoreau while checking the rich flow of life into Conglomerate. If so, I think you are reversing the process!

I love these rainy days now, much, much. We have had only one day of *black* rain this summer. That made me think! But these bright rains fall "turning the sod to violets."

The memory of the letters abides with me, though I did not read them well. May no wind or heat tarnish these blooms! I feel more confidence, so much of thought gives body to the song.

Yet sadly, like the deserted heart of an old person, echoes mine, as I think what joy was mine in the case thou wottest of[n] what holy mother's joy in this birth of the soul. I felt that transport as when her parents see the thrill of life pass across little Una's heart and arms, and she sighs from fulness of life, and is what they comprehend.

In the case of mein herzens kind, too, was it not a well grounded hope?[1] Had not he all? the exquisite sense, the recreative genius, the

218

capacity for religion planted in an unsullied youth. My love for him was, indeed, pure; how could there come a shadow? I know it will pass? but how could it come? how could aught of Death poison for one sultry day these pure waters?

Father, thou hast taught me to prostrate myself in the dust, even with my brow in the dust and *ask to be taught.* Yes, teach me, and wash by age-long flood of truth from my being each atom over[n] which these demons of time can assert their power.

Thou, my Caroline, hast lived a more simple and temperate life than I. Thou mayst be worthier to aid souls to a pure and enduring service. The angels may never forsake the gardens into which thou hast dared to invite human forms!

It is pleasant for me this morning our family worship. Only Mother, Richard and I. Mother makes her little simple tearful prayer for love and purity. I read a hymn which she chooses. Today it was that fine one of Wesley's

"My God, my strength, my hope."[2]

Where he expresses such deep desire, for the "godly fear" "the sober certainty of waking" *good* His hymns are all marked by this more searching sense of what is needful. The other sacred hymn-men sigh and pant and pray for good, but he knows himself most deeply and largely

"Bold to take up, *firm to sustain,*
The consecrated cross"

Life opens again before me, longer avenues, darker caves, adorned with richer crystals! May we meet there sometimes! May we enrich one another! It is a still fairer orison to say May we strengthen and purify one another!

I love the humility of that letter of Williams where he so quick recognizes the truth: it was the best of all. May such hours become his guardians! These children of the spirit as they multiply enfold as an angel-cloud, their sire, who still walks the earth a mingled nature, a troubled, tempted man. They breathe back into his heart the breath he has given, and thus strengthened[n] for conquest he becomes at last worthy his own best thoughts. Did you copy for William that poem of Ellen's

"Air, give me air,"[3]

I should think he would like that.

I have before me a good Sunday bouquet A water-lily, sent me from Una yesterday (I drank up the whole spirit of that you gave and it withered but this is fresh) A cardinal flower, (that is one of your flowers,) some magnionette and ambrosia that Mamma Emerson gave me at parting and heliotrope that my own Mother gave me this morning!

Do you know that the Sunflower is about to yield from its seeds large quantities of oil and become one of the most "available American products." This oil we will burn in our silver lamps, perfumed with essence of Verbena.

About our future, I know you cannot tell till you have been to Naushon. That place may again suit you and you may want to stay.

I make no point of our going together I have a horror now of giving importance to associating me with another in any way little or great.

If it should suit us both in September and we could be together in harmony, in a beautiful place, and some new plant grow up under my hand, and perhaps under yours, to redeem the hours, so that we might remember the time and place as a portion of *home* it would be joyful and like the hour of Elizabeth and Mary.[4]

But if not so, Ceres is well accustomed to wander, seeking the other Magna Dea, and to be refused the cup of milk by the peasant, and to have snatched from her the princely nursling that she would baptize with fire.[5]

I said, if we do not go together I will go to some old place, but afterward remembered ways in which I could probably ascertain about new places, especially in the Gloucester neighborhood enough to go to them, by myself, if I wish. So either way will speed.

And I remain while the fruit is ripening on the bough thy friend

MARGARET.

ALS (MH: bMS Am 1221 [227]).

in the case thou wottest of] ↑ in the case thou wottest of ↓

atom over] atom ⟨of⟩ over

thus strengthened] thus ⟨?⟩ strengthened

1. *Mein herzen kind:* child of my heart (that is, Waldo Emerson).

2. Both the title (slightly misquoted) and the following line are from Charles Wesley's hymn "Jesus, My Strength, My Hope."

3. From an untitled poem in a privately published volume of Ellen Hooper's verse (MH) which begins:

> Air, give me air,
> I am burthened and would be
> In an upper atmosphere
> Where is purity . . .

4. In her journal for 1844 (MHi), Fuller makes it clear that her reference is to the meeting of Elisabeth, mother of John the Baptist, and her cousin Mary, mother of Je-

sus: "And Mary arose in those days, and went into the hill country with haste, into a city of Juda; And entered into the house of Zacharias, and saluted Elisabeth. And it came to pass, that, when Elisabeth heard the salutation of Mary, the babe leaped in her womb; and Elisabeth was filled with the Holy Ghost" (Luke 1:39–41).

5. The second Homeric hymn, "To Demeter," tells of the goddess's wanderings in search of her daughter, Persephone, who had been abducted by Hades. Demeter nursed Demophoön, son of Celeus, by day, but by night she hid him in the fire to make him immortal. Her plan, however, was interrupted (*Hesiod, the Homeric Hymns, and Homerica*, ed. Hugh Evelyn-White [London, 1920], pp. 289–323).

478. To Sarah Shaw

[15? August 1844]

Dear Sarah,

I have the vanity to fancy that on your reading table and Sarah's and Anna's may already be found copies of "Summer on the Lakes"[1] I therefore send sets of the etchings made by S. Clarke for the book and wh came too late to be put in the first copies that were sold. I had a few struck off for myself to give my friends and they can be put in just as well after the book is bound as before. The places where they belong are marked on the backs.

You see my "bark is worse than my bite" I have not been able to visit you as I threatened. Cant you come here? I shall be in Cambridge till 15th Sept, your friend though in haste

MARGARET F.

ALS (VtMiM). *Addressed:* Mrs F. Shaw.
1. Probably Sarah Shaw Russell and Anna Blake Shaw, Sarah's sisters-in-law.

479. To Georgiana Bruce

Cambridge 15th August 1844.

Dear Georgiana,

I was greatly entertained and instructed by the Journals. Continue, I beg, to note for me the salient traits of every day. If you really think me capable of writing a Lehrjahre for women, (and I will confess that some such project hovers before me) nothing could aid me so much as the facts you are witnessing

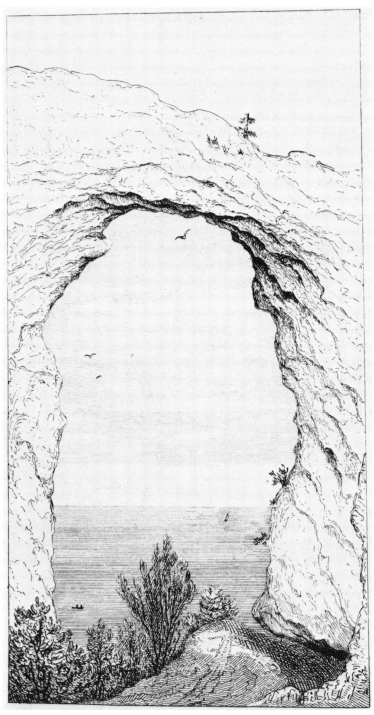

"Mackinaw Island." Etching by Sarah Clarke. Courtesy of the Pennsylvania State University Libraries.

For these women in their degradation express most powerfully the present wants of the sex at large.[1] What blasphemes in them must fret and murmur in the perfumed boudoir, for a society beats with one great heart.

I grieve much that you did not preserve their letters; pray copy if they write you more.

Hope you will stay a year, if circumstances continue as favorable as now. Dully as the days may pass they bring such a scope for observation and thought as can scarcely occur again.

When I can, I will send "The Fairy Queen" to the address you mention, also a set of etchings for "Summer on the Lakes," of which Hecke I believe gave you a copy. They are only in part of the edition, as they make the copies more expensive and I have had some struck off for myself. They are from sketches made by my friend Sarah Clarke on the journey, also etched by her. They can be put into the book as well after binding as before.

I expect soon to publish a more ample version of the Great Lawsuit and if I do, will send you that instead of the number of the Dial which has somehow gone astray to one of the numerous readers who patronized that "noteworthy but unattractive periodical" by borrowing.

I do not attempt to write you a real letter, as I am not well and pressed by various engagements. We break up housekeeping the 20th Septr, there are many affairs to transact. I have something I wish to write and the headach demon is faithful to his prey. But if you write, you will get an answer in some shape, or some time

Meanwhile I shall pay for this sheet as containing only a few lines to thank—

My regards to Mrs Johnson. If I should be on the North River any time in the autumn as is not impossible, I should like to come to Sing Sing. How long could I stay, and what see without disturbing the circle of arrangements?

MARGARET F.

Why dont you write a little narrative of your life on the St Francis.[2] It would not be like writing a journal the Past displays the clear lineaments of objective reality and difficult hills with their tangled forests lie like blue floating islands on the horizon. But perhaps you would rather keep it for a part of[n] your religion

---

ALS (ViU). Published in part in Kirby, *Years of Experience,* p. 207.

for a part of] for ↑a part of↓

1. Some of the prisoners at Sing Sing.

2. Bruce devoted chap. 3 of *Years of Experience* to her life in Melbourne, a village on the St. Francis River in Canada's Quebec province.

480.   To William H. Channing

[1? September 1844?]

[   ] Give me such content as this— And keep awhile the very bliss[n]

You often tell me what to do when you are gone, if you survive me, will you not collect my little flower-pieces, even the insignificant ones. I feel as if from Mother I had received a connexion with the flowers; she has the love, I the interpretation. My writings about them are no fancies but whispers from themselves.

I am deeply taught by the constant presence of any growing thing. This apple-tree before my window I shall mourn to leave. Seeing fruit-trees in a garden is entirely another thing from having this one before my eyes constantly, so that I cant help seeing all that happens to it. But I shall write out the history of our acquaintance and give you a copy.

O how beautiful will be our lives the moment they cease to be per-plexed and harried. Then every accessory will be pertinent, drawn to us by affinity and and reacting on us pleasantly as marriage with con-genial thought. Names and titles too will be quite free from what is adventitious and ugly. I think something of this natural harmony ap-pears now amid a thousand obstacles. It pleases that Raphael and M. Angelo should have recd the archangelic names; it seems inspiration in the parents. So that Swedenborg should bear the name of Emman-uel and Kant, too. The name of Beethoven's mother does not seem without meaning.—[1] In writing yesterday, I observed the names of Mary and Elizabeth meeting again in the two queens with some plea-sure[2] William is the Conqueror. Perhaps it is from such associations that I thought from earliest childhood I could never love one that bore another name. I am glad it was Shakespeare's. Shelley chose it for his child.[3] It is linked with mine in ballad as if they belonged together, but the story is always tragic. In the Douglas tragedy the beauty is more than the sorrow.[4] In one of the later ones the connec-tion is dismal In glided Margaret's grimly ghost and stood at William's feet![5] So shall I never have to reproach thee.

It is pretty with you that the names of Frank and Fanny meet so naturally from the two sides, names of the fosterers of your best lives.[6] At one time when you called Julia "our sweet sister" I thought she might be to me in place of my little sister Julia[7]

ALfr (MB: Ms. Am. 1450 [53]). Published in part in Higginson, *MFO*, pp. 97–98, 101. *Addressed:* William H. Channing / Care W. C. Russell Esq / New York City. *Postmark:* Cambridge MS Sep 2. *Endorsed:* Sept 1844.

the very bliss] the ↑ very bliss ↓ *The entire sentence has been canceled by a later hand.*

1. Maria Magdalena Keverich. Fuller was fascinated by the figure of Mary Magdalene.

2. Fuller, who was then writing *Woman in the Nineteenth Century*, called Elizabeth I and Mary Stuart "types, moulded by the spirit of the time, and placed upon an elevated platform to show to the coming ages, woman such as the conduct and wishes of man in general is likely to make her . . ." (*Woman in the Nineteenth Century*, ed. Joel Myerson [Columbia, S.C., 1980], p. 52).

3. William Shelley, the poet's son, was born on 24 January 1816 and named for his grandfather, William Godwin. The boy died on 7 June 1819 (Newman Ivey White, *Shelley* [London, 1947], 1:426, 2:92).

4. Sir Walter Scott's "Douglas Tragedy," published in his *Minstrelsy of the Scottish Border* (London, 1802). In the ballad William slays Margaret's father and brothers.

5. From David Mallet's "Margaret's Ghost":

> Twas at the silent solemn hour,
>   When night and morning meet;
> In glided Margaret's grimly ghost,
>   And stood at William's feet.

One of the best-known English ballads, the poem was written about 1759 (Thomas Percy, *Reliques of Ancient English Poetry*, ed. Henry B. Wheatley [London, 1886], 3:308–12).

6. Channing's children bore family names: Francis Allston was named for his grandfather, Francis Dana Channing; Frances Maria (Fanny) was named for her mother, Julia Maria, and her maternal grandmother, Maria Verplanck Allen (Higginson, *Descendants of the Reverend Francis Higginson*, p. 32; Edmund J. Cleveland and Horace G. Cleveland, *The Genealogy of Cleveland and Cleaveland Families* [Hartford, Conn., 1899], p. 1769).

7. Channing's wife, Julia Allen Channing, and Fuller's sister Julia, who died in infancy.

481. To Sarah Shaw

Sunday 1st Septr 1844.

My dear Sarah,— Sunday is to me in my way a very holy day. If there are words that require to be spoken with the assurance of pure love and calmness, I wait to see if I can speak them on that day. Therefore I have deferred answering your note.

If you can feel towards me as a Mother, after knowing me so long, I should not be afraid to accept the sacred trust, only I should say, my child, my dear daughter, we are all children together. We are all incompetent to perform any duty well except by keeping the heart bowed to receive instruction *every moment* from the only wisdom. I may have seen more, thought more, may be advanced in mental age beyond you, as you beyond your Anna,[1] and she in turn knows more than the flowers, so that she can water them, when they cannot get water for themselves. But though we are not useless to one another, we cannot be very useful to one another either,[n] other than by clearing petty obstructions from the path which leads to our common home, and cheering one another with assurances of a mutual hope.

The Virgin was made worthy to be the mother of Jesus by her purity. We do not suppose she foresaw intellectually all that was needed for his career. But she commended him to the Spirit that had given him to her. With like desire, if not from the same consecrated life, I could wish good to thee who I believe in thy own wishes and a heart uncorrupted, though, perhaps, frail, worthy of great good.

I advise you not to deal too severely with yourself. There is, probably, a morbid tinge in you, though very little compared with[n] others of your family. Treat it, as I do my headach demons, evade, rather than fight with it. Do not spend time in self-blame so much as solicit the communion of noble and beautiful presences.

No doubt you were married too young and have got to bear a great deal in growing to earthly womanhood with your children. But that is nothing either to you or to them compared with the evils of fancying one self really grown up, because a certain number of years are passed. The children may now have fair play, if not the highest advantages.

You do really need some employment that will balance your life and be your serene oratory when you need one. I will talk of this when we meet. Frank asked me to come when we leave this house (the 19th or 20th) and make you a little visit. I should like much to do that and then we will say *the rest.*

I am desirous for Octr and Novr to go to some beautiful and solitary place, where walking about would be pleasure and excitement enough so that I may give myself undisturbed to some writing and study I have in view. I think a good deal of a place on the North River, but if I do not go *there,* of some bold spot on the sea-shore. Will Sarah R. let me know about that place at Manchester where she was.[2] I have thought I might like to go there from what I heard. I suppose it seems public where *you* were. I want a little description of the spot, the money terms and whether I could go if I want to. Cannot one of you ride over to see me by the 10th or 12th and if you cannot will you write. It would give me great pleasure to have the mosses if you continue to wish to give them to me. It is beautiful to have them pass from the sea to the white paper. I *have* thought of you this summer and always with love as your face beamed on me the first thing in the morning or as you held the dear child and her little hand clasped the cross. You and the children must string the Rosary, together.

We will all be Catholics, but we will grow worthy to worship the Mother and Child by not asking too much aid of them. Our Credos shall be resolute endurance of the forlorn hours, our Pater Nosters and Aves acts of faith and love. And so to your father and my father who is "able to keep us from falling," dear Sarah, I commend you—

On reading over my letter I feel as if I assumed age and wisdom more than is natural to me. But you addressed me as Minerva and I easily took the pedestal. Yet I *am* old enough to know surely that if we persist in aspiration He will not leave us comfortless and what more need a Mother in Israel know?

The association of Undine with these ugly books[n] pictures the course of too many lives.[3]

AL (MH: bMS Am 1417 [176]). *Addressed:* To / Mrs Sarah Shaw / West Roxbury, / there be delivered.

another either,] another ↑ either ↓,
compared with] compared ⟨th⟩ with
ugly books] ugly ⟨B⟩ books

1. The Shaw children were Anna (1836–1923), Robert Gould (1837–63), Susanna (1839–1926), and Josephine (1843–1905). A fifth child, Ellen, was born in 1845 (*Sturgis of Yarmouth*, p. 52; *Boston Daily Evening Transcript*, 24 August 1923; Bradford Adams Whittemore, *Memorials of the Massachusetts Society of the Cincinnati* [Boston, 1964], p. 547).

2. Sarah Shaw Russell.

3. Friedrich de La Motte-Fouqué's *Undine* (Berlin, 1811) is a Romantic fairy tale.

482. To Richard F. Fuller

Cambridge, Sept 20th 44.

My dear Richard,

You will not expect more from me at this time of stress than a few lines just to acquaint you with the leading facts of our condition.

We have got through better than we expected, though Mother and I are both much fatigued. Griffin managed the affairs admirably, was quiet and efficient, Abby, too, did very well in extremis—of pinch.

Mother continues very unwell. I trust you will indeed feel a desire to show her devotion. Without gentle and judicious care to shield her from annoyance, instead of heedlessly inflicting it upon her, she will not remain with us long. The reed is tired of bending to a rude wind and will now easily be uprooted.

We have two excellent letters from Arthur. He is in good spirits and his difficulties decreasing. Still, he thinks you did wisely not to come, and has secured an assistant on his own terms who is likely to do well.

Neither from him or W. H. do answers come which enable to finish the deeds with Mr Lamson;[1] this is a trouble. I have decided to go to N. Y and try it, at least for some months.[2] I feel clear now about doing this.

Have your note safe and shall transfer it to George Kuhn. If you write to me the 29th Septr and address the letter to Canton I shall receive it there. Afterwards write to Mother or write to her *then,* unless you have something special to say to me.[n]

I have suffered much from headach and lost much time. Last week I went to Cohasset for two or three days. There was a noble sea at that time. Since, I have been getting better, but my eyes are much affected.

Your letter was sent to Dr W. He has found the vol. of Diodorus.[3]

Mr and Mrs L. came on Sunday and left Anna with me for the night. I saw her with more leisure and pleasure than any other time and Mother too saw and was extremely pleased with her, of course. She made many inquiries about you. They feel very confident of going to Greenfield.[4]

I can no more now, dear R, and probably cannot again for a month. Then will write at leisure. I am going to[n] the North River 5th Octr Affecy yours

M. F.

ALS (MH: fMS Am 1086 [9:107]); MsC (MH: fMS Am 1086 [Works, 2:731–35]). *Addressed:* Richard F. Fuller / Greenfield / Mass. *Postmark:* Cambridge Sep 23[?].

to say to me] to ⟨do for⟩ ↑ say to ↓ me
going to] going ↑ to ↓

1. The Fullers were selling the Cambridgeport home to Rufus Lamson (1809–79), a Cambridge mason who became a prominent landowner. William Henry and Arthur had sold their portions of the estate to their mother in July, but the papers were not filed until November. Ellen, Margaret, and Mrs. Fuller sold their shares directly to Lamson for a combined price of $2,050 (Middlesex Registry of Deeds, bk. 453; William J. Lamson, *Descendants of William Lamson of Ipswich, Mass., 1634–1917* [New York, 1917], pp. 134, 205).

2. Earlier in the summer, Horace Greeley had offered Fuller a job as his book review editor on the *New-York Daily Tribune*. Her salary was reputed to be $500 a year (Margaret Fuller 1844 journal, MHarF; Anne Weston to Caroline Weston, [27 January? 1845?], MB).

3. Dr W is Robert Wesselhoeft; Diodorus is probably Diodorus Siculus of Agyrium, who wrote a history of the world in forty volumes.

4. Fuller's visitors were the Ellis Loring family. Richard, then studying law with George Davis in Greenfield, fell in love with Anna Loring.

483. To Maria Rotch

Cambridge 25th Septr
1844.

My dear Maria,

Here at your Aunt's this night I find my self unexpectedly in possession of an hour's leisure, and think it is the now or never for me to write to you. Your letter was very pleasing to me. I prize your affece remembrance and shall take always the same interest in your progress through life and in life. Now you are in a scene of more varied charms and instructions than, under the circumstances, England could afford you. I hope and think you will make these of permanent value, and[n] wish you may now be cheered by association with good friends. Write me while in Italy, if you can, such a letter as your last, only *dont cross*. Your handwriting bears it very well, but still there is too much labor for my irritable head in reading crossed pages.

I have just left the house in Ellery St. not without regret, for there many still, and some bright days have been mine. But Richard has taken his degree and gone into a law office, so that all connection between me and the College bell having ceased, I shall like to get beyond reach of its clang.

R. has gone into an office where he has for fellow student one Henry Davis whom he chooses to designate as "Maria's friend," though I believe you knew him only at parties.[1] R. took quite a high rank in his class, and is, every way, improved and improving. Mother is much out of health. She is gone to board for a while in a quiet place, where I hope she may get better. She has had, of late, more care and bustle than are good for her health. Ellen and Ellery are still in Concord, they are happy in a little daughter, born my birthday, named Margaret and known by the pet name of Greta. She is a sweet baby, a clear brunette, with delicate features and large dark blue eyes, which have, young as she is, a contemplative and almost melan-

229

choly expression. I hope she will continue as engaging for Ellen's sake whose heart is engrossed by her.

I am going to pass the autumn in the country on the North River and in December to N. York to try that city for the winter with a view to living there, if my position suits me. I am to *edit*[n] the literary department of the N. Y. Tribune. If you remember Mr Greeley, one of the editors, such an arrangement may not seem to you seducing, but as a's not gold that glitters, so some things that do not glitter may turn to gold. It is a position that offers many advantages and may be turned to much good. I cannot expect, however, to remain free from the usual foibles of Editors and I warn you that, if you write me anything good, it is likely to figure as "interesting communications from a foreign correspondent" in the columns of *my department.* Your friend Anna with her family are removed to a house at some distance from the fashionable region of Boston.[2] Economy obliged to this for two or three years, as they have forestalled their income; but I do not think they will find it a disadvantage. Their friends were real friends, who valued them and not their house and will willingly go a good way to see them. Anna, we suppose, is much better, but she is such a hypochondriac, it is impossible to tell. She is indisposed to the exertions which those around think would do her good. Mr Whelpley is really an interesting young man, pale, handsome, refined, melancholy, with an array of wicked relatives, he may answer as the hero of a small romance all but his name, that we must acknowledge to be plebian.[3] Your ancient acquaintance here have known no important changes. *This* house is even sadder than last winter. Mrs Farrar[n] [   ] It is a great pleasure to her to get your letters; Continue—

And now, dear Maria, I have at least answered all your questions Write again to care Horace Greeley New York, and I will answer when I can. With love to your mother I remain affecly Your friend

S. M. F.

ALS (MH: fMS Am 1086 [9:103]). *Addressed:* Miss Maria Rotch / [not in Fuller's hand] aux soins de Monr J. Glaenzeir / No 14 Boulevard Poissonière / à Paris. *Postmarks:* Liverpool Oc 15 1844. Forwarded from / Harndens / Package Express and Foreign / Letter Office / No 8 Court St Boston. Forwarded by / Harnden & Co / No 20 Water St / Liverpool.

value, and] value ⟨to you⟩, and
to *edit*] to *edit*⟨e⟩
Farrar] *Here several lines have been canceled by a later hand and not recovered.*

1. Richard's classmate Henry Tallman Davis (1823–69), son of John and Susan Tallman Davis of Boston, was admitted to the bar in 1847 but practiced only briefly before becoming a career officer in the army (William T. Davis, *Professional and Industrial History of Suffolk County* [Boston, 1894], 1:433; Edward Wheelwright, *The Class of 1844, Harvard College, Fifty Years after Graduation* [Cambridge, Mass., 1896], pp. 80–82).

2. The Lorings.

3. Probably though not certainly James Davenport Whelpley (1817–72), who had graduated from Yale in 1833 and who was engaged in "literary pursuits" in 1844. He became a doctor but left medicine to edit the *American Whig Review*. His "wicked relatives" were probably Presbyterians, for his father, Philip M., and his grandfather, Samuel Whelpley, were Presbyterian clergymen. The reference may, however, be to his brother, Philip Melancthon Whelpley (Charles Alexander Nelson, ed. *Genealogy of the Morris Family: Descendants of Thomas Morris of Connecticut* [New York, 1911], p. 155; *Statistics of the [Yale] Class of 1837* [New Haven, 1850], p. 43; *Appletons' Cyclopaedia*).

484. To Sarah Hodges

Cambridge
27th Septr 1844.

My dear Sarah,

I am highly gratified with this mark of regard from your Aunt and yourself.[1] It will remind me daily of thoughts that have been very pleasant to me. I hope I may sustain the same relation to my little niece and namesake that your aunt does to you, may aid with fostering love the birth and growth of her mind and share with her the fruits and flowers of two seasons.

The desk is the very thing of all in the world I should be most pleased to receive. I have reced[n] connected with my writing, many gifts the marks of affection that will, I feel, never grow cold, for it is based on the common possession of heavenly hopes. Of these the desk will be the recipient, and I hope to keep it with me always. Its beauty and completeness will make it my companion, such[n] as the good sword of the warrior was to him at an earlier day.

I think, dear Sarah, you cannot go amiss in Fenelon and know not that I could choose unless the volumes were before me. When you want a change try *St Martin*.[2] In Goethe the Iphigenia and Tasso would now reward your patient attention and the thoughtful poems by Schiller, such as "The Artist," stimulate the thinking powers.[3] I have not time now for more. Your sweet little bouquet I shall take with me. The white carnation seems like you. With love and now farewell to your Aunt and yourself

S. MARGARET FULLER.

ALS (MC).

I have reced] I have ↑ reced ↓

my companion, such] my companion, ↑ such ↓

1. Margaret Manning Hodges (1805–87) married George Choate (1796–1880) of

Salem in 1825. In 1844 both the Hodges and the Choate families were living in Cambridge, as was William Henry Fuller (*Hodges Family*, pp. 44, 52, 55).

2. François de Salignac de La Mothe-Fénelon (1651–1715) was a French philosopher and writer. Louis-Claude de Saint-Martin (1743–1803) was a French mystic philosopher influenced by Jacob Böhme.

3. Goethe's *Iphigenie auf Tauris* is a verse play in five acts; his *Torquato Tasso* is another verse play dating from about the same time (1790). Fuller translated *Tasso* in the mid–1830s but never published it. Schiller's *Die Künstler* is a long philosophical poem affirming a belief in moral progress (*OCGL*).

485. To [?]

[Autumn 1844]

"From the brain of the purple mountain"[1] flows forth cheer to my somewhat weary mind. I feel refreshed amid these bolder shapes of nature.[2] Mere gentle and winning landscapes are not enough. How I wish my birth had been cast among the sources of the streams, where the voice of hidden torrents is heard by night, and the eagle soars, and the thunder resounds in prolonged peals, and wide blue shadows fall like brooding wings across the valleys! Amid such scenes, I expand and feel at home. All the fine days I spend among the mountain passes, along the mountain brooks, or beside the stately river. I enjoy just the tranquil happiness I need in communion with this fair grandeur.

ELfr, from *Memoirs*, 2:132–33.

1. Fuller quoted the same Tennyson line in letter 378.

2. On 1 October, Fuller and Sturgis went to Fishkill Landing, New York, for a vacation. Here Fuller completed *Woman in the Nineteenth Century* (Margaret Fuller 1844 journal, MHi).

486. To [?]

[Autumn 1844]

The boldness, sweetness, and variety here, are just what I like. I could pass the autumn in watching the exquisite changes of light and shade on the heights across the river. How idle to pretend that one could live and write as well amid fallow flat fields! This majesty, this calm splendor, could not but exhilarate the mind, and make it nobly free and plastic.

El, from *Memoirs*, 2:133.

487. To Christopher P. Cranch

Fishkill Landing N. Y.
[Autumn 1844]

Dear fellow pilgrim and mountain pastor,

I cannot suffer that Mr. Churchill should be indebted to you for the douceur rendered necessary on account of my age and infirmities.[1] Rarely have I disbursed the needed fee with such satisfaction. What a delightful unity on that day, how fine the lights upon the hills and river during our first drive. How alluring the scene of the Sketch; then the deep solitude of the cave, only relieved by the social harmonies from below! How beautiful our feet upon the mountain as we descended, sweetly human our intercourse with the laborers of the Brick Yard, and the return home, with its happy mixture of ride and walk! so that your pencil alone can do justice, but neither will we forget what we cannot express. We have now enjoyed together two entertainments each perfect in its way.

When the genius of Bellini
Gave forth its sorrowing tones
Through the croak of battelini
For the ear of Mrs. Jones,
We from good-humored Knickerbocken height
Saw Fashion rouging in the candle light
And laughed while Music shrieked and swooned in fright.
Now we had chosen another point of view
Ideal cavern on the mountain height
From which we Nature's windings may pursue
And choose the colors for a fresh delight
Recast by art in combinations new: —
She* veils her brow at once with mist so thick
Mixes the river and the earth for brick,
And mocks at Art's expected juggling trick.

*Nature is here alluded to.

MsCfr (MB: Ms. Am. 1450 [59]).

Christopher Pearse Cranch graduated from the Divinity School in Cambridge in 1835 but was never ordained. An artist and a poet, he devoted his life to the arts. He lived for years in Italy, where he and his wife were Fuller's close friends. He wrote for both the *Western Messenger* and the *Dial (DAB)*.

1. Which Mr. Churchill Fuller mentions is not clear, for the family was large and prominent in the Fishkill area.

488. To Richard F. Fuller

[I] Fishkill Landing
15th Octr 1844.

My dear Richard, I was much pleased to see from your letter to Mother that you were well content with abode, companions, and head lawyer; Now I should like a full letter to myself giving a clearer look into the Mind. Direct to me here and be careful to write *Fishkill Landing*, as Fishkill is another place some miles distant.

I found Mother more pleasantly situated than I had expected. The view from her room was pleasant, and the carpet made it look comfortable. But I suppose she will never sit there. She seemed a little better. Aunt Abba was full of kindness and I hope will persist to show it by gentleness and consideration in little things. They were all much pleased by your letter, justly observing it was a "very pretty" one

The last face I saw in Boston was Anna Loring's, looking after me from Dr Peabody's steps. Mrs P. stood behind her some way up nodding adieux to the "darling" as she addressed me, somewhat to my emotion They seemed like a frosty November afternoon, and a soft summer twilight when Night's glorious star begins to shine. I had only time to bid Anna a hasty farewell. They then intended going to Greenfield and have, I trust, done so ere this. Write me about it.

A bundle sent by Ellen I left with them and requested Mrs Farrar to procure and send you Mr Emerson's address of 1st August.

I had a very agreeable visit from Dr Wesselhoeft. He showed himself desirous of assisting me to procure foreign intelligence for the Tribune and gave me advice about my arrangements, not practicable under the circumstances, but excellent in itself. He sent through Von Raumer a copy of my translation to Dr Eckermann.[1] I think his friendship will be of real value to you. The full look of his eye commands respect and affection.

Can I tell you how much I enjoy being here in this scene of majestic beauty, away from hacknied human thoughts and petty cares. I felt regret at leaving Boston, so many marks of friendship were shown me, at the last[n] so many [II] friendships true, though imperfect, were left behind. But now I am so glad to be enfranchised for a few weeks and left to the society of Nature and the current of my own thoughts.— It is pleasanter than at the West in this that I have a well-ordered quiet house to dwell in and nobody's humor, but my own, to consult— From my windows I see, over the tops of variegated trees, the river with the purple heights beyond and a few minutes walk brings me to its lovely shore. Sails glid[e] past continually, and the great boats stride onward with echoing steps, making waves[n] of their own, whose rush relieves the more stealthy sound of the river ripples. If I go back in the country, there are mountain paths, and lonely glens and rushing streams with many-voiced waterfalls. Such you have also at Greenfield, though less wild and beautiful.

I have, however, had only three days yet of positive leisure. These were of the finest October weather.[n] Now we have had two or three days of rain which I have employed in writing up my letters. As soon as this is done I shall give myself up entirely to rambles in the open air, which I much need to renovate my strength. I am not very well and do not feel as if my mind had had leisure *enough* for a long time. The premature exhaustion of my forces makes me require a great deal of time now for the mind to lie fallow before it can produce its natural harvest.— Mr Greeley has taken a beautiful place near N. Y. If this home should be as pleasant within as without I should much enjoy living there. But things did not look promising for that when I was in N. Y. So I shall try to make the most of my present life, which is more in my own power.

Farewell dear Richard. Remember me with much regard to George Davis. Ever your friend as well as sister

MARGARET.

I: ALfr (MH: fMS Am 1086 [9:124]); II: ALfrS (MH: fMS Am 1086 [9:107a]). MsCfr (MH: fMS Am 1086 [Works, 2:737–39, 779–83]). Published in part in *Memoirs*, 2:132. *Addressed:* To / Richard F. Fuller, / Greenfield, / Mass. *Postmark:* Oct 15.

me, at the last] me, ↑ at the last ↓
making waves] ma⟨de⟩king waves
October weather.] October ⟨leisure⟩ ↑ weather ↓ .

1. Friedrich Ludwig Georg von Raumer (1781–1873) traveled widely and wrote on history, law, and economics. His *Geschichte Europas*, which he began in 1832, was not completed until 1850. Johann Peter Eckermann was Goethe's secretary from 1823 until the poet's death in 1832. He published *Gespräche mit Goethe in den letzten Jahren seines Lebens*, which Fuller translated in 1839 as *Eckermann's Conversations with Goethe*. Eckermann lived in Weimar until his death in 1854.

489. To Georgiana Bruce

Fishkill Landing,
20th Octr 1844.

Dear Georgiana,

In consequence of the many changes of place I have made of late your package has only very lately reached me. I have read it with great interest The two characters are such as I have had least opportunity of knowing.[1] Satira's idealizing of herself in the face of cruellest facts belongs to the fairest, most abused part of feminine Nature.

Eliza's account of her strong instinctive development is excellent, as clear and racy as Gil Blas.—[2] I suppose these women have spoken with more spirit and freedom than any whites would; have they not?

You say few of these women have any feeling about chastity. Do you know how they regard that part of the sex, who are reputed[n] chaste? Do they see any reality in it; or look on it merely as a circumstance of condition, like the possession of fine clothes? You know novelists are fond of representing them as if they looked up to their more protected sisters as saints and angels!

I was prevented by attacks of headach from finishing the pamphlet on Women in August. I hope to do it here, as I remain till Decr At present, however, I pass all the fine weather in the open air, and grow strong daily. Meanwhile every hint from you will be of use to my thoughts. And I shall have an oppory to talk with you, for if Mr Channing goes to Sing Sing next Sunday as he expects, I shall go too; if I hear from him that any unforseen cause prevents, I shall still come another day. Caroline Sturgis, who is with me here, will come too.

I am much pleased by your plan of going to Illinois in the spring.[3] You are much more likely to find a fit sphere there than at the South. But of this, too, I will talk when I come, rather than write now, as writing is not good for me, and I am like to have so much to do, that I must avoid all I can.

One thing I wish to say however, lest the time of my seeing you should be delayed. You said you would write an account of your past, if I asked it. I do ask, if you can do it freely. The record, if written with any thing like the force and vivacity you tell it, and with[n] care for arrangement and finish would be in itself of much value, and bring[n] to you the sort of discipline you have desired. And I should think this winter of seclusion, before entering on a new and various life, might be the very, or the only time for it.

I will now say farewell for this time. If I do not come a letter will reach me here by post, or a parcel would addressed to Mr Van Vliet's boarding house. But I shall probably come.

Your friend

S. M. FULLER—

I was at Brook Farm a few hours before I came away, but had no chance to see things fairly. The wheels seemed to turn easily, but there was a good deal of sound to the Machinery; it did not move quite as effortless and sweet as we dream that angel harpings will.

ALS (CSt). Published in part in Kirby, *Years of Experience*, pp. 211, 218. *Addressed:* Miss Georgiana Bruce / Sing Sing / State of New York. *Postmark:* Fishkill Landing / Oct 21. *Endorsed:* S M. Fuller / Oct—22nd 44.

are reputed] are ⟨so⟩ reputed
and with] and ⟨written⟩ with
and bring] and ⟨be⟩ bring

1. Georgiana Bruce apparently sent Fuller a set of journals from some of the women prisoners at Sing Sing.

2. Alain-René Lesage, *The Adventures of Gil Blas of Santillane*, is a picaresque novel, first published in 1715–35.

3. Bruce went to Cincinnati, not Illinois, in 1845 (Kirby, *Years of Experience*, p. 227).

490.   To Elizabeth Hoar

Oct 20 [28?] 1844

We have just been passing Sunday at Sing Sing. We went with William Channing: he staid at the chaplain's we at the prison. It was a noble occasion for his eloquence and I never felt more content than when at the words "Men and Bretheren," all those faces were upturned like a sea swayed by a single wind and the Shell of brutality burst apart at the touch of love divinely human. He visited several of them in their cells and the incidents that came were moving.

On Sunday they are all confined in their cells after 12 at noon that their keepers may have rest from their weekly fatigues, but I was allowed to have some of the women out to talk with and the interview was very pleasant. They were among the so called worst, but nothing could be more decorous than their conduct, and frank too. All passed much as in one of my Boston Classes. I told them I was writing about Woman and as my path had been a favoured one I wanted to ask some information of those who had been tempted to pollution and sorrow. They seemed to reply in the same spirit in which I asked. Several however expressed a wish to see me alone, as they could then say *all*, and they could not bear to before one another: and I intend to go there again, and take time for this. It is very gratifying to see the influence these few months of gentle and intelligent treatment have had on these women: indeed it is wonderful, and even should the State change its policy, affords the needed text for treatment of the subject.

MsCfr (MH: bMS Am 1280 [111, pp. 116–18]). Published in part in *Memoirs*, 2: 144–45; published entire in *JMN*, 11:479, and Chevigny, p. 335.

In her letter of 20 October to Georgiana Bruce, Fuller mentions plans to visit Sing Sing next Sunday (26 October). On 23 November she wrote Richard that she had visited three weeks since (which would have been 26 October). Thus Emerson misdated this letter, which was probably written soon after Fuller's return to Fishkill.

491. To The Women Inmates at Sing Sing

[Early November? 1844]

My Friends:

After my visit, which, though short, was sufficient to inspire great interest in your welfare and hope for your improvement, I wrote to some of the ladies of Boston on your account, and they will send you books which may, I hope, encourage the taste for reading which it gave me pleasure to hear that so many of you show. Should you acquire a habit of making good books your companions they will form your minds to a love of better pleasures than you have hitherto possessed. In those cases—and they are the greater number—where a naturally good disposition has been obscured by neglect in childhood and a want of proper food for the mind and heart, the wheat will have a chance to grow up and the tares to be choked by acquaintance with pure thoughts and the better purposes for which life was intended by its Giver.

I wrote in your behalf to several of the best and loveliest women I know, for I was sure that these would be the most eager to do any thing in their power to aid their unhappy sisters. I hope you will accept these books as a token that, though on returning to the world you may have much to encounter from the prejudices of the unthinking, yet there are many who will be glad to encourage you to begin a new career, and redeem the past by living lives of wise and innocent acts, useful to your fellow-creatures and fit for beings gifted with immortal souls. Among these you may depend on

Yours with friendliest good wishes,

S. M. FULLER.

EL, from Kirby, *Years of Experience*, pp. 212–13.

492. To William H. Channing

[3? November 1844]

[   ] remarks. These latter, however, you probably heard, wher-

238

Sing Sing Prison, Ossining, New York. From *American Scenery*, ed. N. P. Willis (London, 1840); courtesy of the Pennsylvania State University Libraries.

ever you were. Indeed I have for sometime back commissioned the angelic messenger with one advice to you of especial importance [   ]

Alone myself I have begun the day, by reading Waldo's book.[1] (Out-doors I cannot. I read it one day high up in the mountain side amid a bed of large loose stones that seemed only held together by the vines; wings rustled near. It seemed so much less feeling than nature, instead of being more so, as man should be. But even Confucius is too civic and limitary for outdoor reading.) But the Essays did not chime with in-door life either this morning. Then I wrote these lines to the Apollo on my pin which I like to wear these Jew ordained Sundays.

> I thank the hand which gave this gift to me
> The Delphian image of my destiny.
>   'Tis not the Sun-God, radiantly calm.
> Whose tameless wheels over this worldlet run,
>
>   Calling to life the poison as the balm,
> White birds to worship, wily snakes to shun.
>   'Tis not the Pythian with shaft just sped,
> Avenging sunbeam from that spotless fire,
>
>   Form of stern loveliness, a beauteous dread,
> The sounding bow more than the sounding lyre.
>   It is the Shepherd Singer, heavenly sweet,
> At sight of whom mild flocks and rustic men
>
>   Left their green pastures when his snowy feet
> Turned rather downward through the rocky glen,
>   To where the beach, with ocean wild and wide
> A larger consciousness of life supplied.
>
>   It is the Shepherd Singer, heavenly sad,
> Who vainly loved so many lovely forms;
>   They answered not, or, answering, fell mad,
> And whitest halcyon boded darkest storms;
>
>   Imprisoning bark must fondest bosom wrong,
> And naught is left the Singer but his Song.
>
>   It is enough,—melodiously sad!
> More than enough,—harmoniously glad!
>
>   Earth strings the lyre, but not from earth alone
> Findst thou vibration for its faintest tone.

240

Love filled the eye, but, if beheld too near,
We lose the diamond lustre of the tear.
    When into Genius Love flows back again
One lyric flame from breasts of many men,
    We see the Son back to his home aspire
The Delphian baptized in his own life's fire.
    Thus the Anointed pleases well his Sire,
Soul Poem for the Universal Lyre.

It is enough to frighten versifiers though to be called on by Mrs De Wint.[2] She came and brought a copy of the annual[n] [   ] It was well you [   ] equal to the o[   ] works also. [   ] April night [   ]citement [   ] dentalist [   ] were out [   ] friend it, [   ] to Mrs. W[   ] it decla[   ] Transcen[   ] "if moth [   ] see Mrs [   ] Storey w[   ] and have [   ] would [   ] give it [   ]

ALfr (MB: Ms. Am. 1450 [54]). *Addressed:* To / William H. Channing / City of New York. *Postmark:* New York Nov 5.

you were] you ⟨are⟩ were
the *Annual*] *This and the preceding sentence have been canceled by a later hand.*

1. Emerson's *Essays: Second Series* was published by James Munroe in October 1844. He noted in his journal for 15 October that he had sent a copy to Fuller (Rusk, *Letters of RWE*, 3:264; *JMN*, 9:128).

2. Christopher Cranch's mother-in-law was Caroline Amelia Smith (1795–1852), granddaughter of John and Abigail Adams, who married John Peter De Windt (1787–1870) of Fishkill (*New Letters of Abigail Adams, 1788–1801*, ed. Stewart Mitchell [Boston, 1947], n.p.).

493. To William H. Channing

Sunday eveg
17th Novr 1844.

At last, my dear William, I have finished the pamphlet.[1] The last day it kept spinning out beneath my hand. After taking a long walk early on one of the most noble exhilarating sort of mornings I sat down to write and did not put the last stroke till near nine in the evening Then I felt a delightful glow as if I had put a good deal of my true life in it, as if, suppose I went away now, the measure of my foot-print would be left on the earth. That was several days ago, and I do not know how it will look on revision, for I must leave[n] several days more between me and it before I undertake that, but think it will be much better than if it had been finished at Cambridge, for here has been no headach, and leisure to choose my hours.

It will make a pamphlet rather larger than a number of the Dial, and would take a fortnight or more to print. Therefore I am anxious to get the matter *en train* before I come to N. Y. that I may begin the 1st Decr for I want to have it out by Christmas. Will you then see Mr Greeley about it the latter part of this week or the beginning of next. He is absent now, but will be back by that time and I will write to him about it. Perhaps he will like to undertake it himself.

The estimate you sent me last summer was made expecting an edition of fifteen hundred, but I think a thousand will be enough. The writing, though I have tried to make my meaning full and clear, requires, shall I say? too much culture in the reader[n] to be quickly or extensively diffused. I shall be satisfied if it moves a mind here and there and through that others; shall be well satisfied if an edition of a thousand is disposed of in the course of two or three years

If the expense of publication should not exceed a hundred or even[n] a hundred and fifty dollars, I should not be unwilling to undertake it, if thought best by you and Mr G. But I suppose you would not think that the favorable way as to securing a sale.

If given to a publisher I wish to dispose of it only for one edition. I should hope to be able to make it constantly better while I live and should wish to retain full command of it, in case of subsequent editions.[n] [   ] to be made up before coming here. If Mr. G. really did expect him to write whig editorials, that, I agree with you, he could not do, but I do not think he has ascertained Mr. G's design, and he will go home without doing so.[2]

[   ] seeing him, for the [   ] But I ha[   ] lives none with whom I stand at present in mental relations who does not know the whole of my though[t] about him E said he could alter nothing, still it [   ]

Last night I kept dreaming of you delivering your discourse I heard whole sentences and many tones of voice so I had the benefit of this day's utterance before those who heard it perchance

Adieu dear friend.

ALfr (MB: Ms. Am. 1450 [55]). Published in part in Higginson, *MFO*, pp. 201–2, and Wade, pp. 567–68.

    must leave] must ⟨put⟩ ↑ leave ↓
    culture in the reader] culture ↑ in the reader ↓

or even] or ↑ even ↓

editions.] *The remainder of the sheet has been cut away.*

1. The New York firm of Greeley & McElrath published *Woman in the Nineteenth Century* in February 1845.

2. Her subject is Ellery Channing, who was working for Greeley's paper. Emerson described the greeting Channing got in New York: "Greeley, sick & prostrate, was just leaving the city—he threw to Channing some broadest general directions, & left him to make his own work,—the one thing he could not do." By March 1845 Channing was back home in Concord (Rusk, *Letters of RWE*, 3:268; Robert N. Hudspeth, *Ellery Channing* [New York, 1973], pp. 30–31).

494. To Ralph Waldo Emerson

Fishkill Landing
17th Novr 1844.

I wanted to write, before, dear Waldo, and thank you for the book, but my pen has been a weary with other writing rainy days and evegs and fine days I have spent almost wholly in exercise. This writing has consisted in great part of the never-sufficiently-to-be-talked-of pamphlet, which is at last finished.

I have been happy now in freedom from headach and all other interruption and have spun out my thread as long[n] and many-colored as was pleasing. The result I have not yet looked at; must put some days between me and it first. Then I shall revise and get it into printer's ink by Christmas, I hope.

Your book I have read quite through some of it in the neighborhood of hawks and such like, but will not mar the effect by a few inadequate words. It will be a companion through my life. In expression it seems far more adequate than the former volume, has more glow, more fusion. Two or three cavils I should make at present, but will not, till I have examined further if they be correct.

Your Pentameron I wish I could send now, but am not sure I can be ready.[1] It has been a great pleasure to us to have it The Desatir I want to keep awhile for *Sunday reading*.[2] I will not keep it always.

We go to N. Y. the latter part of next week, and after that Cary will return to Mass in about ten days. We have had a most satisfactory time here so pleasantly together and apart. Ellery shared some of our days on the mountains and can tell you about them, if he will.[n] We have had no social interruptions, and, to me, this tranquillity before the bustle of the winter has been precious. Being out in the open[n] air so much and in such a bold exhilarating scene, books and thought

243

also have had their natural zest,[n] and the seven weeks seem a piece out of the pure blue.

Ellery will bring you this. Probably you will not be surprized to see him back even so soon. He seems to know himself—and be sure that he cannot stay. I have wished he would see Mr Greeley again, and know whether he had all the facts before him but suppose he will not. If it is really just as he supposes, I think, myself, he cannot stay.[3]

I hope you will write to[n] me soon, and as often as you can. I shall feel my separation from almost[n] all that has been companionable to me I suppose when fairly installed in my business life.

Sterling's death was a painful surpriz I thought he would get better and do a little more in our house here.[4]

How is Elizabeth? really well again? Some one spoke of her as having a cough In a letter to me, she[n] spoke of a journey southward;—how far South? I wish it might be to Washington and Baltimore An entire change of scene and association would do her good. Caroline directed a letter to her to the care of your brother William in N. Y. After I know where she is, I shall write to her again, if I have leisure.

Give love to Lidian and Mamma and please mention whether the latter is again quite well.

I enclose a little poem written here which I wish you would have put with the Fourth[n] July ones; you will then have a complete inventory of my emblems and trappings *"in case of death."*[n] Have you safe those I gave you of the All Saints Day etc? I cannot find my copy and though I presume it is only mislaid, feel uneasy lest they should pass out of existence, for to me they are the keys of dear homes, in the past. So I commend them to your care and if I do not find mine, shall by and by have another copy taken of them

Ever affecy yours

MARGARET.

Cranch, Caroline, William and I received our copies of the book at the same time and sat solemnly each with a copy in hand drawing our fates. Suddenly we saw the comic of the scene and laughter was full if not loud.

ALS (MH: bMS Am 1280 [2376]). Published in part in Higginson, *MFO*, p. 201; published entire in Rusk, *Letters of RWE*, 3:269–70. *Addressed:* To / R. W. Emerson / Concord / Mass. *Endorsed:* Margaret F / Nov. 1844.

as long] as ⟨?⟩long
if he will.] if ↑ he ↓ you will.
the open] the ⟨?⟩open

natural zest,] natural z⟨?⟩est,
write to] write ↑ to ↓
from almost] from ↑ almost ↓
me, she] me, ↑ she ↓
the Fourth] the ⟨oth⟩ Fourth
trappings *"in case of death."*] trappings. ↑ *"in case of death"* ↓

1. Walter Savage Landor, *Pentameron and Pentalogia* (London, 1837).
2. Emerson owned a copy of *The Desâtîr or Sacred Writings of the Ancient Persian Prophets* (Bombay, 1818) (Harding, *Emerson's Library*).
3. The details are obscure, but Channing did return to New York and the *Tribune*.
4. The Irish poet John Sterling (1806–44) died on 18 September *(DNB)*. Fuller twice reviewed Sterling's work: *Dial* 2 (1841):135 and 4 (1844):327–49.

495. To Sarah Shaw

Fishkill Landing
20th Novr 1844.

My dear Sarah,

Two months have passed since I was with you, passed with winged swiftness, yet that swiftness has not been as that of the arrow straight to one mark, but rather as that of the bee who finds time to stop wherever he can collect his honey. Happy and blessed have been the weeks of seclusion, the society of the mountains, so bold and so calm, the long mountain paths that suggest the enchantments of nature, the spells of wisdom waiting in the secret for the approach of patient steps; the river so grand and fair with its two thousand sail, each moving softly as an angel's thought, and looking, *in the distance,* as spotless and glittering; and its great boats advancing now and then[n] with a triumphant stride, like some[n] noble discovery breaking in upon the habitual course of human events to inform and extend it.— Then, after the days of exercise, how pleasant the evenings of study or writing by the bright wood fire. The days come to an end solid and unbroken by frivolity or conflict.

Next week it ends and I return from this pleasant life of the *free nun* to the busy rushing world. But I am willing; after such a pleasant time I feel refreshed for the melée and willing to take my share of the press of life.

If you send the box by the 28th to the office of the N. Y. Tribune directed to me Care Horace Greeley, the friendly warmth of your gifts will defend my heart from the cold, as I walk the wide streets of the stranger and meet their foreign gaze.

It pleases me much to combine you two in one gift. I shall think of all that is pleasantest, of my Sarah "the Mother" and of her frank and loving intercourse with me. I shall think of Frank, *the* Frank, and his wise plans for the good of injured men.— Cary says the Forbes s also are anxiously plotting such means of reform.[1] So if Jesus came here, he would not find all unjust stewards.[2]

Say to Anna that her swift and warm response gave me joy. I shall write to her when I have leisure. Love to Sarah.[3] In the spring she gave me violets, in the autumn grapes, was not that expressive of the promi[se] given by her grand nature? Good angels tend it to its proper flower and fruit!

I wish you would write to me fully of yourself and of the children. And tell me also *the news,* which no one writes us. We heard J. King and W. Story were dangerously ill, but not the result.[4] Now in the distance I want some facts as well as thoughts from my friends.

As to the letter for[n] Dr Elliot, I am so well now, it seems as if I should never more be ill, but I suppose the old causes may bring on the old results, and I want some refuge in case of violent assault from my enemy, so should like the letter to use in case of need.[5]

Is the St. with you and if so, how does the plan prosper? I did what I could for you by persuading the Farrars to try her, but in a few hours Mr F. pronounced her a "well intentioned woman of tolerable manners[n] but weak and silly." So, of course, she would not answer there. Of other things, too, you were to write me.

I have enjoyed being with Cary. Our relation has been entirely pleasant, and to me often profitable.

Adieu, dear Sarah, give kisses to the gay little troop, especially the opera dancer, whose inventions it makes me laugh to recollect Always your friend

M. F.

ALS (MH: bMS Am 1417 [177]). Published in Wade, pp. 569–70. *Addressed:* To / Mrs Sarah Shaw / Care F. G. Shaw Esq / West Roxbury / Mass. *Postmark:* Fishkill Landing N. Y. Nov 21.

and then] and the⟨m⟩n
like some] ⟨?⟩like some
letter for] letter ⟨from⟩ ↑ for ↓
tolerable manners] tolerable manners⟨"⟩

1. Probably John Murray Forbes (1813–98) and his wife, Sarah Hathaway Forbes. Forbes, a railroad financier who owned Naushon Island, where Fuller and Sturgis vacationed, was active as a reformer *(DAB).*
2. The parable of the unjust steward, Luke 16:1–12.
3. Sarah Shaw's sisters-in-law, Sarah Shaw Russell and Anna Shaw.
4. William Wetmore Story, the son of Judge Joseph Story of Cambridge, was a bril-

liant lawyer who later renounced the law for sculpture and moved to Italy. Despite Fuller's early coldness toward Story, the two became fast friends when she moved to Rome in 1847.

5. Probably Augustus Greele Elliot (1821–1911) of New York City, a Yale graduate who was at that time on the staff at the New York City Hospital (*Greeley Family*, p. 638; *New-York Daily Tribune*, 14 May 1911).

496. To Richard F. Fuller

Fishkill Landing
23d Novr 1844.

Dear Richard,

I think you may by this time like to hear further notices of your sister's position in these circuits and alternations of our lives. Yet I have not to speak of alternations, only of a portion of pleasing peaceful circuit

The *seven weeks* of proposed abode here draw to a close, and have brought what is rarest, fruition of the sort proposed from them. I have been here all the time except that three weeks since I went down to N. Y. and with W. Channing visited the prison at Sing Sing. This was every way good. I went down on a Friday, seeing the Highland pass in bright hues and purple shadows. A woman on board observed to me that she "had come down by the day boat because she was told there were things here worth seeing." I assured her she had not been misinformed and that she was now on the very spot where these things were. I then pointed her attention to the lofty mountain called "the Crow's Nest" she gazed awhile, and then, with a sigh, admitted "Well! this does beat all!"

On Saturday we went up to Sing Sing in a little way-boat, thus seeing that side of the river to much greater advantage than we can in the mammoth boats. We arrived in resplendent moonlight by which we might have supposed the prisons palaces if we had not known too well what was within.

On Sunday W. C. addressed the male convicts in a strain of the most noble and pathetic eloquence. They listened with earnest attention; many were moved to tears, some, I doubt not, to better life. I never felt such sympathy with an audience, as I looked over that sea of faces marked with the the traces of every ill, I felt that, at least, heavenly truth would not be kept out by self-complacency and a dependence on good appearances.

I talked with a circle of women and they showed the natural aptitude of the sex for refinement. These women, some black and all from the lowest haunts of vice, showed a sensibility and a sense of[n] propriety which would not have disgraced any place.

When we returned we had a fine storm on the river clearing up with strong wind, and the mountains in their veils. Since then I have finished at leisure *the pamphlet,* and written one or two trifles, also studied much in evenings, Taylor's translations of the old Greek writers, the Confucious, the Desater, and Alkuna, a Scandinavian mythology, have been my best books.[1] I have also read with great delight Landor's Pentameron, rejoicing to find a book of his that is new to me. One of my few regrets at not having money is that I cannot own all[n] his works. I do own most other[n] book[s] of my contemporaries that I prize. H[ow]ever I have him much by heart and own the Pericles and Aspasia. I hope to get his books reprinted here and then *can* own them.

All the fine weather I have passed in the mountain passes, along the mountain brooks or the river. My mind has not been active, but in quiet happiness lived with this fair grand nature. It has been to me just what I wanted and I will not forget to be grateful.

I have seen almost no people, except those who board[n] in this house. With these my relation has been pleasant and afforded amusing incidents and narratives which you, no doubt, will sometime hear.

I am most unusually well, scarce ever a headach, and do not need to lie down all day. I do just enough for my strength and so do it well, in hours unbroken by petty interruptions.

Ellery was here 3 days one of which he passed in the mountains with us; the meeting was very pleasant. He is now in N. Y whither I also go in two or three days I do not begin with the Tribune till 1st Decr

Write to me there, care H. Greeley. Tell more of your new surroundings and your thoughts. I hope the historical studies continue. That will be something noble and solid I expect to give *myself* now for some time to small things except Sundays

I have little news from Boston and none that would interest you. I suppose Mr and Mrs Motte can tell you a good deal.[2] Farewell dear Richard, I shall have little time to write, but will when I can and am ever affecy yr sister

M.

Have you read Mr E's new volume?

ALS (MH: fMS Am 1086 [9:108]); MsCfr (MH: fMS Am 1086 [Works, 2:739–49]). Published in part in *Memoirs,* 2:144–45, and *WNC,* p. 373. *Addressed:* Richard F. Fuller / Greenfield / Mass. *Postmark:* Fishkill Landing N. Y. Nov 25.

The Memoirs *version badly mixes the letter with that of* 10 December 1845 *to Richard Fuller.*

a sense of] a ↑ sense of ↓
own all] own ↑ all ↓
own most other] ↑ own ↓ most ↑ other ↓
who board] who b⟨?⟩oard

1. Thomas Taylor (1758–1835) was a self-taught neoplatonist who was much admired in the United States. Fuller probably read his *Classical Tracts* (London, 1831) or *The Mystical Initiations; or, Hymns of Orpheus* (London, 1787).
2. Probably Mellish I. Motte and his wife, Mary Ann. Motte was the Unitarian minister in Greenfield in the 1850s (*Heralds*, 3:259).

497. To Charles K. Newcomb

Fishkill Landing
25th Novr 1844.

My dear Charles,

I have thought of you very often here and wished you were with me. You would have been perfectly happy as I have in the company of the mountains They are companions both bold and calm; they exhilarate and they satisfy. Being close on the great river too so long has been the realazation of a dream, and this has been my life. Though I have studied books and thought thoughts yet *this* has been my life.

Of this life I have nothing to say so that all my writing is only as a word of affection from the distance which you said would be pleasant.

Caroline and I have had a very harmonious relation, so that I have not been prevented as you feared I might from enjoying my peace of mind. She has been friendly, sisterly, and enough of a companion. We have lived much apart, but enjoyed the thought that each was present here.

Your Mother wrote that early in the winter she should come with you to N. Y. Of this we shall be glad. I hope it may be when Ole Bull is there or some good music. I am going now to the City in a day or two. I dread it; the civic life from which so long I have been excused, yet am willing for a sacred seven weeks tranquillity have been granted here, and now, all round me is turned corpse-like cold; The river from blue to lead, the mountains from purple to gray. Adieu, dear Charles

I do not ask you to write, only because it would be useless, I know. Ever yours,

M.

ALS (MH: fMS Am 1086 [10:143]). Published in part in *Memoirs*, 1:264. *Addressed:* Charles King Newcomb / Brook Farm.

498. To [?]

[December 1844]

This place is, to me, entirely charming; it is so completely in the country, and all around is so bold and free.[1] It is two miles or more from the thickly settled parts of New York, but omnibuses and cars give me constant access to the city, and, while I can readily see what and whom I will, I can command time and retirement. Stopping on the Haarlem road, you enter a lane nearly a quarter of a mile long, and going by a small brook and pond that locks in the place, and ascending a slightly rising ground, get sight of the house, which, old-fashioned and of mellow tint, fronts on a flower-garden filled with shrubs, large vines, and trim box borders. On both sides of the house are beautiful trees, standing fair, full-grown, and clear. Passing through a wide hall, you come out upon a piazza, stretching the whole length of the house, where one can walk in all weathers; and thence by a step or two, on a lawn, with picturesque masses of rocks, shrubs and trees, overlooking the East River. Gravel paths lead, by several turns, down the steep bank to the water's edge, where round the rocky point a small bay curves, in which boats are lying. And, owing to the currents, and the set of the tide, the sails glide sidelong, seeming to greet the house as they sweep by. The beauty here, seen by moonlight, is truly transporting. I enjoy it greatly, and the *genius loci* receives me as to a home.

ELfr, from *Memoirs*, 2:150–51.

1. Fuller is describing Horace Greeley's home on Turtle Bay in New York City.

499. To Georgiana Bruce

[December? 1844]

I will get you, if any friend has it here, Goethe's "Correspondence with a Child" (more properly it should be named, "A Child's Correspondence with Herself")."[1] I send this number of "Günderode." The remainder I hope to publish if ever I have time and money.

I was very sorry you could not hear Ole Bull. He played that night, in compliance with a request made him by note, "Ciciliano e Tarentelle," the most romantic of all his pieces, and the audience encored it, so at last I have heard it enough.[2] [   ] I think Beethoven was just what he needed to be at that period of his experience. For so vast a soul there was wonderfully little of the grotesque in his character. He understood all through nature. You ask if I can conceive of orchestral music greater than his. I cannot. My whole soul is filled and borne onward with his. The biographical notices are good, I think, considering that they are made by small men, speaking of one so very great. They make no petty attempt to measure him.

Cannot you send me more about those women, or are you willing that I should transmute it into my own forms? I was greatly entertained and instructed by the journals. Continue, I beg, to note for me the salient traits of every day.

You will need some apprenticeship to teach you to be careful of your health. It is so very unnatural to guard against harm; yet it is a pity to let the body become a clog, instead of a pliant vestment and organ to the spirit.

Your true friend but worthless correspondent,

MARGARET F.

ELfr, from Kirby, *Years of Experience*, pp. 205–6.

1. Bettina von Arnim's spurious *Briefwechsel mit einem Kinde,* published in 1835, was widely read and admired. The book purported to be the correspondence between von Arnim and Goethe.

2. Bull began his New York concerts on 18 December at the Italian Opera House. Fuller reviewed the performance in the *Tribune* on 20 December *(New-York Daily Tribune,* 17 and 20 December 1844).

500.   To Ralph Waldo Emerson

New York.
3d Decr 1844.

Your letter, my dear Waldo, greeted my arrival here, and though your pen had wandered somewhat wildly and lazily over the paper, yet I followed more than once the traces of its course. As to your indolence I applaud it it is the state that ought to follow a process so unnatural as the reading of proofs. I consent to be forgotten and neglected as long as shall be necessary.

The letter to Caroline is also recd and shall reach her. We are now at some distance from one another, but shall meet once more before she goes.

I do not feel like writing, either;—my "views" as they say in N. E. are too unsettled. In two or three weeks, I shall know which way the East lies from this spot, then, then, dear companion, and light of my thoughts, you shall hear from

MARGARET.

ALS (MH: bMS Am 1610 [50]). *Addressed:* R. W. Emerson / at Mr Adams's / Boston.

501. To William H. Channing

[4 December 1844]

I shall venture to counsel when plain matters of fact are before us, though my real confidence must be in a ceaseless prayer that your enthusiasm may be tempered to a steady and milder glow, though perhaps never subdued.

ELfr, from Frothingham, *Memoir of William Henry Channing*, p. 193.

502. To James F. Clarke

New York,
Dec 12th 1844.

Dear James,

I write to ask a favor of you. Cranch has sent[n] two pictures to Miss Peabody's on sale. I fear they will be seen to great disadvantage in her dingy room, and told him I would write to some friend in B. about it. Will you, if desirable, have them by and by, seen in some other house also? Will you, if they strike you favorably, mention them and get them looked at?[n] If they can be sold, the money is very desirable to him, but it is still more important, that he should have a chance to be seen properly; because, if people get prejudiced against him in the beginning, his pictures would[n] have no chance for a long time. To me it seems that his progress in the time is surprizing.

252

I desired them to send you a number of the Tribune, containing my piece on Mr E. which, I thought, might interest you.[1] I wish you would sometimes send me numbers of the Xn World, in which you write articles that are important to you, as I shall not otherwise see it.[2] And write to me, now and then, if you have time. We would not lose sight of one another. With love to Anna, your friend ever

MARGARET.

ALS (MH: bMS Am 1569.7 [465]). *Addressed:* Rev J. F. Clarke / Boston / Mass. *Postmark:* Boston Mass. Dec 19.

has sent] has se⟨?⟩nt
looked at?] looked ⟨a⟩at?
pictures would] pictures ⟨c⟩would

1. "Emerson's Essays," *New-York Daily Tribune,* 7 December 1844, Fuller's first review for Greeley's paper. Fuller said of her friend that he "imprisons his reader only to free him again as a 'liberating God.'" While positive, the essay was unusually reserved, given the close friendship between author and subject.

2. In January 1843 Clarke and some of his parishioners founded the *Christian World,* for which the minister not only wrote more than 250 essays and poems but later served as publisher and editor (Arthur S. Bolster, Jr., *James Freeman Clarke: Disciple to Advancing Truth* [Boston, 1954], p. 164).

503. To Elizabeth P. Peabody

New York 26th Decr 1844.

Dear Elizabeth,

I wished to earlier answer your good letter, but my life begins to be crowded and, à l'ordinarie,—pain in the side or spine follows much exertion. I am obliged to be especially careful not to write too much.

I like my position very well; think I can fill it, and learn a great deal in it. This scene brings me many fresh impressions.

Let me answer, in brief, to the most interesting part of your letter. Probably, I have, as you say, a large share of prudence by nature. It has not, however, been large enough to save me from being much disappointed, in various relations, by a want of delicacy and tenderness from those who had seemed capable of it. But, perceiving similar faults in me, and yet knowing my heart capable of pure and intelligent love, I believe them so, too, and that we shall all be better, and do better as we grow.

The tone of your letter was so mild, and its spirit so comprehensive, that I felt as if you *must* be nearer peace than I had ever expected to find you in this world. Yet your tendency to extremes, as to personal attachments, is so strong, I am afraid you will not wholly rise above it.

The persons whom you have idolized can never, in the end, be ungrateful, and, probably, at the time of retreat they still do justice to your heart. But, so long as you must draw persons too near you, a temporary recoil is sure to follow. It is the character striving to defend itself from a heating and suffocating action upon it.—

A little, only a little less of this in you would give your powers the degree of fresh air they need. Could you be as generous and sympathetic, yet never infatuated; then the blur, the haste, the tangle would disappear, and neither I nor any one could refuse to understand you.

I admit that I have never done you justice. There is so much in you that is hostile to my wishes, as to character, and especially as to the character of woman. How could I be quite candid? Yet where I have looked at you, truly, I have also looked steadily, and always feel myself in your debt that you cordially pardon all that must be to you repressing—and unpleasant in me.

To the care of the fair spirit that sometimes looks out so full through your features and your conduct I commend you. It must finally give you back all your friends.

As to Gunderode, I should like much to have the copies boxed up, after having been counted, you reserving some on sale, and sending me *ten,* which I will distribute from time to time. Should I ever get a name, probably I may be able to finish the translation on good terms, but shall, at present, do nothing about it.

As the copy-right was taken in your name, I also wish a writing from you relinquishing any title to it. And in the same letter, acquaint me how much is still due you, for the expenses for publication. I will not pay you till it is convenient, but *then* I wish to do so, and it is right I should. The ten copies I should be very glad to have the day before New Year's day and with them 2 sets of the etchings I left for sale with you. A set of these makes a pretty present.

My pamphlet on woman is in press at last, and you will receive it ere very long.

Can you with all convenient speed, send the enclosed to B. Randall, and have that to Mrs. F. put into the Post Office. Remember me to your mother and know me all yours in friendliest good will,

MARGARET.

MsC (MH: fMS Am 1086 [Works, 3:261–69]); MsCfr (MB: Ms. Am. 1450 [126]). Published in part in Chevigny, pp. 134–35; published entire in Wade, pp. 571–72.

504. To Anna Loring

Eveg of
26th Dec 44.

My dear Anna,

I often want to hear from you and still no letter comes. Do write me a good one. I want to know now how you all are at the happy home. I cannot get any one to write me whether John King has recovered and of Jane and the baby. Will you tell me too of Maria White's wedding which takes place this evening?[1] And the great Fair that is going on now if you are interested in it this year, tell me about that.[2] And let me know what Miss Martineau writes and copy her address that I may write to her from here. I wish to join my voice to the jubilee of her friends. And tell me, beside all[n] these things, those about yourself which you know will interest me.

Now I have given you a good stint but if you love me, as I think you do, you will make the exertion to do it all for me.

Do you see any of my writings in the Tribune. The Christmas day address I thought would interest you.[3] I have just passed my Christmas at Sing Sing and wish I could tell you about it.

Perhaps you will come to N. Y. and pass a night with me here in my little bed and a day afterward in seeing this sweet place. It is just such an one as you would like, so secluded and picturesque. The water view is most lovely. It is almost happiness to live in so sweet a place.

With love to Father and Mother I here close my bait for a letter from Anna to

MARGARET

ALS (MWelC).

beside all] beside⟨,⟩ all

1. Maria White married James Russell Lowell on that day (Delmar R. Lowell, *The Historic Genealogy of the Lowells of America from 1639 to 1899* [Rutland, Vt., 1899], p. 121).

2. The annual antislavery fair opened in Boston on 24 December at Amory Hall. Anna's mother, Louisa Loring, was one of the managers (*Liberator,* 20 December 1844).

3. In "Christmas," *New-York Daily Tribune,* 25 December 1844, Fuller comments on rituals, art, education, and the relationships between men and women.

505. To Samuel G. Ward

N. Y. 29th Decr, 1844.

I wish you a happy new year, dear Sam and Anna, and many happy years, and that they may come better and better.

Last year, at this time, we were listening to Rakemann, and some of those strains haunt my memory often. I hope we may hear some music, together, when you come here. That is only one little month from this, and if it be like the last, it will go like lightening.

I have been once to the opera, and once to a concert by the same corps; it is not well worthy the name of music. All Donizetti and such like, poor flimsy melodies, and performed in the common-place Italian manner, vivacity gesticulation, bold[n] clear sonorous singing, but no genius and no passion.

I have been at Ole Bull's concerts, heard his Niagara and Solitude of the Prairie, with both of which I am much pleased. The Philharmonic have not yet given a concert, but will the 11th.[1] Many thanks about Mr Habicht, but, after writing to you, I decided to subscribe with a friend, with whom I shall go regularly.[2]

My life here is a queer one and presents a good many daily obstacles of a petty sort, but I find the way to get along. I like the position; it is so central, and affords a far more various view of life than any I ever before was in. My associates think my pen does not make too fine a mark to be felt, and may be a vigorous and purifying implement. I cannot judge so well of this, but I begin to find the level here. I shall be much employed for some time in visiting public institutions and writing short pieces on such subjects as are thus suggested to me. This will suit me well.

I doubt whether I shall put much outlandish matter into the paper; it is emphatically an American journal. Its readers want to know about our affairs and our future. I shall illustrate from the past, and European life, but shall not dwell much upon them.

I like Mr Greeley much. He is a man of the people, and outwardly unrefined, but he has the refinement of true goodness, and a noble disposition. He has, in his own range, great abilities. We have an excellent mutual understanding.

The people who are brought in my way in his house, are new to me and represent what I have seen least of. I form, for myself, some pleasant acquaintances, whom I shall see mostly at their own houses.

Ellery seems to be going on well. I see him little, as he is engaged all times but Saty, but he writes me funny notes from the office giving me fatherly advice as to my literary course. I gave him the money in a way you would have approved. I saw he needed it, as he probably, as yet, gets none for his work, and I assure you he was touched to the heart. A beautiful light fell across his features.

Ever affectionately your

MARGARET.

ALS (MH: bMS Am 1465 [923]). *Addressed:* To S. G. Ward Esq / Lenox / Mass. *Postmark:* New York Dec 30. *Endorsed:* 1844 / S. M. Fuller / Dec. 29.

gesticulation, bold] gesticulation, ⟨loud⟩ bold

1. In her review Fuller praised the Haydn Symphony no. 2 and commented favorably on the quality of the orchestra and on the sophistication of the audience, but she fumed about the lack of fresh air in the building (*New-York Daily Tribune,* 18 January 1845).

2. Claudius Edward Habicht (d. 1883), who was born in Sweden, worked for a time in Boston with Sam Ward at Baring Brothers. In 1848 he became the consul in New York City for Norway and Sweden. Fond of music, he was known in New York for his soirees at his 16th Street home (*New York Times,* 30 March 1883).

506. To William H. Channing

New Year's eve [1844]

I forgot to ask you, dear William, when we shall begin our round of visits to the public institutions I want to make a beginning, as, probably, one a day and once a week will be enough for my time and strength.

Now is the time for me to see and write about these things, as my European stock will not be here till Spring.

Should you like to begin with Blackwell's Island, Monday or Tuesday of next week?[1]

I had much in my mind to say to you this evening, but a visitor has come between. Perhaps it is no matter, I[n] feel as if something new, *and good* was growing. Neither your dark hour nor the pang of sadness that seizes upon me at moments can shake my faith that not only a general, but just now a special good is growing.

I find in my last spring journal these lines of which I had a faint remembrance as you were telling your dream

Boding Raven of the breast,
Dost call the Vulture to thy nest?
Through broken-hearted trusting love
That Vulture may become a Dove,
— Yet scare the Vulture from my breast.
These days have brought too much unrest,
Let the humble Linnet sing
Of the assured, if distant, Spring,
While I baptize in the pure wave,
Then prepare a deep safe grave.
Where the plighted hand may bring
Violets from that other Spring,

Whence the soul may take its flight
Lark-like spiral seeking light
Seeking secure the source of light.

drittissimo calle, I seek said Petrarch but the spiral is the highest form of human ascent."

I have copied exactly from the page. And can I leave thee, my friend, while this wonderful harmony subsists between our minds? Shall words and shadows have power to repel me? Never.

ALfr (MB: Ms. Am. 1450 [57]). Published in part in Higginson, *MFO*, p. 207.
matter, I] matter, ⟨Let⟩ I

1. Fuller first wrote of her visits to Blackwells Island on 19 March in her essay "Our City Charities: Visit to Bellevue Alms House, to the Farm School, the Asylum for the Insane, and Penitentiary on Blackwell's Island." Highly critical of the conditions she found, Fuller reserved her harshest comment for the political system: "It is a most crying and shameful evil, which does not belong to our institutions, but is a careless distortion of them, that the men and measures are changed in these institutions with changes from Whig to Democrat, from Democrat to Whig" (*New-York Daily Tribune,* 19 March 1845).

INDEX

Abraham, John, 31, 33n, 44, 45n, 46n
"Adagio Religioso" (Bull), 201
"Address Delivered in Concord on the Anniversary of the Emancipation of the Negroes in the British West Indies" (Emerson), 213, 216n
Adventures of Gil Blas of Santillane, The (Lesage), 236, 237n
Aeneid, The (Vergil), 74
"Affliction" (G. Herbert), 49n
Alcott, A. Bronson, 34, 35n, 52n, 55, 60, 61n, 102n, 104, 113, 125n, 134n, 178, 212; Fuller on, 49–50
Alcott, Abigail May, 52n, 102n, 108, 212
Allen, Maria Verplanck, 33n, 225n
Allen, William, 33n
Allston, Washington, 37n, 177, 180n
Ames, Joseph Alexander, 39, 40n
Ames, Sarah Clampitt, 40n
Anti-Slavery Fair, 255
Arnim, Bettina Brentano von, 5, 52n, 60
Arnim, Joachim von, 123n
Association (Brisbane), 175n
Athelwold (Smith), 161n

Bailey, Philip, 195n
Balch, Joseph Williams, 64, 65n
Ballads and Other Poems (Longfellow), 58, 59n
Bancroft, Elizabeth Davis, 38, 39n
Bancroft, George, 39n
Barker, Jacob, 124, 189

Bartlett, Miss, 205
Bartlett, George, 39n
Bartlett, Mary Gorham, 39n
Bassett, Miss, 158
Beethoven, Ludwig von, 36, 122, 168, 173, 251
Beethoven, Maria Magdalana Keverich von, 224, 225n
Bell, John, 171, 174n
Bible, 50, 67, 74, 77, 99, 114, 121, 140, 154, 172, 220, 221n, 246
Borrow, George, 59n, 60
Bradford, George Partridge, 117
Braham (Abraham), John, 31, 33n, 44, 45n, 46n
Bremer, Frederika, 138
Brentano, Clemens, 123n
Briggs, Charles, 190, 192n
Brisbane, Albert, 52, 174, 175n
Brook Farm, 37n, 41, 42n, 76, 77, 82, 83, 87, 94, 97, 111–13, 125, 144, 145n, 161, 201, 208n
Brougham, Henry Peter, 103, 104n
Browning, Robert, 104
Brownson, Orestes Augustus, 124n, 175n
—letter to, 174
Bruce, Georgiana, 207, 208n
—letters to, 210–11, 221–23, 235–37, 250–51
Buchanan, Joseph Rodes, 177–78, 180n
Buckminster, Joseph Stevens, 177, 180n

Bull, Ole Bornemann, 201, 249, 251, 256
—works of: "Adagio Religioso," 201; "Ciciliano e Tarentelle," 251; "Niagara," 256; "Solitude of the Prairie," 256
Burditt, Cordelia, 153
Burditt, James, 153
Burditt, Mary, 153
Burley, Susan, 101, 103
Burr, Aaron, 178
Bussey, Benjamin, 38, 39n
Bussey, Judith Gay, 39n

Cabot, Hannah Jackson, 188
Cabot, Joseph S., 39n
Cabot, Samuel, Jr., 188
Cabot, Samuel, Sr., 188n
Caldwell, John, 38, 39n
Carlyle, Thomas, 125n, 128, 129n
—works of: *Chartism*, 128, 129n; *Past and Present*, 125n, 128, 129n; *Sartor Resartus*, 129n
Cary, George Blankern, 132, 134n
Cary, George, Sr., 134n
Cary, Helen Paine, 134n
Ceres, 220
Channing, Barbara, 41–42
—letter to, 202
Channing, Ellen Fuller, 6, 31, 33n, 34, 35–36, 38, 41, 44, 46, 70, 82, 84, 86, 94, 95, 103, 118, 132, 152, 153, 172, 187, 191, 196–97, 202, 208, 217, 229, 234
Channing, Ellery, 6, 33n, 34, 35, 44, 50, 63, 70, 79–80, 82, 84, 86, 94, 96, 103, 104n, 110, 111n, 117, 118, 136, 145n, 146, 148, 159, 162n, 172, 181, 182, 196–97, 206, 229, 243; Fuller on, 46, 71, 80, 87, 95, 114; in New York City, 242, 243, 244, 248, 256
—works of: "Dirge," 97, 98n; "The Earth," 136, 138n; "The Youth of the Poet and the Painter," 136, 138n
Channing, Frances Maria, 224–25
Channing, Francis Allston, 68, 224–25
Channing, Francis Dana, 225n
Channing, Julia Allen, 33n, 225
Channing, Margaret Fuller, 6, 187, 196–97, 202, 204, 208, 211, 217, 229–30
Channing, Mary Elizabeth, 38, 39n, 41, 42n

Channing, William Ellery, 33n, 97, 98n, 102, 106–8, 177, 199
Channing, William Henry, 6–7, 32, 33n, 50, 70, 98, 120, 128, 129n, 170, 219, 236, 237, 244, 247
—letters to, 42–43, 67–68, 69, 72–75, 80, 90–92, 99, 141–42, 153–55, 182, 193, 198–99, 223–24, 238–42, 252, 257–58
Charles O'Malley, the Irish Dragoon (Lever), 32, 33n
Charters, Alexander, 130, 131n
Charters, Ellen Boomer, 131n
Charters, James B., 131n
Chartism (Carlyle), 128, 129n
Cheney, Mary, 127n
Cheney, Silas, 127n
Chickering, Jonas C., 32, 33n
Child, Lydia Francis, 183
—letter to, 183
Choate, George, 231n
Choate, Margaret Hodges, 231
Christian World, 253
"Christmas" (Fuller), 255
Chromatography (Field), 171, 174n
Churchill, Mr., 233
"Church-Porch, The" (Herbert), 80, 81n
"Ciciliano e Tarentelle" (Bull), 251
Clarke, Abraham, 126, 127n
Clarke, Anna Huidekoper, 101
—letter to, 101
Clarke, James Freeman, 7, 39, 40n, 53, 54n, 67n, 101n, 106, 161n, 177–78, 180, 190, 198; Fuller on, 119–20
—letters to, 79, 111, 185, 252–53
Clarke, Marianna Elizabeth, 42
Clarke, Marianne Mackintosh, 36, 37n, 42, 44
—letter to, 152–53
Clarke, Rebecca Hull, 126, 127n, 205
Clarke, Sarah Ann, 36, 37n, 38, 60, 137, 143, 147, 177–78, 180, 181, 185, 196, 198, 221, 223
—letter to, 123
Clarke, Thomas, 37n
Clarke, William Hull, 125, 190, 191, 204, 205
Cleverly, Asa P., 31, 33n, 35
Cleverly, Rebecca Whiton, 33n, 38, 44
Codman, Catherine Amory, 205, 206n
Codman, Henry, 206n
Codman, Mary Cushing, 205, 206n

Codman, Stephen, 206n
Coleridge, Samuel Taylor, 159
"Comus" (Milton), 49n
Conant, Augustus Hammond, 190, 192n, 204, 206n
Confucius, 67, 240, 248
"Conservative, The" (Emerson), 97, 98n
Conversations (Fuller), 5, 6, 40n, 97, 99, 101, 108, 114, 152, 161, 162–63, 183–84, 185, 187, 193
Conversations with Goethe (Eckermann, trans. Fuller), 164n, 234, 235n
Cours de l'histoire de la philosophie (Cousin), 86, 87n
Cousin, Victor, 86, 87n
Cranch, Christopher Pearse, 244, 252
—letter to, 233
Crane, Abigail, 33n, 234
Crane, Charles P., 32, 33n, 43, 45n
Crane, Elizabeth, 33n
Crane, Nancy Weiser, 32, 33n
Crane, Peter, Jr., 165–66, 167n
Crane, Peter, Sr., 166
Crane, Simeon, 33n
Cumming, Alfred, 113
Cumming, Elizabeth Randall, 32, 33n, 36, 113, 119
Curtis, Burrill, 211
Curtis, George, 211n
Curtis, George William, 211
Curtis, Mary Burrill, 211n
Cyropaedia (Xenophon), 64, 65n

Daguerre Exhibition, 195, 196n
Dante, 102–3, 104n, 144, 145n, 194, 195n
Davis, Charles, 39n
Davis, Eliza Bussey, 39n
Davis, George T., 106n, 229n, 234
—letter to, 104–6
Davis, Henry Tallman, 229, 230n
Davis, John, 230n
Davis, Susan Tallman, 230n
De l'humanité, de son principe, et de son avenir (Leroux), 124n
Desâtîr or Sacred Writings of the Ancient Persian Prophets, The, 243, 245n, 248
"De vita coelesti, ex iisdem principiis conjectura" (E. Herbert), 109, 110n
"De vita humana philosophica disquisitio" (E. Herbert), 109, 110n
De Windt, Caroline Smith, 241

De Windt, John Peter, 241n
Dial, 32, 33n, 70, 97, 123, 136–37, 138, 148, 160, 161n, 183. *See also* Emerson, Ralph Waldo, and *Dial*; Fuller, Margaret, and *Dial*.
"Dialogue" (Fuller), 209, 210n
Digby, Kenelm, 110, 111n
Diodorus Siculus, 228
"Dirge" (Ellery Channing), 97, 98n
Discourse of Matters Pertaining to Religion, A (Parker), 68n
Discourses of Sir Joshua Reynolds, The (Reynolds), 171, 174n
Discourses on Painting and the Fine Arts (Reynolds), 171, 174n
Dix, Dorothea, 58, 59n, 60
Domenichino, Il, 70, 71n, 217
Donizetti, Gaetano, 256
"Dora" (Tennyson), 80
Dorr, Charles Hazen, 33n
Dorr, Thomas Wilson, 74
Dorr Rebellion, 72–74
Dos niños comiendo fruta (Murillo), 87, 88n
"Douglas Tragedy, The" (Scott), 224, 225n
Dresel, Otto, 195n
Dwight, John Sullivan, 45
—letter to, 45

Eames, Charles, 38, 39
"Earth, The" (Ellery Channing), 136, 138n
Eastlake, Charles L., 171, 174n
Eckermann, Johann Peter, 234, 235n
"Edith" (Newcomb), 78, 79n, 94, 201
Elements of Psychology (Cousin, trans. Henry), 87n
Eliot, William Greenleaf, 191, 192n
Elisabeth (mother of John the Baptist), 220, 221n
Elizabeth I, 224, 225n
Elliot, Augustus Greele, 246, 247n
Elssler, Fanny, 199
Emerson, Charles C., 48n
Emerson, Edith, 98, 99n, 161, 175, 207, 210
Emerson, Edward Waldo, 208, 209n, 211, 217
Emerson, Lydia Jackson (Lidian), 59, 83, 84, 96, 98, 113, 152, 176
Emerson, Ralph Waldo, 5, 7, 32, 33n, 39, 40n, 75, 113, 119, 142, 151, 185,

Emerson, Ralph Waldo (*cont.*)
201, 206, 212, 240, 253; and birth of
son, 208, 211, 217; and *Dial*, 57–58,
60, 61n; Fuller on, 52–53, 91–92;
Fuller's visits to, 34, 90–92, 148; lectures, 108, 114, 115n, 120, 182. *See
also titles of individual lectures.*
—letters to, 49–54, 57–60, 69–71, 77,
83–84, 92–93, 96–98, 101–4,
110–11, 121, 123–24, 128–31,
136–38, 143–44, 152, 159–61,
163–64, 175–80, 181–82, 196, 207,
209–10, 213–16, 243–44, 251–52
—translation of: *Vita Nuova*, 102–3,
104n, 144, 145n
—works of: "Address Delivered in Concord on the Anniversary of the
Emancipation of the Negroes in the
British West Indies," 213, 216n;
"The Conservative," 97, 98n; *Essays:
Second Series*, 209, 210n, 240, 241n,
243, 253; "Gifts," 137, 138n; "The
Humble Bee," 177, 179n; "Manners,"
32, 33n; "Man's Relation to Nature,"
39n; "New England," 108, 109n–
10n; "Nominalist and Realist," 125n;
"Ode to Beauty," 148, 149n; "Saadi,"
97, 98, 99n; "Threnody," 179n; "To
Rhea," 137, 138n; "Woodnotes," 142;
"The Young American," 179, 180n
Emerson, Ruth Haskins, 220
Emerson, Susan Haven, 149n, 158,
159n
Emerson, Waldo, 42–43, 48, 114, 157,
175–77, 217, 218–19
Emerson, William, 149n, 244
—letter to, 158–59
"Emerson's Essays" (Fuller), 253
"Entertainments of the Past Winter"
(Fuller), 58, 59n
Ernest (Lofft), 104
Essays: Second Series (Emerson), 209,
210n, 240, 241n, 243, 253
Euripides, 64

Faerie Queene, The (Spenser), 223
Farrar, Eliza Rotch, 38, 40n, 57, 61, 64,
83, 90n, 114, 119, 120, 122, 139,
141n, 145, 146, 169, 191, 192n, 208,
230, 234, 254
Farrar, John, 40n, 76, 82, 83, 90n, 114,
119, 120, 122, 198, 204, 246

Faust (Goethe), 110, 111n, 155
Felton, Cornelius, 109n
Fénelon, François de Salignac de La
Mothe-, 231, 232n
Festus (Bailey), 194, 195n
Field, George, 171, 174n
Flaxman, John, 171, 174n
Fletcher, Nathaniel, 33n
Fletcher, Sarah, 33n
Forbes, John Murray, 246
Forbes, Sarah Hathaway, 246
Forbes, William Hathaway, 99n
Forsyth, Joseph, 171, 174n
Fourier, François-Marie-Charles, 52n,
170
Francis, Abigail Allyn, 163
—letter to, 162–63
Francis, Convers, 191, 193n, 198, 204
Freeman, Eliza Sturgis, 39n
Freeman, Nathaniel, 39n
Freeman, Russell, 38, 39n
Freeman, Tryphosa, 39n
Fruitlands, 102n, 212
"Fruitlands" (Lane), 137, 138n
Fuller, Abraham Williams, 31, 33n, 36,
82, 187–88, 191, 205
Fuller, Arthur Buckminster, 6, 31, 33n,
47, 48n, 63, 64, 85, 86n, 145, 158,
228; and Belvidere School, 158,
159n, 190–91, 192n, 204, 206n
—letters to, 189–92, 202–5
Fuller, Cornelia, 32, 33n, 35, 41, 44, 47
Fuller, Edward Breck, 197
Fuller, Ellen Kilshaw. *See* Channing,
Ellen Fuller.
Fuller, Eugene, 31, 32, 33n, 36, 38, 44,
64, 72, 145, 187–88
Fuller, Frances Hastings, 6, 32, 33n, 35,
36, 37n, 38, 41, 43–44, 45, 47
—letter to, 187–88
Fuller, Henry Holton, 31, 33n, 35, 36,
37n, 64
Fuller, Julia, 225
Fuller, Lloyd, 34, 35n, 36, 41, 60, 61,
62n, 63, 65, 71, 76, 82, 146, 189, 191,
200, 204
Fuller, Margaret: and *Dial*, 5, 50,
53–54, 57–58, 60, 76, 83n, 106, 144;
health of, 31, 36, 41, 49, 55, 105,
118–19, 123, 133, 150, 162, 164–65,
167, 169, 173, 179, 228, 235, 243;
lyrical expressions of, 48, 62–63, 66,
69, 77–78, 86, 88–90, 96, 219;

Fuller, Margaret (*cont.*)
   moves to New York, 6–7, 229n, 230,
      242, 243, 245, 249; reading of, 64,
      67, 86, 93, 124, 156; visits West, 5–6,
      59, 82, 123, 124
—opinions of: on beauty, 43, 66, 80,
      81, 86, 90, 93; on emotions, 47, 55,
      69, 85, 86, 105–6, 164–65, 179; on
      friendship, 47–48, 52–53, 56, 66,
      72, 91–92, 93, 96, 99, 105–6, 111,
      112–13, 253; on Indians, 130,
      132–33, 134–35, 137; on mind, 64,
      86, 155; on music, 31–32, 45, 67,
      103, 114, 122, 168, 173, 251, 256; on
      nature, 75, 77–78, 79, 80, 81, 90, 92,
      130–31, 132–33, 134–35, 137,
      143–44, 169, 213, 224, 232, 234,
      243–44, 245, 249; on women, 157,
      197, 213, 225n, 226, 236, 237, 238;
      on writing, 47, 58–59, 78, 80, 96,
      103, 159–60, 198–99, 202, 209, 242,
      256
—translations of: *Conversations with
      Goethe*, 164n, 234, 235n; *Die Gün-
      derode*, 5, 50–52, 60, 174n, 250, 254
—works of: "Christmas," 255;
      "Dialogue," 209, 210n; "Emerson's
      Essays," 253; "Entertainments of the
      Past Winter," 58, 59n; "The Great
      Lawsuit," 6, 123, 124n, 199, 223;
      "Life on the Prairies," 209, 210n;
      "Our City Charities," 258n; "Romaic
      and Rhine Ballads," 97, 98n; *Summer
      on the Lakes, in 1843*, 5, 159–60, 185,
      196, 197, 198, 199, 200, 202, 204,
      206–7, 221, 223; "The Two Her-
      berts," 209, 210n; *Woman in the Nine-
      teenth Century*, 5, 6, 223, 225n, 232,
      236, 237, 241–42, 243, 248, 254
Fuller, Margaret Ellen, 187, 188n
Fuller, Margarett Crane, 34, 46, 50, 55,
      60, 61, 62, 63, 72, 82, 85, 86, 118,
      132, 133, 152, 165, 172, 187, 204,
      205, 219, 220, 227–28, 229, 234
—letters to, 31–32, 35–39, 41–42,
      43–45
Fuller, Mary Fletcher, 32, 33n
Fuller, Mary Stone, 36, 37n, 38, 44
Fuller, Richard Frederick, 6, 31, 33n,
      41, 48, 118, 172, 176, 200, 204,
      229n; and Harvard, 65n, 132, 191
—letters to, 34, 40, 61–62, 63–65,
      71–72, 81–82, 85–86, 132–33,

   145–46, 181, 208, 227–28, 234–35,
      247–48
Fuller, Timothy, 34, 35n, 64, 85, 86n,
      105, 156, 166, 188n
Fuller, William Henry, 31, 33n, 35,
      37n, 38, 44, 187, 228
Fuller, William Williams, 32, 33n
Fuseli, Henry, 171, 174n

Gay, Joshua, 39n
Gay, Sarah, 39n
Geschichte der Literatur der Gegenwart
      (Mundt), 129n, 138
Geschichte der neueren deutschen Kunst
      (Raczyniski), 109n
Geschichte Europas (Raumer), 235n
Gifford, Mary, 56, 57n, 169
Gifford, Tabitha, 57n
Gifford, Warren, 57n
"Gifts" (Emerson), 137, 138n
Godwin, William, 225n
Goethe, Johann Wolfgang, 68, 128,
      155, 160, 163, 231, 250
—works of: *Faust*, 110, 111n, 155;
      Iphigenie auf Tauris, 231, 232n;
      Torquato Tasso, 231, 232n; *Wilhelm
      Meisters Lehrjahre*, 68; *Wilhelm Meisters
      Wanderjahre*, 68
Goethes Briefwechsel mit einem Kinde (B.
      von Arnim), 250, 251n
Grattan, Eliza O'Donnel, 38, 40n
Grattan, Thomas Colley, 38, 40n
"Great Lawsuit, The" (Fuller), 6, 123,
      124n, 199, 223
Greaves, James Pierrepont, 212
Greeley, Horace, 6, 52, 127n, 191,
      193n, 200, 229n, 230, 235, 242, 244,
      250; Fuller on, 256
Greeley, Mary Cheney, 126, 127n
Greene, William Batchelder, 33n
Greenough, Horatio, 39, 40n
Greville, Fulke (First Baron Brooke),
      93
Günderode, Die (B. von Arnim, trans.
      Fuller), 5, 50–52, 60, 174n, 250, 254

Habicht, Claudius Edward, 256, 257n
Hall, Edward Brooks, 184
Hall, Louisa Park, 185n
Hamlet (Shakespeare), 156
Handbook of the History of Painting, A
      (Kugler, trans. Eastlake), 171, 174n
Handel, George Frederick, 31, 67

Harrington, Helen Griswold, 204, 206n
Harrington, Joseph, 204, 206n
Hawthorne, Nathaniel, 5, 40n, 58, 70,
   71n, 211, 217; Fuller on, 65–66, 70
—letter to, 115–17
Hawthorne, Sophia Peabody, 40n, 70,
   71n, 117n, 188, 217
—letter to, 65–66
Hawthorne, Una, 188, 189n, 210, 211,
   217, 218, 220
Hedge, Frederic Henry, 7, 162n
—letter to, 106–9
Henry, Mr., 64
Herbert, Edward (baron of Cherbury),
   108–9, 110
Herbert, George, 47, 49n, 57, 80, 81n
—works of: "Affliction," 49n; "The
   Church-Porch," 80, 81n
Herodotus, 86
Hibes, Mr., 188
Higginson, Thomas Wentworth, 39n
Hinds, Ebenezer Pierce, 204, 206n
Hinshaw, Mr., 132–33
*Histoire de la vie et des ouvrages de Ra-
   phaël* (Quatremère de Quincy), 171,
   174n
*Histoire de la vie et des ouvrages
   Michel-Ange Bonarroti* (Quatremère de
   Quincy), 171, 174n
Historical Sketches of the Old Painters
   (Lee), 190, 193n
History of Painting in Italy, The (Lanzi),
   171, 174n
*History of the Rise, Increase, and Progress
   of the Christian People Called Quakers,
   The* (Sewel), 122
Hoar, Elizabeth Sherman, 7, 49, 64, 84,
   103–4, 148, 155, 161, 176, 189, 217,
   244; Fuller on, 48, 76
—letters to, 46–48, 54–55, 68, 79–80,
   101, 113–14, 118–19, 125–26,
   185–87, 237
Hodges, Elizabeth Donnison, 174n
Hodges, Richard, 174n
Hodges, Sarah, 172, 174n
—letter to, 231
"Hollis Street Council" (Parker), 97,
   98n
Homer, 80, 220, 221n
Hooper, Ellen Sturgis, 96, 98n, 180,
   219, 220n
Horace, 40
Howe, Miss, 188

Howe, Julia Ward, 191, 193n
Howes, Elizabeth Burley, 39n, 103
Howes, Frederick, 39n
Howes, Susan, 38, 39n, 103
Howitt, Mary, 138n
Howitt, William, 124
Huidekoper, Harm Jan, 101n
"Humble Bee, The" (Emerson), 177,
   178n
Hunt, Benjamin Peter, 138n

"Ideale, Die" (Schiller), 48n
*Imaginary Conversations of Literary Men
   and Statesmen* (Landor), 93
Ingham, Charles C., 108, 109n
Iphigenie auf Tauris (Goethe), 231, 232n

Jackson, Charles T., 37n
Jackson, Marianne, 36, 37n, 185
James, Henry, Sr., 151
—letter to, 151
James, Margaret Walsh, 152n
Jean Paul (J. P. F. Richter), 98, 99n
"Jesus, My Strength, My Hope" (Wes-
   ley), 219, 220n
Johnson, Mrs., 223

Kant, Immanuel, 224
Keats, Emma, 34, 35n
Keats, George, 34, 35n, 36
Kerner, Justinus, 124
King, Alice, 188, 189n, 255
King, Jane Tuckerman, 87, 88n, 114,
   119, 126, 128, 129n, 188, 246, 255
—letter to, 217
King, John Gallison, 127n, 255
Kinslay, Miss, 36
Knaben Wunderhorn, Des (A. von Ar-
   nim), 122, 123n
Knapp, Jacob, 42
Kugler, Franz, 171, 174n
Kuhn, George, 36, 37n, 41, 145, 191,
   228
Kuhn, Nancy Weiser (daughter), 113,
   118
Kuhn, Nancy Weiser (mother), 36, 37n,
   63, 65
Künstler, Die (Schiller), 231, 232n

La Motte-Fouqué, Friedrich, 227n
Lamson, Rufus, 228
Landor, Walter Savage, 93, 194n
—works of: *Imaginary Conversations of
   Literary Men and Statesmen,* 93; *The*

Landor, Walter Savage (*cont.*)
—works of (*cont.*)
  Pentameron and Pentalogia, 243, 245n,
  248; *Pericles and Aspasia*, 194, 248
Lane, Charles, 102n, 104, 108, 114,
  125n, 136–37, 170, 172; Fuller on,
  113, 179
—letters to, 211–12, 218
Lane, William, 102n
Lanzi, Luigi Antonio, 171, 174n
Lawrence, Mr., 85
Lawrence, Stilman, 40
*Lectures on Painting Delivered at the Royal
  Academy* (Fuseli), 171, 174n
Lectures on Sculpture (Flaxman), 171,
  174n
Lee, Hannah Farnham, 193n
Leroux, Pierre, 124n
Lesage, Alain-René, 237n
Lessing, Karl Friedrich, 108, 109n
Letters from New-York (Child), 183
Lever, Charles James, 33n
*Life of Edward Lord Herbert of Cherbury,
  Written by Himself, The*, 108, 110
"Life on the Prairies" (Fuller), 209,
  210n
Little, Charles Coffin, 198n
—letter to, 197–98
Little and Brown Co., 198
—letter to, 200–201
Livermore, George, 191, 193n
"Locksley Hall" (Tennyson), 80
Lofft, Capel, the younger, 104, 156,
  157n
—works of: *Ernest*, 104; *Self-Formation*,
  156, 157n
Longfellow, Frances Appleton, 59n
Longfellow, Henry W., 58, 59n, 60,
  103, 161n
—letter to, 122
—works of: *Ballads and Other Poems*, 58,
  59n; *The Spanish Student*, 161n
Loring, Anna, 228, 229n, 230, 234, 255
—letter to, 195
Loring, Ellis Gray, 195n, 212, 228, 230
Loring, Louisa Gilman, 195, 228
Loring, Thacher, 197n
Lowell, Charles Russell, 168n
Lowell, James Russell, 255
Lowell, Maria White, 255

Mackintosh, Dorcas, 37n
Mackintosh, Peter, 37n

Maglathlin, Bartlett, 193n
Maglathlin, Henry Bartlett, 191,
  193n
Maglathlin, Maria Chandler, 193n
Mann, Horace, 40n, 159n
Mann, Horace, Jr., 188, 189n
Mann, Mary Peabody, 40n, 188
"Manners" (Emerson), 32, 33n
"Man's Relation to Nature" (Emerson),
  39n
"Margaret's Ghost" (Mallet), 224,
  225n
Marston, John Westland, 161n
Martineau, Harriet, 177, 180n, 255
Mary, mother of Jesus, 220, 221n, 226
Mary Stuart, 224, 225n
May, Samuel J., 158, 159n
Meditations for Private Hours (Dix), 58,
  59n, 60
Memoir of William Ellery Channing
  (William Henry Channing), 97, 98n
Merchant of Venice, The (Shakespeare),
  126
Mesmerism, 177–79, 180, 181–82, 201
Messiah (Handel), 31, 67
Metcalf, Charles R., 61, 62n, 63
Metternich, Klemens Wenzel von, 38,
  40n
Michelangelo, 224
Milnes, Richard Monckton, 103
Milton, John, 47, 49n
"Morte d'Arthur" (Tennyson), 80
Motley, Maria Davis, 38, 39n
Motley, Thomas, 39n
Mott, James, 121n
Mott, Lucretia Coffin, 120, 121n
Motte, Mary Ann Alger, 248, 249n
Motte, Mellish I., 248, 249n
Mulliken, George Samuel, 205, 206n
Mundt, Theodor, 129n, 138
Murillo, Bartolomé Esteban, 87

"Napoleon" (Presbury), 58, 59n, 60
Neighbours, The (Bremer), 138n
Newcomb, Charles King, 50, 52n, 70,
  71n, 87, 115–16; Fuller on, 78
—letters to, 75–76, 77–78, 93–94, 95,
  125, 201, 206–7, 249
—works of: "Edith," 78, 79n, 94, 201;
  "The Two Dolons," 50, 52n, 70, 71n,
  76, 78
Newcomb, Charlotte, 75, 76n
Newcomb, Elizabeth, 75, 76n

Newcomb, Rhoda Mardenbrough, 72, 75, 76, 95, 125, 184, 249
"New England" (Emerson), 108, 109n–10n
"Niagara" (Bull), 256
"Nominalist and Realist" (Emerson), 125n
"Notes from the Journal of a Scholar" (C. Emerson), 137, 138n
"Notes on Art and Architecture" (Ward), 137, 138n
Nouveau Monde industriel et sociétaire, Le (Fourier), 175n

Observations on Italy (Bell), 171, 174n
"Ode to Beauty" (Emerson), 148, 149n
"Ode upon the Question Moved" (E. Herbert), 109, 110n
Odyssey, The (Homer), 80
Oliver, Daniel, 188n
"On Death" (Shelley), 165, 167
"Our City Charities" (Fuller), 258n

Pan, 202
Paracelsus (Browning), 104
Paradise Lost (Milton), 47, 49n
Park, John, 185n
Parker, Theodore, 54, 68, 97, 98n, 121n, 160, 162n; Fuller on, 120
—works of: *A Discourse of Matters Pertaining to Religion*, 68n; "Hollis Street Council," 97, 98n
Parsons, Anna, 179n
Parsons, Anna Quincy Thaxter, 177–79, 180, 181–82, 201
Parsons, Nehemiah, 179n
Past and Present (Carlyle), 125n, 128, 129n
Patrician's Daughter, The (Marston), 161n
Patton, Mr., 204
Peabody, Elizabeth Palmer (daughter), 52n, 53, 54n, 59n, 161, 174, 180, 252; Fuller on, 58, 60, 253–54
—letter to, 253–54
Peabody, Elizabeth Palmer (mother), 38, 40n, 234
Peabody, Nathaniel, 38, 40n, 234
Peabody, Sophia. *See* Hawthorne, Sophia Peabody.
Pentameron and Pentalogia, The (Landor), 243, 245n, 248
Pericles and Aspasia (Landor), 194, 248

Petrarch, 114, 258
Philip Van Artevelde (Taylor), 161n
Pierpont, John, 121n
Plato, 67, 93
"Poet's Mind, The" (Tennyson), 77, 79n, 232
Presbury, Benjamin Franklin, 59n
Presbury, Sarah Pratt, 59n
Presbury, Seth, 59n
Present, The, 5, 142, 143, 170
Prichard, Jane Hallett, 84
Prichard, Moses, 84
"Prophecy—Transcendentalism—Progress" (Saxton), 160, 162n

Quatremère de Quincy, Antoine, 171, 174n

Rackemann, Frederick William, 32, 33n, 36, 103, 172, 256
Raczyniski, Atanazy, 109n
Randall, Belinda, 32, 33n, 36, 119, 172, 174n, 254
Randall, Hannah Adams, 172, 174n
Randall, John, Jr., 70, 71n
Randall, John, Sr., 33n, 71n, 172, 174n
Randall, Maria, 32, 33n, 128, 129n
Rape of Europa, 70
Raphael, 78, 195, 224
Raumer, Friedrich Ludwig Georg von, 234, 235n
Remarks on Antiquities, Arts, and Letters during an Excursion in Italy (Forsyth), 171, 174n
Reynolds, Joshua, 171, 174n
Rice, Charlotte, 41n
Rice, Edward, 40, 41n
Rice, William, 41n
Richter, Jean Paul Friedrich [pseud. Jean Paul], 98, 99n
Ripley, George, 41, 42, 62, 76, 160
Ripley, Sophia Dana, 36, 37n, 41, 42, 61, 62, 76, 108
Robert, Mr., 187
Robinson Crusoe (Defoe), 191
Rogers, William Matticks, 37n
"Romaic and Rhine Ballads" (Fuller), 97, 98n
Rotch, Ann Waln, 122n, 148
Rotch, Francis Morgan, 147, 148n
Rotch, Francis, Sr., 122n
Rotch, Maria, 122, 141
—letters to, 146–48, 170–73, 229–30

Rotch, Mary, 59, 69, 70, 71, 74, 103
—letters to, 56–57, 62–63, 119–20, 121–22, 139–41, 168–70
Rousseau, Jean-Jacques, 156
"Rumors from an Aeolian Harp" (Thoreau), 97, 98n
Rural and Domestic Life of Germany, The (Howitt), 124
Russell, George Robert, 42n
Russell, Sarah Shaw, 41, 42n, 221, 226, 246

"Saadi" (Emerson), 97, 98, 99n
Saint-Martin, Louis-Claude de, 231, 232n
Saint-Simon, Comte de (Claude-Henri de Rouvroy), 124, 125n
Sarto, Andrea del, 202
Sartor Resartus (Carlyle), 129n
Saxton, Jonathan Ashley, 162n
Schadow, Wilhelm von, 108, 109n
Schelling, Friedrich Wilhelm, 109, 110n
Schiller, Johann Christoph Friedrich, 46, 48n, 231
"Schloss am Meere, Das" (Uhland), 108, 109n
Schneider, Colonel, 135–36
Scott, Walter, 225n
Seherin von Prevorst, Die (Kerner), 124, 198
Self-Formation (Lofft), 156, 157n
"Sermon on the Character and Ministry of the Late Rev. William Ellery Channing, D.D., A" (Hedge), 106–8, 109n
Sewel, William, 122
Shakespeare, William, 108, 126, 224
—works of: *Hamlet*, 156; *The Merchant of Venice*, 126; *The Two Gentlemen of Verona*, 108, 110n
Shattuck, Amelia, 39n
Shattuck, Eleanor Elizabeth, 38, 39n
Shattuck, George, 39n
Shaw, Anna, 211n, 226, 227n
Shaw, Anna Blake, 32, 33n, 46, 67, 87, 180, 221, 246
Shaw, Elizabeth (daughter), 188
Shaw, Elizabeth (mother), 42n
Shaw, Ellen, 227n
Shaw, Francis, 39, 40n, 209, 226, 246
Shaw, Josephine, 168, 227n
Shaw, Robert Gould (father of Francis), 33n, 42n

Shaw, Robert Gould (son of Francis), 227n
Shaw, Sarah Sturgis, 7, 39, 209
—letters to, 127, 168, 221, 225–27, 245–46
Shaw, Susanna, 227n
Sheafe, Jacob, 159n
Sheafe, Margaret, 158, 159n
Sheafe, Mary Haven, 159n
Shelley, Percy Bysshe, 165, 167, 224, 225n
Shelley, William, 224, 225n
Silenus, 202
Sing Sing Prison, 221–23, 236, 237, 247–48
Smith, William Henry, 161n
"Social Tendencies" (Lane), 137, 138n
Socrates, 67
"Solitude of the Prairie" (Bull), 256
Spanish Student, The (Longfellow), 161n
Sparks, Jared, 40n
Spenser, Edmund, 126, 127n
Sterling, John, 159, 161n, 244, 245n
Stevens, Abby, 124, 131, 208, 227
Stevens, Anne, 124, 189, 208
Stimson, Abigail Clarke, 183
—letter to, 183–84
Stimson, John H., 184
Storer, Elizabeth Howe, 217
Storer, Robert Boyd, 217n
Storer, Sarah Hoar, 217n
Story, William Wetmore, 246
Strafford (Sterling), 160, 161n
Sturgis, Caroline, 7, 45, 47, 50, 79n, 96, 103, 119, 123, 193, 198, 199, 236, 244, 246, 249, 252; Fuller on, 46, 78
—letters to, 56, 72, 87, 94, 193–94, 196–97, 200, 218–20
Sturgis, William, 40n, 46n, 123
Sue, Marie-Joseph (Eugène), 207
Sullivan, James, 199
Summer on the Lakes, in 1843 (Fuller), 5, 159–60, 185, 196, 197, 198, 199, 200, 202, 204, 206–7, 221, 223
Sumner, Charles, 38, 40n
Swan, Joshua, 174n
Swedenborg, Emanuel, 224
Sylvain, James, 199
Symonds, Mrs., 38

Tappan, Caroline Sturgis. *See* Sturgis, Caroline.
Tappan, Lewis, 121n

Tappan, William Aspinwall, 121
Taylor, Henry, 159, 161n, 248, 249n
Taylor, John, 159n
Tennyson, Alfred, 5, 77, 79n, 80, 81n, 87, 91, 92n, 106, 151, 232
—works of: "Dora," 80; "Locksley Hall," 80; "Morte d'Arthur," 80; "The Poet's Mind," 77, 79n, 232; "The Two Voices," 80; "Ulysses," 80, 91, 92n
Thoreau, Cynthia Dunbar, 84
Thoreau, Henry David, 83n, 97, 160, 162n, 208, 210, 218
—letter to, 148–49
"Threnody" (Emerson), 179n
"To Rhea" (Emerson), 137, 138n
Torquato Tasso (Goethe), 231, 232n
Tracy, Albert H., Jr., 151n
Tracy, Albert H., Sr., 131, 132n
—letters to, 139, 149–50, 155–57
Tracy, Francis Walsingham, 151n
Tracy, Harriet Norton, 150, 151n
Trauernde Königspaar, Das (Lessing), 108, 109n
"Triformis" (Clarke), 159, 161n, 185
Tuckerman, Gustavus, 88n
Tuckerman, Jane. *See* King, Jane Tuckerman.
Twice-Told Tales (Hawthorne), 58
"Two Dolons, The" (Newcomb), 50, 52n, 70, 71n, 76, 78
Two Gentlemen of Verona, The (Shakespeare), 108, 110n
"Two Herberts, The" (Fuller), 209, 210n
"Two Voices, The" (Tennyson), 80

Uhland, Ludwig, 108, 109n
"Ulysses" (Tennyson), 80, 91, 92n
Undine (La Motte-Fouqué), 227
Universal Yankee Nation, 64, 65n

Vergil, 40, 74
Vieuxtemps, Henri-François-Joseph, 173, 174n
Vita Nuova (Dante, trans. Emerson), 102–3, 104n, 144, 145n
"Voyage to Jamaica" (Hunt), 137, 138n

Walker, Catharine Bartlett, 39n
Walker, James, 38, 39n
Walker, John, 39n
Walker, Lucy Johnson, 39n

Wayne, Anthony, 177, 180n
Ward, Anna Barker (daughter), 32, 33n
Ward, Anna Barker (mother), 32, 33n, 36, 39, 50, 103, 114, 136, 180, 188; Fuller on, 47
—letters to, 164–67, 189
Ward, Lydia Gray (daughter of Samuel), 6, 124
Ward, Lydia Gray (mother of Samuel), 33n, 124
Ward, Mary, 32, 33n, 38
Ward, Samuel Gray, 5, 32, 33n, 36, 37, 39, 40n, 50, 70, 97–98, 103, 124, 146, 159, 173, 180, 188, 209; Fuller on, 47, 88–90
—letters to, 88–90, 134–36, 255–56
Ward, Thomas Wren, 33n
Watson, Elizabeth, 33n
Watson, Mary, 33n
Watson, William, 33n
Weeks, Jordan and Co., 32, 33n, 54n
Wesley, Charles, 219
Wesselhoeft, Ferdinande Hecker, 174n
Wesselhoeft, Minna, 173, 174n
Wesselhoeft, Robert, 145, 146n, 169, 173, 174n, 217, 228, 234
Wheeler, Charles Stearns, 110n
Whelpley, James Davenport, 230, 231n
Whelpley, Philip M., 231n
Whelpley, Philip Melancthon, 231n
Whelpley, Samuel, 231n
Whipple, Mr., 188
White, George, 120
Whiting, Ann, 188
Whiting, Hannah, 188n
Whiting, William, 188n
Whittier, Simeon Chase, 205, 206n
Wilhelm Meisters Lehrjahre (Goethe), 68
Wilhelm Meisters Wanderjahre (Goethe), 68
William the Conqueror, 224
Williams, Charles H. S., 130, 132n
Willis, Nathaniel Parker, 200, 201n
Willson, Edmund B., 190, 192n
Willson, Martha Butterick, 192n
Woman in the Nineteenth Century (Fuller), 5, 6, 223, 225n, 232, 236, 237, 241–42, 243, 248, 254
Women inmates at Sing Sing Prison, letter to, 238
"Woodnotes" (Emerson), 142
Wright, Henry G., 102n, 104

Xenophon, 64, 65n, 67, 68n

"Young American, The" (Emerson), 179, 180n
Young Lady's Friend, The (Farrar), 191, 192n

"Youth of the Poet and the Painter, The" (Ellery Channing), 136, 138n

Zelter, Karl Friedrich, 163, 164n
Zincali, The (Borrow), 58, 59n